"The author has written a book that is b
needed topic: the relationship of the old covenant to the new. I believe this work
will not only fill a needed gap in Christian literature but will be extremely helpful
and useful to believers. The failure to understand the relationship of the old
covenant to the new is probably one of the most important areas where Christians need good help—and they will receive good help here."

Peter J. Gentry, Donald L. Williams Professor of Old Testament Interpretation,
The Southern Baptist Theological Seminary

"Many readers of the Old Testament struggle to understand all of those random,
bizarre, strict, and oppressive laws. What's a Christian to do? Start by reading
Todd's *Sinai and the Saints*. Todd offers his readers engaging stories, provocative
insights, and a compelling interpretation that offers a way forward—one that
makes sense of the law and helps people understand it in light of Jesus and the
rest of Scripture."

David T. Lamb, Allan A. MacRae Professor of Old Testament, Biblical Theological
Seminary, author of *God Behaving Badly* and *Prostitutes and Polygamists*

"Addressing highly relevant questions, especially in the area of ethics, Todd provides an exceptionally helpful guide to the complex issue of how Christians
should view Old Testament law as authoritative Scripture. His approach, which
is accessible to nonexperts, draws on the best of modern scholarship, offering,
among other things, an insightful discussion of the relevance of the Ten Commandments for twenty-first-century Christians. Anyone grappling with how to
approach the laws of Exodus to Deuteronomy from a Christian perspective will
find this book an invaluable introduction."

T. Desmond Alexander, director of postgraduate studies,
Union Theological College, Belfast

SINAI AND THE SAINTS

READING OLD COVENANT LAWS FOR THE NEW COVENANT COMMUNITY

JAMES M. TODD III

IVP Academic

An imprint of InterVarsity Press
Downers Grove, Illinois

InterVarsity Press
P.O. Box 1400, Downers Grove, IL 60515-1426
ivpress.com
email@ivpress.com

InterVarsity Press® is the book-publishing division of InterVarsity Christian Fellowship/USA®, a movement of students and faculty active on campus at hundreds of universities, colleges, and schools of nursing in the United States of America, and a member movement of the International Fellowship of Evangelical Students. For information about local and regional activities, visit intervarsity.org.

Scripture quotations, unless otherwise noted, are from The Holy Bible, English Standard Version, copyright © 2001 by Crossway Bibles, a division of Good News Publishers. Used by permission. All rights reserved.

While any stories in this book are true, some names and identifying information may have been changed to protect the privacy of individuals.

Cover design: Faceout Studio
Interior design: Dan van Loon
Image: open Bible: © TokenPhoto/iStockphoto

ISBN 978-0-8308-5162-1 (print)
ISBN 978-0-8308-9176-4 (digital)

Printed in the United States of America ♾

Library of Congress Cataloging-in-Publication Data

Names: Todd, James M., 1981- author.
Title: Sinai and the saints : reading old covenant laws for the new covenant community / James M. Todd III.
Description: Downers Grove : InterVarsity Press, 2017. | Includes bibliographical references and index.
Identifiers: LCCN 2016046184 (print) | LCCN 2016048576 (ebook) | ISBN 9780830851621 (pbk. : alk. paper) | ISBN 9780830891764 (eBook)
Subjects: LCSH: Jewish law | Bible. Pentateuch--Criticism, interpretation, etc. | Bible. Penteteuch--Relation to the New Testament. | Christianity and law.
Classification: LCC BS1225.6.L3 T63 2017 (print) | LCC BS1225.6.L3 (ebook) | DDC 222/.106--dc23
LC record available at https://lccn.loc.gov/2016046184

| P | 25 | 24 | 23 | 22 | 21 | 20 | 19 | 18 | 17 | 16 | 15 | 14 | 13 | 12 | 11 | 10 | 9 | 8 | 7 | 6 | 5 | 4 | 3 | 2 | 1 |
| Y | 34 | 33 | 32 | 31 | 30 | 29 | 28 | 27 | 26 | 25 | 24 | 23 | 22 | 21 | 20 | 19 | 18 | 17 |

To Maisy, Lily, and Isaac,

whose love, joy, smiles, and hugs inspire me

to be a better man.

CONTENTS

PREFACE   ix

INTRODUCTION: What Do I Do with All These Laws?   1

  1 Which Laws Are We Discussing?   11

  2 What Are My Options? Approaches to the Old Covenant Laws   30

  3 "In the Beginning," Not "Thou Shalt Not"   45

  4 The Rest of the Story (Part 1): Israel at Sinai   56

  5 The Rest of the Story (Part 2): Before and After Sinai   72

  6 "Thou Shalt Not Remove Them":
     What About the Ten Commandments?   89

  7 Does This Mean I Can Do Whatever I Want?   108

  8 Why Should We Read the Laws?   127

  9 Can I Have the Good News? The Hope of the Pentateuch   152

CONCLUSION: Back to the Beginning: The Law in the Early Church
  and the Contemporary Church   177

APPENDIX A: How Should Christians Use the Hebrew Bible
  to Address Homosexuality?   183

APPENDIX B: The Second Commandment and Images in Worship   193

APPENDIX C: Challenges to My Position   199

BIBLIOGRAPHY   207

SCRIPTURE INDEX   215

PREFACE

As a professor of biblical studies, I have discovered that my students' ability to read, know, and appreciate the Old Testament often hinges on their understanding of its laws and their role in the biblical story. I have written this book to help students better understand the purpose and function of these laws in the biblical story. I also pray that this book helps many other Christians engage the Old Testament in more depth.

This book is an introduction to the topic and not an academic treatise. I have assumed that my readers have a basic knowledge of the biblical story. For readers who are interested in pursuing the topic with more depth, I reference other works on particular issues in my footnotes. Also, the bibliography contains numerous works that give more academic treatments on the topic and works that discuss closely related topics.

The material in this book comes out of several years of course lectures, sermons, and other teaching opportunities. The role of the Old Testament laws in the Christian's life is one of the most complicated areas of Christian theology, so I approach the topic standing on the shoulders of many who have engaged this issue before me. I hope my research and creative presentation of the material will help others better understand the Old Testament and its continuing role in the modern Christian's life.

Writing a book takes a team of faithful supporters, and God has certainly blessed me with such a team. My interest in this topic began as I sat in Dr. John Sailhamer's Old Testament Theology class at the beginning of my master's program. Dr. Sailhamer challenged me to think about the Pentateuch's message by paying close attention to the book's structure. His imprints are throughout this book. Many of my thoughts in this book arose out of conversations with Jonathan Chandler, a friend and former copastor. Two of my colleagues, Mark Rapinchuk and Rusty Osborne, have been great resources for me as I have wrestled with the complicated issues in this book. Working with such wise men is a great honor and privilege. Dylan Parker, a former student, read the manuscript and gave me valuable feedback. I also thank my dean, Eric Bolger, for his support during this project. My wife, Christina, and my three children, Maisy, Lily, and Isaac, have been extremely gracious to me, as I have spent countless hours during the summers and school breaks writing away in the basement. David McNutt and the team at IVP have been more than helpful in this process. David's grace, kindness, and availability impressed me at every turn in the process. Finally, I thank Christ, whose grace has sustained me throughout the entire process.

INTRODUCTION

WHAT DO I DO WITH ALL THESE LAWS?

It is a familiar story, perhaps one in which you have found yourself. It is the beginning of a New Year and thus time for new goals. Like many Christians, one of your goals is to read the entire Bible in one year. As you begin reading, you are enamored by the familiar stories of creation, Adam and Eve, the flood, Abraham, Isaac, Jacob, Joseph, and Israel's exodus. Moreover, you stumble across stories that had fallen deep in the bottomless pits of your memory, stories of excitement, adventure, and, to be honest, some gruesomeness. Your confidence level soars, and nothing can stop you! That is, until you leave the exodus story and read about the Israelites' trek across the wilderness to Mount Sinai (Ex 19:11). At first, it feels like the excitement of the story will continue as you read about the burning mountain, upon which the thunder, lightning, and fire of God's presence appear. Yet, while reading of Israel's time at a literal mountain, you have hit a mountain of your own—that is, a mountain of laws!

Much like the work required to climb a real mountain, your Bible reading plan begins to feel like hard work instead of pleasure; verse after verse of laws have replaced the exciting stories of action and adventure. The thighs and calves of your attention span begin to burn as you read numerous chapters of laws. In fact, for many Christians, this mountain marks the end of good intentions and the frustration of yet another New Year's goal gone awry. Many are able to make it successfully through the detailed instructions (Ex 25–31) and subsequent construction of the tabernacle (Ex 35–40) but are unable to push through the numerous laws of Leviticus. Others make it through the tabernacle and the laws of Leviticus but falter once they hit the census at the beginning of Numbers (if only they knew how close they were to leaving the mountain).

Although you love God's Word and want to read all of Scripture, you find it difficult to read the laws day after day. What adds to the difficulty is that many of the laws are hard to understand because of the vast differences between the culture of the ancient Israelites and our modern culture. For example, one of the most repeated commands in these early books of the Bible is the command not to boil a kid goat in its mother's milk (Ex 23:19; 34:26; Deut 14:21). The command probably referred to the practice of milking the mother goat, killing the kid goat, and boiling the meat of the kid goat in the mother's milk.[1] My question is, who would be tempted to do this? Or should we interpret this as many Jews do and not eat dairy products and meat together in the same meal? Or perhaps you are okay with this command, but the one that really gets you is the command to build a parapet around the roof of one's house (Deut 22:8). After you look up what a parapet is in the dictionary, you once again are puzzled as to why anyone would be on your roof in the first place.

Maybe you are the person who has some knowledge of ancient Near Eastern (i.e., the region where the events of the Bible took place) cultural practices, so you are aware of the cultural reasons for these laws, but you struggle with how to apply these laws to a modern culture. Like any good Christian, you want to apply the Bible to your own life in a meaningful way, but as you read, you quickly realize that if you were to obey many of these commands, you would stick out like a polar bear on South Beach.

For example, should Christians follow the dietary laws (Lev 11)? How does a modern woman apply the commands relating to purification after childbirth (Lev 12)? How should Christians follow the principles for cleansing their homes of mildew (Lev 14)? Should Christian farmers leave some of their harvest for the poor (Lev 19:9)? Should Christian men not cut the hair on the sides of their head (Lev 19:27)? Should Christians wear clothes made of two kinds of material (Lev 19:19)? Are women forbidden to wear jeans (a common interpretation of Deut 22:5)? We could keep going, but hopefully you get the point. Christians must answer these important questions in a consistent and logical manner.

---

[1] See Douglas K. Stuart, *Exodus*, New American Commentary 2 (Nashville: Broadman & Holman, 2006), 539-40, for support and interaction with alternative interpretations.

Let's go one step further. Some of the laws seem natural for modern Christians to obey, but the various types of punishments associated with breaking these commands seem out of place in our modern context. For example, the punishment for breaking many of the Ten Commandments is death (see Ex 31:14; Deut 13; 22:20-22). Or how about the command for parents to take the lead in stoning their rebellious son to death (Deut 21:18-21)? On what basis do we obey the commandments but dismiss the associated punishment? Again, this is an important question for Christians who strive to interpret the Bible consistently.

I do not know if you can relate to these struggles, but many Christians wrestle with the simple question, what do I do with all these laws? They want to obey God's Word, but when it comes to the laws, they do not even know where to start. Add into the mix the many different perspectives and interpretations pastors and scholars give, and we have a recipe for discouragement and surrender. In all actuality, some readers, after reading the previous paragraphs, might be ready to throw in the towel on this subject right now. If that is you, then keep reading for just a few more pages, and let's see if I can convince you otherwise.

WHO CARES?

The knee-jerk reaction for many of us when we encounter controversial or complicated issues is to walk away from the topic with a laissez-faire attitude. Why bother discussing an issue that Christians have not resolved in the span of two millennia of church history? What makes us think we can provide solutions to such difficult problems? If these are the types of questions running through your mind right now, this section is for you. Let's look at two key reasons why Christians must have an appropriate understanding of how to interpret the laws in the Old Testament.

The Old Testament laws and the voice of the church in culture. American culture is currently in one of the biggest cultural shifts since this country's conception. In my eyes, the old moral order is quickly eroding as the waters of a new moral revolution wash down the hill of America's moral landscape. One of the hot-button issues in this culture shift is homosexuality and, more specifically, gay marriage. I mention this topic here not because I expect to resolve the matter completely but because it can illustrate for us the relevance of understanding the role of the Old Testament laws in the Christian life.

Since I have a great interest in the Old Testament and the Christian application of this part of the Bible, I have paid close attention to the debates over the (im)morality of homosexuality and gay marriage. Numerous Christian leaders appearing on talk shows and news networks have given their opinion on homosexuality and gay marriage. Countless debates have transpired on Facebook pages, blogs, and other media outlets. Such pervasive debate has revealed a great divide in our culture, even between many Christians and their respective denominations.

Very often, the Old Testament laws come up in this discussion, and unfortunately, many times Christians do not deal methodically and consistently with these laws when articulating their positions. Many Christians quote Leviticus 18:22 ("You shall not lie with a male as with a woman; it is an abomination") as the key verse for the topic. While turning to the Scripture for answers to key topics is praiseworthy, I am often embarrassed by the scarcity of a reasonable explanation for why this verse applies to all people at all times and other verses in the same book do not (e.g., dietary laws [Lev 11] and laws forbidding people to wear clothing made of two kinds of material [Lev 19:19]). Without a doubt, there are exceptions, but at the level of the average Christian, it is rare for someone to articulate competently his or her reason for obeying the prohibition of sexual immorality in Leviticus 18:22 and not the prohibition of wearing clothing made of two types of fabric in Leviticus 19:19.

If Christians are going to have any voice in the broader culture, we must be able to explain how we differentiate between those things that are permissible and those things that are not. In fact, advocates of homosexuality and gay marriage often call out Christians for their inconsistency in picking and choosing Old Testament laws. At times, these opponents may be acting out of their own ignorance of how to interpret the Bible. However, they may honestly want answers regarding why many Christians pick and choose which laws still apply and which laws do not.

I will give two examples from American culture to illustrate my point. In an episode (season two, episode three) of NBC's television show *The West Wing*, President Bartlet enters the room of a talk-radio reception during the final hour of midterm election day. As he begins to address the radio hosts, he notices a woman sitting in the midst of his audience. President Bartlet pauses for a second and then continues his speech. However, it becomes apparent that he cannot ignore the woman's presence without comment, so he stops, points to her, and asks, "I'm sorry, you are Dr. Jacobs, right?" After receiving an affirmative answer, he begins to push her regarding her conservative radio show, eventually getting to his major point. He has a problem with her calling homosexuality an abomination. Facetiously, he tells her, "I like your show. I like how you call homosexuality an abomination."

Confidently, she replies, "I don't say homosexuality is an abomination, Mr. President. The Bible does."

He responds, "Yes it does. Leviticus—"

She retorts, "18:22."

He says, "Chapter and verse," pauses, and then begins to attack her views. His diatribe is as follows:

> I wanted to ask you a couple of questions while I had you here. I'm interested in selling my youngest daughter into slavery as sanctioned in Exodus 21:7. She's a Georgetown sophomore, speaks fluent Italian, and always clears the table when it was her turn. What would a good price for her be? While thinking about that, can I ask another? My Chief of Staff, Leo McGarry, insists on working on the Sabbath. Exodus 35:2 clearly says he should be put to death. Am I morally obligated to kill him myself or is it okay to call the police? Here's one that's really important, 'cause we've got a lot of sports fans in this town. Touching the skin of a dead pig makes one unclean (Leviticus 11:7). If they promise to wear gloves, can the Washington Redskins still play football? Can Notre Dame? Can West Point? Does the whole town really have to be together to stone my brother, John, for planting different crops side by side? Can I burn my mother in a small family gathering for wearing garments made from two different threads? Think about those questions, would you?[2]

President Bartlet's speech, as written by the show's producers, underscores, among other things, the significant place of the Old Testament laws in the cultural debate over homosexuality. This episode aired in the year 2000, but the same sentiments have surfaced multiple times since then.[3]

---

[2]Aaron Sorkin, "The Midterms," *The West Wing*, directed by Alex Graves, aired October 18, 2000; quoted from www.imdb.com/title/tt0200276/faq?ref_=tt_faq_1#.2.1.6.

[3]The episode itself continues to come up in discussions about the issue. For example, on September 9, 2015, *CNN Tonight* anchor Don Lemon replayed the clip in an interview with

We find a more recent example in the sports world. When Jason Collins became the first athlete in a major American team sport to announce publicly that he was gay (April 2013), the topic of homosexuality became a staple on sports shows (and has continued to be so as other athletes have made similar announcements). For example, ESPN's *Outside the Lines* immediately tackled the issue and even allowed a Christian to outline his perspective. On April 29, 2013, an ESPN analyst interviewed LZ Granderson, an ESPN columnist, and Chris Broussard, an ESPN NBA analyst. At one point in the interview, the host highlighted that Jason Collins identified himself as Christian and asked Broussard, a professing Christian, to share his thoughts on such a claim. Broussard's response was one of the best Christian responses I have heard.[4] He not only highlighted other common sexual sins but also stated that anyone living such a lifestyle is choosing to live in open rebellion against God.

Of course, Broussard's comments garnered significant attention as numerous individuals criticized his response. One such critique came the same evening from Kelly Dwyer, a sportswriter for Yahoo Sports. Dwyer, taking issue with Broussard's comments, wrote the following:

> The Bible, through many translations, sects, and testaments, says quite a few things. It has been used as a basis to defend slavery, segregation, the oppression of women's rights, and laws forbidden the consumption of shrimp scampi—found in the same Leviticus portion of the Bible that forbids a man to lay with another man. It also says quite a few things about fabric blends and working on Sundays, something Chris Broussard often flaunts in his clear "open rebellion to God."[5]

Dwyer's reaction to Broussard reveals a deep confusion over why some Old Testament laws apply today and others do not. Even though Broussard said nothing about Leviticus in his comments, Dwyer took the opportunity to highlight Broussard's supposed hypocrisy. I am not greatly concerned that unbelievers (I assume) are unable to interpret the Bible properly; what

---

Matt Bevin, a gubernatorial candidate in Kentucky. See www.cnn.com/videos/tv/2015/09/09/matt-bevin-gay-marriage-cnn-tonight-don-lemon.cnn. Accessed September 10, 2015.

[4]Quoted in Kelly Dwyer, "ESPN's Chris Broussard Clarifies His Views on Jason Collins: 'I Don't Agree with Homosexuality. I Think It's a Sin,'" Yahoo Sports, April 29, 2013, http://sports.yahoo.com/blogs/nba-ball-dont-lie/espn-chris-broussard-clarifies-views-jason-collins-don-221941033.html.

[5]Ibid.

concerns me is that many Christians would be unable to give a reasonable rebuttal of President Bartlet's and Kelly Dwyer's challenges. Would you be able to give an answer to these challenges?

I could give more examples from both the media and personal conversations of how the Old Testament laws come up repeatedly in discussions about homosexuality and many other moral issues;[6] instead, I want to stress the importance of having a method to deal with ethical issues addressed by these laws. For too long, many Christians have haphazardly followed the pick-and-choose method whereby they decide which Old Testament laws apply to them based on what suits their fancy at a particular point in their lives. As Christians, we have a responsibility to interpret God's Word consistently in a way that does not undermine the good news we proclaim to the world. A failure to interpret God's Word consistently in these important dialogues often results in confusion and accusations of hypocrisy.

The Old Testament laws and the message of the Bible. "Don't miss the forest for the trees." We often use this common expression to remind ourselves to keep the big picture in view, even when we focus on the details of a matter. Such an adage is beneficial in many areas of life, especially biblical interpretation. The Bible is such a long book that people often get lost in the details and never grasp the big picture. In other words, many Christians know numerous individual Bible stories but have no idea how these smaller stories fit together in the big story.

When one reads the Bible, there is a constant interaction between the smaller stories and the one big story. For example, the story of David and Goliath is one episode in the larger story of David's life and, even more importantly, in the larger story of the books of 1 and 2 Samuel. One needs a basic knowledge of the big story in order to make sense of the smaller stories, *and* the smaller stories always enhance and challenge our understanding of the big story.

One of the most significant stories in the Bible is the story of God giving his laws to Israel at Mount Sinai. This story takes up all or parts of Exodus, Leviticus, Numbers, and Deuteronomy. Additionally, this story echoes throughout the rest of the Old Testament and much of the

---

[6]For example, the topic of Christians and tattoos frequently involves a discussion of the laws in Leviticus.

New Testament. It is therefore very difficult to understand the message of the Bible without a working knowledge of how the laws fit into the story of the Bible.

MOUNT SINAI

A mountain located in the Sinai Peninsula upon which God appeared to Moses and the Israelites. Traditionally, Jebel Musa, which is home to the Monastery of St. Catherine, has been identified as Mount Sinai.

If we just use the New Testament as an example, we discover that Jesus and the apostles often discussed the issue of the Old Testament laws. In the Sermon on the Mount, Jesus commented on several of the laws found in the Old Testament and urged his followers to go beyond the laws in their actions (Mt 5:21-48). While much of his discussion of the Old Testament laws was concentrated in the Sermon on the Mount, many of Jesus' other teachings and actions relate to the laws. For instance, while participating in one of his regular pastimes—debating with the Pharisees—Jesus would often challenge the religious leaders' understanding of the laws (and their own traditions), particularly that of the Sabbath.

What to do with the Old Testament laws continued to be a question after Jesus' ascension. The question of the laws takes a central role in the story of the new, expanding church in the book of Acts. In particular, when the early Jewish Christians realized that God had accepted the Gentiles, a great controversy arose in the church over whether Gentiles were required to keep the laws and, in particular, be circumcised (Acts 15, see esp. v. 5).

The question of the Old Testament laws occupies a central position in Paul's explanation of the gospel of God to the church in Rome. Although Paul's discussion of the Old Testament laws in Romans is his most detailed, he addresses the issue in several of his other letters (e.g., 2 Cor 3; Eph 2:11-22; Col 2:8-23; 1 Tim 1:8-11), in particular the letter to the Galatians. The other apostles cannot escape this issue either, as several of them devote attention to the laws (e.g., in Hebrews and James 2:8-13).

Since the issue of the Old Testament laws is such a major topic throughout the Bible, one can argue that we cannot understand the Bible unless we understand the function of these laws in the biblical story. Dodging the discussion of the Old Testament laws inevitably results in an ignorance of key portions of the biblical story and an inability to understand properly many of the Bible's key teachings.

THE PURPOSE OF THIS BOOK

Whether you struggle with what to do with the Old Testament laws and thus need no motivation to keep reading, or whether you have tried to avoid this topic for a while and I have successfully convinced you of its importance, I invite you to keep reading. My goal in this book is to provide answers to the questions I have raised (and some more that I will raise later) in a way that is easy to understand, informative, and helpful for reading the Bible.

This is a very practical book. Throughout, I offer some important principles and teachings on one of the most important endeavors of every Christian's life: reading the Bible. The God of the universe has revealed himself to us in the Bible and in so doing has chosen to communicate with us by means of a written text. It is therefore essential for every Christian to know not only *what* the Bible states but also *how* to interpret its content properly; this content includes the Old Testament laws.

My approach in this book is different from most books on the role of the Old Testament laws in the Christian's life. Most jump straight into the New Testament and evaluate what Jesus, Paul, and the other apostles had to say about the topic. My starting point is the Old Testament. Since the laws under consideration are in the Old Testament, it makes sense to me to start there and then make our way into the New Testament's teachings. In this regard, I will use the New Testament in a confirmatory role.

I hope that when you have finished reading this book, you will have a better understanding of the biblical story and be equipped to give reasonable answers regarding the role of the Old Testament laws in the lives of modern Christians. We have lots of ground to cover in order to get a good view of the landscape. Therefore, before we jump into the how-to, we must first identify the laws we will be discussing.

ONE

WHICH LAWS ARE WE DISCUSSING?

Definitions are very important in life. Although we often take our shared understanding of words for granted in everyday life, certain events can quickly remind us how important a proper understanding of words is. One such event is learning a new language. Anyone who has traveled internationally and attempted to speak a foreign language has probably experienced the awkward laughs of native speakers when he or she has used the wrong word in a sentence. Even if you have not traveled internationally, you have probably been on the laughing side of this equation at some point in your life.

Using the wrong word when interacting with someone who speaks a different language can be rather humorous, but in more serious matters, definitions carry much more weight. As we have already noted, this book's topic is an important issue for Christians, and as we will demonstrate in the next chapter, it is controversial. Hence, much more is at stake in the present task than a foreigner's choice of the wrong word. So, let's begin by defining our terminology.

THE MEANING OF "TORAH"

Many of us properly associate the English word *law* with specific rules given by a government for its citizens. Most countries have a variety of laws dealing with anything from traffic to property to criminal activity. We can categorize these laws in numerous ways and sometimes designate them statutes or legislation (collectively).

Many Christians, upon reading the word *law* in their English translations of the Bible, associate their common understanding of the English word with the biblical text. Although the meanings of the biblical text and the modern usage of the word *law* might be the same, we should not assume so until we have consulted the original languages.

Since the Old Testament was written in Hebrew (with a sprinkling of Aramaic, primarily in Daniel and Ezra), we have to look beyond the English translation to the Hebrew word under consideration. For the most part, the Hebrew word translated "law" throughout the Old Testament is *torah*. This Hebrew word has a broader meaning than simply "rule," just as our English word *law* has a broader meaning. For example, we often use *law* to refer to those who enforce the law ("Don't get in trouble with the law"). According to standard Hebrew lexicons, *torah* has two primary meanings: (1) general instruction and (2) particular instruction (i.e., a rule).[1] Even though the second definition overlaps with our modern understanding of "law," we rarely think of "law" as general instruction. However, the Hebrew Bible often uses the word *torah* in such a manner (e.g., Deut 1:5; Prov 1:8; 4:1). Therefore, when we read the word *law* in our English Bibles, we must be cognizant of the different meanings of the Hebrew word *torah*.

How then do we know which meaning a biblical author intends? As with any word that has multiple meanings, the context in which the word is used determines the meaning of the word. Let's look at another English example. The word *chair* can refer to either the person who leads a committee or an object upon which one sits. We determine the meaning of the word simply by reading the sentence in which the word is used. We use the same process with the Hebrew word *torah*.

Since this book focuses on the particular instructions given to Israel in specific portions of the Old Testament, the word *torah* in many of our discussions will involve the second meaning—that is, rules or specific instructions.[2] This word has several synonyms in the Old Testament. Genesis 26:5 provides a good sampling of these synonyms. In this verse, the Lord states concerning Abraham: "Abraham obeyed my voice and kept my

---

[1] Francis Brown, S. R. Driver, and Charles A. Briggs, *The Brown-Driver-Briggs Hebrew and English Lexicon* (Peabody, MA: Hendrickson, 1996), 435. Ludwig Koehler and Walter Baumgartner, *The Hebrew and Aramaic Lexicon of the Old Testament* (Leiden: Brill, 2002), 1:1710-11; quotation from 1711.

[2] I will discuss the other meaning of *torah* (i.e., "instruction") in a later chapter.

charge, my commandments, my statutes, and my laws." Thus, when the Old Testament authors refer to specific laws, they often use the words "commandment" (*miṣwâ*), "statute" (*ḥōq* or *ḥuqâ*), and "judgment" (*mišpāṭ*) (see Deut 4:8) interchangeably with "law" (*torah*).

THE LAWS UNDER CONSIDERATION

Linguists typically distinguish between the meaning (concept reflected in the dictionary) and the referent (the person, place, or thing to which a word refers) of a word. For instance, the Hebrew word *yiṣḥāq* means "he laughs." In the book of Genesis it refers to Abraham's son Isaac, but in my family it refers to my son Isaac. The meaning of the Hebrew word has not changed, but the possible referents have. If someone uses the word *Isaac* in our house, the context of the conversation determines whether that person is referring to Isaac Todd or Isaac, the son of Abraham. In a similar manner, whenever we encounter the word *law* or *laws* in the Bible, we have to determine which law or laws the biblical author is referencing.

A precise identification of the law(s) under consideration is essential for a proper analysis of the Christian's obligation to the Old Testament laws. Christians often make general references to "God's law(s)," "biblical law(s)," or "God's commandment(s)" without specifying which laws they have in mind. Such generalities are not helpful.[3] For example, when Jesus says in John 14:15, "If you love me, you will keep my commandments" (he makes similar statements in vv. 21 and 23), we must identify his commandments. Is it every command in the Bible? Is it the commands in the New Testament?

---

[3]Unfortunately, biblical scholars sometimes make this mistake. For example, Willem A. VanGemeren ("The Law Is the Perfection of Righteousness in Jesus Christ," in *Five Views on Law and Gospel*, ed. Wayne G. Strickland [Grand Rapids: Zondervan, 1996], 40) quotes the NIV's translation of 1 Cor 7:19 ("Keeping God's commands is what counts") to critique those who draw a distinction between the laws that Moses gave and the new covenant. VanGemeren fails to clarify which commands Paul is referencing in this verse. Jerram Barrs (*Delighting in the Law of the Lord: God's Alternative to Legalism and Morality* [Wheaton, IL: Crossway, 2013]) sometimes identifies God's law as all the commands in the Bible (1), sometimes as the laws written on the hearts of all people (290), and sometimes as the laws in the Old Testament (308-11). In all fairness to Barrs, he considers all of these different laws expressions of the same law of God. However, he applies them in different ways (e.g., he advocates finding principles from the Old Testament laws [315-18]), thus evidencing that differences do exist between these various categories. Book titles also demonstrate this lack of clarity. For example, Joe Sprinkle, *Biblical Law and Its Relevance* (Lanham, MD: University Press of America, 2005), and Thomas R. Schreiner, *40 Questions About Christians and Biblical Law* (Grand Rapids: Kregel, 2010).

Is it just the commands that Jesus gave during his time on earth? If our obedience to these commandments measures our love for him, then we had better know which commandments he wants us to obey. To alleviate some of vagueness of this discussion, I will identify the specific laws that we will examine for the rest of the book.

Did you know that the first commands God gave in the Bible were not the laws given to Israel at Mount Sinai (beginning in Exodus 20)? God gave his first law, often termed the creation mandate, to the first human beings, Adam and Eve. Genesis 1:28 records this first command: "Be fruitful and multiply and fill the earth and subdue it, and have dominion over the fish of the sea and over the birds of the heavens and over every living thing that moves on the earth." As the Creator and king of the universe, God gave his vice regents a specific task to perform, a task integrally related to his creation of humankind in his image.

God gave Adam a second law or command after placing Adam in the Garden of Eden: "You may surely eat of every tree of the garden, but of the tree of the knowledge of good and evil you shall not eat, for in the day that you eat of it you shall surely die." (Gen 2:16-17). Of course, Adam (along with his wife, Eve, and thanks to the serpent) failed to obey this law and rebelled against his king, thus opening the floodgates of sin and making it necessary for God to give more laws.

If we fast-forward a few chapters, more commands appear after Noah exits the ark. Just before giving Noah permission to eat meat (Gen 9:3), God repeated the creation mandate to Noah and his sons (Gen 9:1). God also commanded Noah not to eat meat with blood and gave a law regarding the punishment of murderers (Gen 9:4-6). As we continue reading the Old Testament, we encounter various laws and commands given to numerous individuals and nations. In each instance, the responsible reader must interpret and apply such laws according to their context.

In my introduction, I mentioned the "Old Testament laws" on several occasions. I presented the laws in such a manner to avoid confusing my readers in the introduction, but my topic is actually narrower than the Old Testament laws. This book focuses on the group of laws given to Israel at Mount Sinai and throughout their journey from Sinai to the Promised Land (Ex 20–Deut). God did not give these laws to all humanity; he gave them to a specific group of people at a specific time in a specific place for a specific purpose. These laws are part of a covenant that God made with his chosen people Israel after he delivered them from the oppressive hand of Pharaoh (Ex 1–15).

Before looking at this particular covenant, it is important to understand covenants in the ancient Near East. Modern Christians often use the word *covenant* to describe marriage. In so doing, they emphasize the sacred seriousness of the marriage commitment in contrast to lesser commitments one might make (e.g., a commitment to go to the store with a friend). This understanding of a covenant parallels covenants in the ancient world. Covenants were common in the ancient Near East and consequently the Bible. Much like the way we sign modern contracts, individuals and nations formalized their agreements with a covenant, which was a binding agreement between two parties. The Bible records covenants between individuals (1 Sam 20:16-17), kings and individuals (Gen 21:31-32; 26:28-31), kings (2 Kings 16:7-9), God and individuals (Gen 15), and God and nations (Ex 19–24). The covenant God makes with Israel at Sinai falls under the final category.

EXCURSUS: THE OLD COVENANT AND ANCIENT NEAR EASTERN VASSAL TREATIES

Yahweh's covenant with Israel at Sinai reflects many elements in Hittite vassal treaties of the second millennium BC. These treaties were made between a powerful king (the suzerain) and a subject king (vassal). They often highlighted the suzerain's benevolent actions toward the vassal and outlined the stipulations for the vassal. A typical suzerain-vassal treaty contained the following elements:[4]

1. Identification of Covenant Giver

2. Historical Prologue

3. Stipulations

4. Provision for Deposit and Periodic Public Reading

5. List of Witnesses

6. Blessings and Curses

---

[4]Taken from George E. Mendenhall and Gary A. Herion, "Covenant," in vol. 1 of *Anchor Bible Dictionary*, ed. David Noel Freedman (New York: Doubleday, 1992), 1180-82.

The Pentateuch gives evidence of adapting such treaties by the form and wording of certain sections in the Sinai legislation. Scholars have identified parallels with these treaties in Exodus 20–24 and the book of Deuteronomy. These parallels are important because they provide another metaphor by which to understand Yahweh's relationship with Israel. As their suzerain, Yahweh provided his vassal with numerous benefits, which served as the basis for the people's allegiance to him.

TITLES OF THE COVENANT

Names and titles communicate something about the person or thing to which one assigns them. Many parents (especially in the ancient world) recognize the significance of a name and therefore carefully consider the name they assign their child. The best examples of the importance of names come from the Bible itself. Numerous names reflect the parents' desire for the child (Gen 5:28-29), the circumstances of the child's birth (Gen 21:1-7), or the child's appearance (Gen 25:25). The significance of a name or title is not limited to human beings. In the modern world, business owners often give their businesses a name that reflects their mission or highlights certain features of the business. Many hospitals and universities name buildings in honor of donors who make significant contributions to the organization. We even name animals based on a distinguishing characteristic (e.g., great white shark, whitetail deer, and catfish).

Such communicative significance also applies to the titles of the various biblical covenants. Over the years, biblical scholars have assigned several titles to God's covenant with Israel at Sinai, a couple of which come directly from the biblical text. As one would expect, each of these titles highlights a different aspect of the covenant and therefore enhances our understanding of the covenant. Let's look at the four most common titles for this covenant.

The title that appears most frequently in the Bible is "the law" (*torah*). That's right; not only do the biblical authors use the word "law" (*torah*) to refer to individual rules, but they also use it to refer to the entire covenant God made with Israel at Mount Sinai. This dual reference parallels our English word *law*, which we often use to designate both individual laws and the entire group of laws. For example, consider the following sentence: "The law permits certain actions that we would consider immoral." *Law* in this sentence does not refer to one law but the entire system of laws. Once again, the context determines whether the word refers to an individual law or the covenant as a whole.

The Old Testament authors use the Hebrew title "law" (*torah*) (see Deut 4:8; 27:26; 28:58; 33:10; 2 Chron 6:16; 14:4) along with other terms. The New Testament authors, on the other hand, adopt the Greek word *nomos* ("law") as their primary term for this covenant. For a good sampling of passages where New Testament authors use "law" to describe the entire covenant, read the books of Romans and Galatians (e.g., Rom 3:19-20; 4:13-15; Gal 3:17-25).

The second and third terms biblical authors use to describe the covenant God made with Israel at Sinai are the *Mosaic covenant* and the *Sinai* (or *Sinaitic*) *covenant*. The former reflects Moses' role as the mediator of the covenant, and the latter relates to the location of the covenant ceremony. Regarding this location, biblical authors sometimes call the mountain Horeb (e.g., Deut 1:6, 19; 4:10; 5:2; 1 Kings 8:9; Ps 106:19; Mal 4:4), so when biblical authors mention a covenant at Horeb, they are referencing the same covenant.[5]

OLD COVENANT AND NEW COVENANT

Old covenant: The covenant God made with Israel at Mount Sinai. Moses served as the covenant mediator.

New covenant: The covenant God made with the church. Jesus initiated the covenant with his blood and serves as the covenant mediator.

The final term biblical authors use to describe this covenant is the *old covenant*. This term highlights the contrast between this covenant and the new covenant. This implicit contrast between old and new reminds me of AT&T's "More Is Better" commercial, which begins with a man sitting in a circle with a group of kids and asking them, "Who thinks more is better than less?" When the kids raise their hands in approval, he asks, "Why?" Of course, the kids give cute answers that I

---

[5]Moses also calls this mountain "the mountain of God" (Ex 3:1; 4:27; 18:5; 24:13).

know were in no way scripted by the producers. The commercial ends with the narrator saying, "It's not complicated. More is better. And AT&T has the nation's largest 4G network." In a similar manner, the title old covenant implies, rightly so, the inferior nature of the covenant God made with Israel at Sinai. Although this title is limited to the New Testament (see 2 Cor 3:14; Heb 8:6), the contrast between the old covenant (mediated by Moses at Sinai and fulfilled by Jesus at the cross) and the new covenant (mediated and inaugurated by Jesus at the cross) begins in the Old Testament (see Deut 30:1-10; Jer 31:31-34; 32:39-41; Ezek 34:25-31; 36:24-38).

Since the Old Testament itself initiates this contrast and points its readers to the new covenant, we must not apply the term *old covenant* to the Old Testament as a whole. Readers with a knowledge of the terminology might be scratching their head at this point because *covenant* and *testament* are often used as synonymous terms. If the old covenant and the Old Testament are two different things, why are their names so similar? Like many of the titles given to the individual books within the Old Testament, the term *Old Testament* is based on tradition. In this case, the tradition began at the end of the second century.[6] Unfortunately, the tradition from which we adopted this title equated the old covenant with the Old Testament. Even today, many Christians do not distinguish between the covenant Yahweh made with Israel at Sinai (i.e., old covenant) and the first thirty-nine books of the Bible (i.e., Old Testament). Historically, other titles have been used to designate these books of the Bible. For example, Jews commonly refer to the Old Testament as the Tanak, a title that reflects the three major divisions of the Hebrew Bible: Torah, Prophets (Nevi'im), and Writings (Ketuvim). Jesus used a similar title in Luke 24:44: "the Law of Moses and the Prophets and the Psalms." For the remainder of this book, I will use the term *Hebrew Bible* to designate these thirty-nine books. Although this term is not perfect (a small percentage of the Hebrew Bible contains Aramaic rather than Hebrew), it alleviates some of the confusion and negative connotations associated with the term *Old Testament*.

---

[6]Ronald K. Harrison, "Bible," in vol. 1 of *International Standard Bible Encyclopedia*, ed. Geoffrey W. Bromiley (Grand Rapids: Eerdmans, 1979), 483.

YAHWEH

The divine name God revealed to Moses in Exodus 3:14. The name appears in Hebrew as four consonants, YHWH (also called the Tetragrammaton), and is based on the phrase "I Am."

HEBREW BIBLE

An alternate title for the Old Testament that reflects the original language in which the books were written.

To better understand the difference between the old covenant and the Hebrew Bible, we need to make an important distinction. John Sailhamer distinguishes between a historical event and the text that records the historical event.[7] For example, George Washington was a historical figure who did many things throughout his lifetime. When someone writes a biography of George Washington, he or she must select certain events from his life based on the aspects of his life that he or she wants to emphasize. In other words, the biographer must interpret his life, which is why two biographies about the same person can have some significant differences. These differences do not necessarily equal contradictions; they can be complementary. For example, one biographer might focus on Washington's public life, while another focuses on his family life. The two biographies will include different stories, and different aspects of Washington's personality will emerge in each biography. These important distinctions apply to more than just biographies; they apply to any attempt to write about historical events.

We should apply the distinction between text and event to the old covenant and the Hebrew Bible. The old covenant was a historical event in which God made a covenant with his people. The Hebrew Bible is a book that records the old covenant and a host of other events. In writing about the old covenant, Moses—in the Pentateuch, the first five books of the Hebrew Bible—chooses which laws and stories from Israel's time at Mount Sinai to record in his book. Through his selectivity and emphases, Moses is not simply telling us that God made a covenant with Israel; he is telling us something about the covenant God made with Israel. In other

---

[7]John Sailhamer, *Introduction to Old Testament Theology: A Canonical Approach* (Grand Rapids: Zondervan, 1999), 36-85.

words, Moses is giving his readers his interpretation of the event (the giving of the old covenant). And since I believe God inspired Moses to write the first five books of the Hebrew Bible, we as readers get the inspired interpretation of the event.[8]

DIVISIONS OF THE OLD COVENANT LAWS

Did you know that the traditional number of laws contained in the books of Genesis through Deuteronomy is 613? Regardless of whether the Jewish scholar Maimonides counted correctly, that is a lot of laws![9] Of course, when we compare them with the number of laws in many modern nations, the number does not seem quite as large. America's federal government can institute that many laws in a year. Many local governments have more laws than the old covenant. Nevertheless, when one is reading Exodus, Leviticus, or Deuteronomy, 613 laws seems like a million!

Whenever we are dealing with such a large number of anything, it often helps to divide the items into smaller and more manageable units. In fact, if you are an obsessively organized person like me, you feel overwhelmed until you subdivide things into smaller groups. Occasionally, I will kick into organize mode at home and reorganize closets, cabinets, and our garage. I have even cataloged my personal library.

Like books in a library, we can group many of the old covenant laws according to their subject matter or other criteria. Organizing the laws in such a manner helps us see the major issues addressed in the old covenant. In what follows, I organize the old covenant laws according to (1) Israel's location when God gave them the various laws and (2) the more specific subdivisions scholars have traditionally proposed.

---

[8]Since the Enlightenment, many scholars have rejected the Mosaic authorship of the first five books of the Hebrew Bible. I affirm the Mosaic authorship of these books because of the testimony of later biblical books (Josh 1:7-8; 2 Kings 14:6; 2 Chron 25:4; 34:14) and Jesus (Mk 12:26; Jn 5:45-46). Moses undoubtedly used sources in the compilation of these books, and later editors probably added some sections (see Num 12:3; Deut 34:1-12), but the majority of the material goes back to Moses.

[9]Maimonides was a twelfth-century (AD) Jewish philosopher who listed the old covenant laws in his *Book of Commandments*. The Babylonian Talmud (Tractate Makkot 23b) divides these laws into 365 negative commands—paralleling the number of days in a year—and 248 positive commands—paralleling the number of human body parts.

Law groups according to the location of giving. God's giving of the old covenant laws to the people of Israel occurs in the biblical text at three major locations. These locations reflect the postexodus journeys of God's people and thus help us understand the larger story recorded in Exodus through Deuteronomy. The first and largest division of laws consists of the laws God gave at Mount Sinai. Israel arrives at Mount Sinai in Exodus 19 (the laws start coming in Exodus 20), and they do not leave until Numbers 10. Thus, Israel's eleven months at Sinai comprise almost fifty-nine chapters of the Hebrew Bible (31.5 percent of the chapters in the Pentateuch).

The laws given to Israel during their journey in the wilderness make up the second major geographical grouping of the laws. Shortly after leaving Sinai, the Israelites rebel against the Lord by refusing to enter the Promised Land (Num 13–14). As punishment for such obstinate rebellion, the Lord condemns his people to wander in the wilderness for forty years (so the generation of perpetrators could die). During this forty-year period, the Lord gives many other laws to his people. These laws are intertwined with stories of Israel's further rebellion in Numbers 15–36.

The final group of laws related to Israel's geographical location consists of the laws Moses gives the Israelites on the plains of Moab. Just before his death, Moses gives a series of sermons to the new generation of Israelites who are at the edge of the Promised Land. The book of Deuteronomy records these sermons. Although Moses gives laws throughout the book of Deuteronomy, chapters 12–26 have the highest concentration of laws (i.e., the law code). In fact, in this section of Deuteronomy, Moses repeats some of the laws Yahweh gave at Sinai and in the wilderness (this is how Deuteronomy, which means "second law," got its name) because he is speaking to a new audience. Since the exodus generation has died, Moses reminds their children of numerous laws (and adds a few new ones) as they prepare to enter the Promised Land.

Figure 1.1 provides a visual representation of the old covenant laws grouped according to the geographical locations we just discussed. The rectangle as a whole represents the first five books of the Bible (Genesis–Deuteronomy), while the smaller boxes represent the narrative portions of these books and the law groups just discussed.

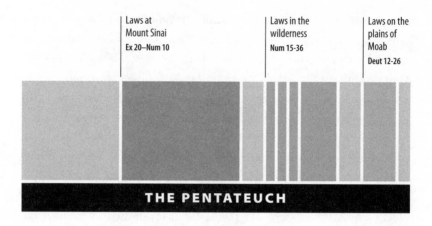

Figure 1.1. Law groups according to place of giving

Law groups according to traditional subdivisions. The second way one can organize the old covenant laws is according to their traditional subdivisions. These divisions are more specific and content-oriented than the divisions based on Israel's geographical location, thus giving us a better picture of the different issues addressed by the old covenant. In what follows, we will explore the various divisions book by book.

Laws in Exodus. The Ten Commandments (also known as the Ten Words—a literal translation of Ex 34:28 and Deut 4:13—or Decalogue) are the first laws Yahweh gives at Sinai and summarize Israel's covenant obligations to Yahweh. Following a brief explanation of the people's fear and their request for Moses to mediate the covenant (Ex 20:18-21), we encounter the second section of laws in Exodus. Scholars typically designate Exodus 20:1–23:33 the Covenant Code because after Moses wrote down everything the Lord said (Ex 24:4), he called this written material "the Book of the Covenant" (Ex 24:7). The Covenant Code contains the basic laws for governing the Israelite nation. These laws deal with servants, punishments for injury, animals, property, the Sabbath, festivals, and several other important issues.

The third major section of laws in Exodus, found in chapters 25–31, contains the instructions for the tabernacle. Two chapters within this section deal specifically with the priesthood. Chapter 28 contains instructions for the priestly garments, and chapter 29 includes the instructions for the consecration ceremony for Aaron and his sons to serve as priests. Several chapters later, we read about the actual construction of the tabernacle (Ex 35–40), although it feels as if we are rereading the instructions because of the numerous parallels between the two sections. This high degree of repetition between the instructions (Ex 25–31) and the description of the tabernacle's construction (Ex 35–40) underscores the tabernacle's significance[10] and the people's complete obedience: "According to all that the LORD had commanded Moses, so the people of Israel had done all the work" (Ex 39:42).

Before leaving Exodus, I must mention the small section of laws in Exodus 34. God gave these laws, which come just before the construction of the tabernacle, to Moses when he renewed the covenant after the people built the golden calf. Since these laws reflect a renewal of the covenant, many of them echo laws in the Ten Commandments and the Covenant Code (Ex 20:1–23:33).

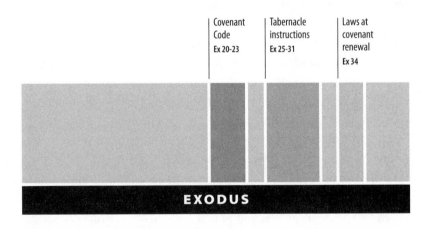

Figure 1.2. The laws of Exodus

Laws in Leviticus. Exodus concludes with Yahweh's glory filling the tabernacle (Ex 40:34-38). Now that the tabernacle is complete, Leviticus 1–7 addresses one of the key activities the priests carried out in the tabernacle courts: the Israelites' offerings. These laws outline regulations for five types of offerings (burnt, grain, fellowship, sin, and guilt) (Lev 1:1–6:7) and give instructions to the priests regarding their administration of these offerings (Lev 6:8–7:38).

The next section of laws appears in Leviticus 11–15. These laws deal with ceremonial cleanliness and address such topics as clean and unclean foods,

---

[10]T. Desmond Alexander, *From Paradise to the Promised Land: An Introduction to the Pentateuch*, 3rd ed. (Grand Rapids: Baker, 2012), 225.

purification after childbirth, skin diseases, mold, and bodily discharges. Since God required Israel to be holy, he gave them specific guidelines regarding ritual purity in their camp. Ritual or ceremonial purity (being "clean") referred to the condition of a person who was fit to enter Yahweh's holy areas (i.e., the camp or tabernacle).[11] Throughout this section of laws, God gives precise distinctions between the clean and the unclean. At the end of this section, Yahweh states his purpose for distinguishing between the clean and unclean. According to Leviticus 15:31, Yahweh was protecting his people from defiling his tabernacle with their uncleanness and thereby incurring his wrath. For this reason, these laws emphasize the priests' role as those who distinguish between the clean and unclean (cf. Lev 10:10).

The largest section of laws in Leviticus is the Holiness Code (Lev 17–26), so named because of the repetition of the phrase "You shall be holy, for I the LORD your God am holy" (Lev 19:2; 20:26) and other similar phrases (cf. Lev 20:7; 21:8; 22:32-33). The laws of the Holiness Code address numerous topics, including the eating of blood, sexual activity, festivals, the Sabbath, and the Year of Jubilee. Most of Leviticus 26 consists of the covenant blessings and curses. In general, these laws relate to the conduct of the whole congregation more than the previous section.

Attentive readers might have noticed that I omitted a couple of chapters in my discussion of the laws in Leviticus: Leviticus 16 and 27. Scholars typically do not group these two chapters, which bracket the Holiness Code, with the larger groups of laws in Leviticus. Leviticus 16 is sandwiched between two of the major law groups and contains the instructions for the Day of Atonement, on which the nation made atonement for their sins. This chapter's literary location highlights the importance of the Day of Atonement.[12] Finally, Leviticus 27 serves as an epilogue for the book and deals with vows and things dedicated to the Lord.

---

[11] Ritual purity was not the same as moral purity; however, a failure to maintain ritual purity was a moral issue. John E. Hartley provides a helpful clarification: "In the routine of daily living, every Israelite became periodically unclean. No shame or harm attended becoming unclean for a brief period of time. The major danger in becoming unclean lay in coming into contact with the holy, for holiness is powerful, consuming all that is unclean. There was a latent moral danger: any person who failed to take the steps leading to ritual purity committed a deliberate sin against God and became subject to the penalties for such a wrong." John E. Hartley, "Holiness," in *Dictionary of the Old Testament: Pentateuch*, ed. T. Desmond Alexander and David W. Baker (Downers Grove, IL: InterVarsity Press, 2003), 426.

[12] Mark F. Rooker, *Leviticus*, New American Commentary 3a (Nashville: B&H, 2000), 45.

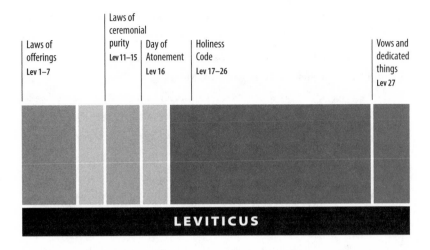

Figure 1.3. The laws of Leviticus

Laws in Numbers. Upon leaving Leviticus, we come to somewhat of a bump in the road when it comes to organizing the old covenant laws, since the laws in the book of Numbers are not in easily discernable units like those in Exodus and Leviticus. In general, we can arrange the laws of Numbers into two major groups. The first group, Numbers 1–10, contains various laws and deals with the arrangement of the camp as Israel prepares for their journey from Sinai to the Promised Land. The second group is scattered throughout the stories of Israel's wilderness journey in Numbers 15–36 and consists of laws addressing a wide variety of issues.

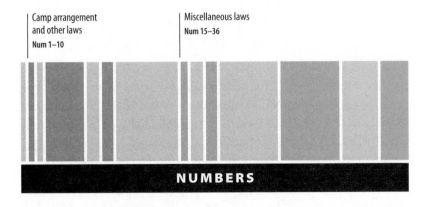

Figure 1.4. The laws of Numbers

Laws in Deuteronomy. The last major section of old covenant laws appears in the book of Deuteronomy. As previously mentioned, there are many laws throughout this book. Most of these laws are interspersed among the more general instructions given by Moses (e.g., "love the Lord," "fear the Lord," "serve the Lord"). However, one section, Deuteronomy 12–26, contains specific laws related to Israel's conduct in the land. Scholars often call this section the Deuteronomic Code. Unlike some of the earlier laws in Exodus–Numbers that deal with Israel's conduct during their journey to the land, the laws in the Deuteronomic Code deal explicitly with Israel's conduct once they take possession of the land (see Deut 12:1). For this reason, Israel was unable to obey many of these laws until they arrived in the land.

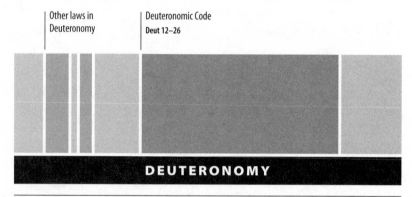

Other laws in Deuteronomy

Deuteronomic Code
Deut 12–26

DEUTERONOMY

Figure 1.5. The laws of Deuteronomy

TYPES OF LAWS IN THE OLD COVENANT

Many of us understand all laws, including biblical laws, in terms of "thou shalt nots." We might call these prohibitions; in the American legal system, they are statutory laws. "Thou shalt not drive over the speed limit." "Thou shalt not take candy from the store without paying for it." "Thou shalt not trespass on thy neighbor's property." These examples represent the way most of us think about these laws. Many people are unaware of another type of law called case law. Case law builds on precedents. When an issue arises that the current statutes do not address, someone (e.g., a judge) has to decide the legality of the matter. Such a decision becomes a precedent for future courts as they seek to interpret similar situations in light of the law. In fact, statutory and case laws are not the only types of laws in the American legal system, but before I get too deep in the murky waters of legal jargon, I will return to the old covenant laws.

Scholars typically categorize the old covenant laws in these same categories. Laws that give an absolute prohibition are apodictic laws. The Ten Commandments serve as a good example of this type of law since they prohibit certain actions in a straightforward manner ("You shall not . . ."). Like the American legal system, the old covenant also contains numerous case or casuistic laws. As noted previously, these laws build on precedent cases and typically appear as if-then statements (the "if" or "when" clause is called the protasis, and the "then" clause is designated the apodosis). Case laws are in many sections of the old covenant. In particular, the first half of the Covenant Code has a high frequency of this type of law. One example is Exodus 21:28: "When an ox gores a man or a woman to death, the ox shall be stoned, and its flesh shall not be eaten, but the owner of the ox shall not be liable."

In addition to the casuistic and apodictic classifications, some scholars give more specific taxonomies of the old covenant laws. These other classifications deal primarily with the topics of the laws and not their forms (as with the apodictic/casuistic distinction). I will discuss the most common of these systems in the next chapter.

EXCURSUS: LAWS IN THE ANCIENT NEAR EAST

Archaeological discoveries have provided scholars with law collections that date from the middle of the third millennium BC to the middle of the first millennium BC. These law collections come from the ancient Near Eastern (ANE) regions of Mesopotamia, Syria, and Anatolia. The major ANE law collections are the Laws of Ur-Nammu (ca. 2100 BC), the Laws of Lipit-Eshtar (ca. 1900 BC), the Laws of Eshnunnu (ca. 1770 BC), the Laws of Hammurabi (ca. 1750 BC), the Middle Assyrian Laws (14th century BC), the Neo-Babylonian Laws (7th century BC), and the Hittite Laws (16th–12th century BC).[13] Of these collections, the Laws of Hammurabi (LH) provide the most significant opportunity for comparison and contrast with the old covenant laws contained in the Pentateuch.

---

[13]Raymond Westbrook, "The Character of Ancient Near Eastern Law," in *A History of Ancient Near Eastern Law*, ed. Raymond Westbrook (Leiden: Brill, 2003), 1:8-9.

ANE law collections are similar to the old covenant laws in two major ways. First, like many of the old covenant laws, the majority of ANE laws appear in casuistic form. Second, the ANE collections contain many laws whose content is similar to the old covenant laws.[14] We find a good sampling of these similar laws when we compare the Laws of Hammurabi with the Covenant Code (Ex 20:22–23:33). Specifically, the law concerning an ox that gores someone (Ex 21:28-32 and LH 250-52) and the law of *lex talionis* (the law of retribution) (Ex 21:23-25 and LH 196-97, 229-32) have the strongest parallels. Yet even these laws differ in some key details.

While scholars have long discussed the implications of the overlap between the old covenant laws and ANE laws, most agree that these similarities result from a common legal tradition and a shared way of life in the ancient Near East. Differences between the various ANE law collections demonstrate that different nations adapted the legal tradition to their contexts. The old covenant laws reflect this larger cultural legal tradition but also demonstrate numerous unique features.

One of the major discussions surrounding the ANE laws is the manner in which they functioned in the everyday lives of the citizens. Scholars typically point to thousands of ANE legal documents that do not reference any official legal collection. Such a phenomenon has led many scholars to conclude that these legal collections served an educational function in the scribal schools. In the case of the Laws of Hammurabi, the prologue and epilogue indicate that it functioned as royal propaganda since Hammurabi highlighted his justice before his people and the gods.

The old covenant laws—with their covenantal context—differ from the ANE laws at this point. Later biblical books, especially the Prophets, indicate that Yahweh expected Israel to obey his covenant stipulations (Is 5:24; Jer 11:2-10; Ezek 16:59). In fact, the Hebrew Bible connects Israel's exile to their failure to obey the old covenant laws (2 Kings 17:13-19; 2 Chron 36:21). Although

---

[14]For an extensive discussion of common laws, see Samuel Greengus, "Law," in vol. 4 of *Anchor Bible Dictionary*, ed. David Noel Freedman (New York: Doubleday, 1992), 245-51.

the old covenant laws highlighted Yahweh's wisdom (and thus functioned in a manner similar to LH), they also functioned as the means by which Israel demonstrated their faithfulness to him. They were not merely royal propaganda or scribal fodder.

THE OLD COVENANT AND THE REST OF THE HEBREW BIBLE

Since the old covenant contains the laws by which the Israelites were to govern themselves in the Promised Land, it plays a significant role in the story after Israel leaves Sinai and enters the Promised Land. For this reason, the authors of the Hebrew Bible's historical books often refer to this covenant as they tell the story of Israel's conquest of the land (Joshua), the nation's life inside the land (Judges–Kings), and the people's return to the land after their exile in Babylon (Ezra–Nehemiah). Additionally, the prophets constantly exhort the people to obey this covenant so that the people might avoid the judgment that Yahweh promised to bring upon them for covenant disobedience. Thus, this covenant provides an important backdrop for the rest of the Hebrew Bible. Without a knowledge of this covenant, one cannot interpret the rest of the Hebrew Bible properly.

A clear understanding of the old covenant laws provides a foundation for addressing the important question, what do I, as a Christian, do with all these laws? It is to this question we now turn, but since interpreters have answered this question in a variety of ways, we are going to look at some common answers Christians give.

TWO

WHAT ARE MY OPTIONS?

APPROACHES TO THE OLD COVENANT LAWS

One of my least favorite things in life is making a major purchase. As much as I hate spending money, I hate even more dealing with the myriad of buying options. I recently had to purchase a vehicle, so I decided to browse the local listings on Craigslist. After looking for an hour, I discovered that I had only looked at the cars that had been posted that day (and I do not live in a major metropolis). Needless to say, I did not look much longer because the options overwhelmed me. What if I bought a vehicle and someone listed a better one the next day? How do I know which vehicle is the best deal? What happens if I buy a lemon? These are the types of questions that were running through my mind and causing my blood pressure to rise.

I know that having options is much better than not having them. If I only had two cars to choose from on Craigslist, I would probably pay more than I should for a vehicle. I would also lose the possibility of getting the exact things I want in a vehicle. When I have more choices, I have a higher chance of finding something that fits my tastes. In the end, even though I hate sorting through all the options, I endure it because I know multiple options benefit me when I make my purchase.

Many believers feel the same way when it comes to interpretive options. They strongly dislike sorting through all the views and figuring out which one best explains the biblical passage or theological issue at hand. Truth be told, many believers do not see the benefit of exploring interpretive options and simply refuse to make the effort. These believers regard controversial discussions as scholarly nonsense that has no impact on their daily lives. Yet, as important as it is to have options when we make major purchases in life, an awareness of our options is even more important when it comes to interpreting the Bible. Whenever we approach a topic that has generated much discussion and a variety of interpretations, we must be aware of all the options on the table. Engaging the various interpretations gives us categories with which we can approach the topic, highlights the key issues in the discussion, and helps us refine (or maybe reject) our own view. When we purchase vehicles, the amount of knowledge we have about automobiles and how they work corresponds directly with our chances of being skunked by a shrewd salesman. A person who does not know what the oil pan looks like will have a hard time checking for engine leaks. Likewise, our knowledge of key issues keeps us from, at worst, being led astray and, at best, being ignorant of the strengths and weaknesses of our position.

For these reasons, we are now going to explore some common views regarding the role of the old covenant laws in the life of the Christian. In my introduction, I outlined several difficult issues related to the modern Christian's interaction with the laws. Each of the views I outline in this chapter represents an attempt to determine systematically and consistently which laws directly apply to Christians and which laws do not. In other words, each approach is dealing with the difficult questions we have already discussed, albeit some better than others.

THE COMMON GROUND

Before discussing the different views, let's begin with the positive. When it comes to their interpretation of the laws, adherents of the major views share some common ground. First, proponents of all the views affirm that the old covenant laws do not serve as the basis for a person's salvation. With Paul, believers have long concluded "that one is justified by faith apart from works of the law" (Rom 3:28). As I will demonstrate later in this book, the old covenant did not address Israel's "spiritual salvation." On the contrary, the covenant concerns Israel's role as God's conduit of blessings among the nations.

Second, each view has some adherents who derive principles from the old covenant laws in order to apply them to modern believers. For example, a variety of interpreters argue that the old covenant gleaning laws teach a principle of God's care for the poor and disenfranchised. As confirmation, these interpreters highlight other biblical authors who underscore this principle (i.e., the Prophets). Therefore, modern believers should also demonstrate care for the poor and disenfranchised. The application of this principle looks much different for modern believers than it did in ancient Israel. I could give many other examples, but the principle approach usually assumes that Christians are not required to obey directly the law(s) under consideration.

A third area of common ground among the different views is the affirmation that the old covenant laws reflect God's character. For example, by reading the old covenant laws, we see God's concern for the poor and disenfranchised. We also learn that he is a holy God who cares about the holiness of his people, a God who is jealous for the affections of his people, a just God who punishes sin and disobedience, a merciful God who provides a means by which his people can approach him, an invisible God who refuses to be represented by images, and the sovereign king who rules over all the nations.

So where lies the great divide? The dividing point for the three views I will discuss is the question of which old covenant laws modern Christians are under. Paul often uses the language of being "under the law" to refer to the law's authority over a person or group. To use a modern analogy, we might use the phrase "under the jurisdiction of the law." Most of us understand the significance of jurisdiction when it comes to law enforcement. For example, my family and I live a significant distance from our extended family. Therefore, we often take long road trips during the summers and holiday seasons. As the son of a truck driver, I have learned a few driving tricks over the years. One thing my dad always preached to me was that whenever you drive through a small town, you have to drive the speed limit. Why? Small-town cops are more likely to give you a speeding ticket than the highway patrol. Generally speaking, the highway patrol will allow cars to drive up to ten miles per hour over the speed limit. However, whenever you enter a small town, you enter the jurisdiction of the city police, who are more likely to give you a ticket for driving five miles per hour over the speed limit. The moral of the story is this: once you leave the jurisdiction of a small town, the city police cannot give you a ticket. For many people, this translates into pushing the gas pedal a little closer to the floor. This idea of jurisdiction helps us understand the differences in the various Christian views of the old covenant laws. Each view has a different understanding of the old covenant's jurisdiction in the believer's life.

Historically, many theologians have delineated three uses of the old covenant laws.[1] The first use of the law is to restrain sin. In this regard, the law was supposed to function like a corral for Israel to keep their actions in check. The second use of the law is to condemn the sinner. In other words, it serves as a mirror that highlights the sinner's depravity and guilt before a holy God. Paul's discussion of the law's purpose in Galatians 3:21-25 serves as a good example of the first two uses of the law. The third use of the law is as a guide for the Christian's life. This third and final use is the dividing line for the various Christian approaches. As you will see, none of the views argues that Christians are under the jurisdiction of all the old covenant laws. So, which old covenant laws should modern Christians use as moral guidance for their lives? Each of the following views answers this question in a different manner. In what follows, I introduce the three most common positions among contemporary Christians. For each approach, I offer a brief overview, key biblical support, and the view's strengths and weaknesses.

MORAL LAW CHRISTIANS

What I will term "Moral Law Christians" affirm that Christians remain under the authority of some old covenant laws.[2] Adherents of this view divide the old covenant laws into three major categories: (1) moral laws,

---

[1] For two brief historical sketches of Christian approaches to the old covenant laws (and the ethical requirements of the Old Testament in general), see Christopher J. H. Wright, *Old Testament Ethics for the People of God* (Downers Grove, IL: InterVarsity Press, 2004), 387-414, and Peter T. Vogt, *Interpreting the Pentateuch: An Exegetical Handbook* (Grand Rapids: Kregel, 2009), 32-42. For a more extensive treatment of the various Christian approaches to the old covenant laws, see Wayne G. Strickland, ed., *Five Views on Law and Gospel* (Grand Rapids: Zondervan, 1996). For a recent overview of the broader theological systems that inform these views, see Peter J. Gentry and Stephen J. Wellum, *Kingdom Through Covenant: A Biblical-Theological Understanding of the Covenants* (Wheaton, IL: Crossway, 2012), 39-80.

[2] This view is typically held by—though not limited to—those who espouse covenant theology. For an introduction to covenant theology, see Michael S. Horton, *God of Promise: Introducing Covenant Theology* (Grand Rapids: Baker, 2006).

(2) ceremonial laws, and (3) civil laws. Moral laws reflect the eternal character of God and thus set forth his standard of right and wrong for all people at all times. Examples of moral laws are the prohibitions against murder, incest, theft, bestiality, homosexuality, and adultery. Ceremonial laws (or cultic laws) deal with the ritual purity of the Israelites before God and their worship of God. Included in these laws are the laws concerning leprosy, eunuchs, dead bodies, skin diseases, unclean foods, sacrifices, and offerings. Civil laws, sometimes called judicial laws, served an important function in the governing of Israelite society. These laws outline the appropriate conduct of the Israelites as they lived as a nation under the rule of God (i.e., a theocracy) and include laws related to kings, prophets, capital punishment, land ownership, debts, and harvesting.

Once adherents of this view classify the various laws, they take an additional step and argue that Christians (and the entire world) must keep the moral laws but not the ceremonial and civil laws. Christ's life and work on the cross provides the primary basis for their dismissal of the ceremonial and civil laws. Jesus fulfilled these types of laws, so Christians are no longer under their authority. They use numerous passages to support their dismissal of these laws (Rom 6:14-15; 7:4-6; 10:4; Gal 3:25; 5:18; Eph 2:14-15; Col 2:14). For example, Paul writes the following in Colossians 2:14: ". . . by canceling the record of debt that stood against us with its legal demands. This he set aside, nailing it to the cross." Paul teases out the full implications of this reality a few verses later when he writes, "These ["a festival or a new moon or a Sabbath" in v. 16] are a shadow of the things to come, but the substance belongs to Christ" (Col 2:17). Since the church now lives under the "substance" of Christ's work, we no longer live in the shadows of the civil and ceremonial laws (cf. Heb 10:1).

All the passages I listed in the previous paragraph teach that Christians are not under the law in general (i.e., the passages do not distinguish between the three types of laws). In their interpretation of these passages, Moral Law Christians limit the law's referents to the civil and ceremonial laws (as opposed to the entire law). For support of their dismissal of the ceremonial laws, they highlight several New Testament examples that specifically teach the dismissal of the ceremonial laws. Jesus himself dismissed the categories of clean and unclean foods in his debate with the religious leaders over ritual defilement (Mt 15:1-20; Mk 7:1-23 [esp. v. 19]). In a similar manner, God used the cleanliness of all foods to convince Peter that the Gentiles were clean, thus leading to the inclusion of Gentiles in the church (Acts 10). Also, Jesus' reference to his body as the temple undermines the centrality of the temple in Israel's worship (Jn 2:19-21). Finally, Hebrews 9–10 provides some of the clearest statements of Christ's elimination of the old covenant sacrificial system.

On a practical level, when Christ instituted his church with members from all tribes and nations, he effectively eliminated the civil laws.[3] Since the church is not a geopolitical entity, the church cannot live under the old covenant civil laws. Even the Jews who lived during the time of the New Testament could not obey many of the civil laws, because they were under Roman domination. To be clear, Moral Law Christians do not use this practical reasoning as their main evidence for their position; their main evidence is Christ's fulfillment of the old covenant and the resultant change in God's redemptive purposes.

Now that I have shown why Moral Law Christians do not submit to the civil and ceremonial laws, let's look at the positive side of their argument. They believe that Christians are under the old covenant moral laws because the New Testament demonstrates a continued relevance of these laws. The New Testament writers repeat nine of the Ten Commandments (they do not repeat the Sabbath) as normative for believers, and Paul affirms the inherent goodness of the old covenant laws (Rom 7:12). Additionally, Moral Law Christians contend that many old covenant laws still apply to all people today because they are timeless commands.

Although the Bible does not explicitly outline these three divisions, Moral Law Christians support their divisions with a few key passages. First, they argue from the old covenant itself that God considered the actions of other nations wrong. For example, Leviticus 18:1-3 contains Moses' exhortation for the people of Israel not to live as the Egyptians and Canaanites. This implicit critique of these other nations demonstrates that their sexual practices (the topic of Lev 18) violated the moral law of God.

---

[3]Theonomists argue that the moral *and* civil laws are still in effect. For an overview of this position, see Greg L. Bahnsen, "The Theonomic Reformed Approach to Law and Gospel," in *Five Views on Law and Gospel*, ed. Wayne G. Strickland (Grand Rapids: Zondervan, 1996). For a fuller treatment, see Bahnsen, *By This Standard: The Authority of God's Law Today* (Powder Springs, GA: American Vision, 2008).

Second, adherents of this view cite the example of Jesus, who made distinctions between the old covenant laws on at least two occasions. In Matthew 23:23 Jesus critiques the scribes and Pharisees for neglecting "the weightier matters of the law." Jesus' reference to "the weightier matters" demonstrates that he made distinctions in the various laws. The second example some Moral Law Christians use is when Jesus delineates the greatest and second-greatest commandments (Mt 22:36-40; Mk 12:28-34; Lk 10:25-28). Matthew and Mark both record Jesus' conversation with a lawyer that began with the lawyer asking Jesus to identify the greatest (or most important) commandment. Jesus did not rebuke the lawyer but answered him with a quotation of Deuteronomy 6:4-5 and Leviticus 19:18. This conversation between Jesus and the lawyer provides further confirmation that both Jesus and at least some first-century Jews made distinctions between the various laws.

The major strength of this view is that it attempts to demonstrate how many of the laws given to Israel have a universal application. Indeed, the New Testament authors repeat many of the old covenant laws and apply them to an audience broader than Israel (e.g., Rom 13:8-10; Eph 6:2-3). In a world that dismisses the Hebrew Bible as outdated and irrelevant, Moral Law Christians emphasize its moral authority in the lives of modern Christians and modern societies.

The major weakness of this view is that proponents are open to the charge of picking and choosing the laws that best fit their own system (i.e., who determines which law is a moral law?), since their categories do not appear in Scripture and, more importantly, the laws are not arranged according to these divisions. For example, Walter Kaiser, a proponent of this position, identifies the Ten Commandments and Leviticus 18–19 as two passages that teach God's moral law.[4] Yet most Moral Law Christians identify several laws in Leviticus 19 as nonmoral laws. In fact, this one chapter contains all three types of law intermingled.[5] Critiquing these categories, Elmer Martens writes concerning Leviticus 19: "In this single speech the stipulations about refraining from image-making (cult

---

[4]Walter Kaiser, "The Law as God's Guidance for the Promotion of Holiness," in *Five Views on Law and Gospel*, ed. Wayne G. Strickland (Grand Rapids: Zondervan, 1996), 198.

[5]Willem A. VanGemeren ("The Law Is the Perfection of Righteousness in Jesus Christ," in *Five Views on Law and Gospel*, ed. Wayne G. Strickland [Grand Rapids: Zondervan, 1996], 31), another Moral Law Christian, acknowledges the "intertwined" nature of these laws in Ex 22.

[ceremonial]), insisting on truth-telling (moral), and prescribing compassionate treatment for aliens (civil) tumble about in chaotic confusion."[6] Furthermore, some laws do not easily fit into just one of the divisions. For example, is the prohibition against putting tattoo marks on oneself (Lev 19:28) a moral law or a ceremonial law? Or what about the command to rise before the elderly (Lev 19:32)?

Second, Jesus' reference to "the weightier matters of the law" (Mt 23:23) is not the same as the divisions that Moral Law Christians propose because Jesus did not divide the laws in order to delineate which laws had eternal relevance and which laws were temporary. After rebuking the Pharisees for neglecting "the weightier matters of the law," he states, "These you ought to have done, without neglecting the others" (Mt 23:23). Jesus rebuked them for only practicing some of the laws; he expected the Pharisees to keep *all* the laws. Consequently, the distinctions Jesus and his fellow Jews drew are not the same as the distinctions that Moral Law Christians draw.

In his critique of Moral Law Christians, Peter Vogt underscores how these divisions do not fit with how the ancient world interpreted reality. He writes, "In the ancient Near East, and in Israel, all of life was seen to have religious significance. . . . It is hard, then, to draw distinctions that would have been foreign to the mind of the original audience."[7] Vogt's criticism gets to the heart of the primary criticism directed toward this view: the lack of biblical evidence for their proposed divisions.

TEN COMMANDMENTS CHRISTIANS

Next, what I will term "Ten Commandments Christians" are very similar to the Moral Law Christians in that they argue that Christians are under the authority of the old covenant moral laws. These views are so similar that we could classify Ten Commandments Christians as a subset of Moral Law Christians. But Ten Commandments Christians separate themselves from Moral Law Christians by limiting the moral law to the Ten Commandments and their repetition/explication in later passages within the old covenant (e.g., Moses repeats or further explains the Sabbath command of Ex 20:8-11 in Ex 23:12; 31:12-17; 34:21; 35:2-3; etc.). So instead of trying

---

[6]Elmer Martens, "How Is the Christian to Construe Old Testament Law," *Bulletin for Biblical Research* 12, no. 2 (2002): 201.
[7]Vogt, *Interpreting the Pentateuch*, 44.

to decide which laws are moral laws throughout the books of Exodus–Deuteronomy, these Christians simply highlight the Ten Commandments as their basic guide to life. On a popular level, this view is probably the most prevalent.

The key support for this interpretation of the laws is the importance placed on the Ten Commandments throughout the Bible. The Ten Commandments are the only laws God gave directly to Israel (Ex 20:1; cf. 20:18-19), written with the finger of God (Ex 32:16) and placed in the ark of the covenant (1 Kings 8:9). They are repeated twice to the Israelites before they enter the Promised Land (Ex 20 and Deut 5) and are considered an adequate summary of the entire old covenant (Deut 4:13). Jesus and Paul both list many of the Ten Commandments as examples of righteous actions before God (Mt 19:18; Mk 10:19; Rom 13:9-10). When something is consistently given this much emphasis, it must be important to God and therefore should be important to Christians.

As for their dismissal of the other old covenant laws, Ten Commandments Christians use the same scriptures and arguments that Moral Law Christians use. Because of Jesus' work and his consequent institution of the new covenant, God's redemptive purposes have shifted. This shift in God's redemptive plan means that the civil and ceremonial laws are no longer operative in the Christian community.

The major strength of this view is that it properly recognizes the Hebrew Bible's emphasis on the Ten Commandments. Second, this position avoids much of the subjectivity that comes when one extends the moral laws to other old covenant laws. The authors of the Hebrew Bible consistently treat the Ten Commandments as a package, and by following their lead, Ten Commandments Christians avoid the charge of picking and choosing laws that best fit their fancy. Finally, like Moral Law Christians, Ten Commandments Christians generally emphasize the continued importance and relevance of the Hebrew Bible for modern believers. For them, the Hebrew Bible is Christian Scripture.

The primary weakness of this view is demonstrated in how proponents deal with the law concerning the Sabbath day. Critics often highlight the New Testament passages that teach that Christians are no longer required to keep the Sabbath (Rom 14:5-8; Col 2:16-17). If Christians are not under the Sabbath law, then at least one of the Ten Commandments is not part of the moral law of God, and the Ten Commandments Christian no longer has a neat package of laws. I devote an entire chapter to the Ten Commandments, so we will return to this point on a deeper level in chapter five.

A second weakness pertains to the New Testament's use of the Ten Commandments. While it is true that the New Testament repeats nine of the ten commands, a closer examination reveals some intriguing facts. First, the New Testament authors only quote the fifth through tenth commandments verbatim. They teach the same concepts contained in the first three commandments, but they do not quote them directly. Second, the New Testament authors never refer to the Ten Commandments as a unit and never quote all of them together in the same passage. Furthermore, when Jesus quotes some of them in his conversation with the rich young ruler (Mt 19:16-22; Mk 10:17-22), he adds another command in both accounts (Mt 19:19 adds Lev 19:18; Mk 10:19 adds "Do not defraud"). Therefore, even though the authors of the Hebrew Bible typically treat the Ten Commandments as a package, the New Testament authors do not follow suit. The New Testament usage demonstrates that Jesus and the New Testament authors did not treat the Ten Commandments as a self-contained unit and sometimes (in the case of Jesus) included other laws in their partial lists of the Ten Commandments.

NO-OLD-LAW CHRISTIANS

The third and final Christian approach to the role of the old covenant laws in believers' lives—the approach I will term "No-Old-Law Christians"— argues that believers are not under the authority of the old covenant laws in any way. Proponents of this approach disagree with the divisions of the Moral Law Christians and the continuing authority given to the Ten Commandments by Ten Commandments Christians. The result is an affirmation that the old covenant ended with Christ's death and resurrection, thus freeing Christians from the obligation to obey the old covenant laws. No-Old-Law Christians do not affirm that Christians are free to do whatever they wish, because the Bible (especially the New Testament) contains many clear guidelines on how Christians should live their lives.

Proponents of this view find their key support in several New Testament passages that teach either that believers are no longer under the law or that Christ abolished the law on the cross (Rom 6:14-15; 7:4-6; 10:4; Gal 3:24-25;

5:18; Eph 2:14-15; Col 2:14). Ephesians 2:14-15 serves as a good example. These verses read, "For he himself is our peace, who has made us both one and has broken down in his flesh the dividing wall of hostility by abolishing the law of commandments expressed in ordinances, that he might create in himself one new man in place of the two, so making peace." No-Old-Law Christians identify "the law of commandments expressed in ordinances" as all the old covenant laws. Attentive readers may have noticed that No-Old-Law Christians use the same verses that Moral Law and Ten Commandments Christians use to support the end of the civil and ceremonial laws. No-Old-Law Christians argue that these passages do not distinguish between law types and that the Bible consistently treats the old covenant laws as a unit. Therefore, we should not limit references to the Christian's freedom from the law to the civil and ceremonial aspects of the law.

Probably the greatest strength of this view is its clear distinctions between the old covenant and the new covenant. Proponents of this view see a clear break between the period of the old covenant and the period of the new covenant at the cross. These clear distinctions remove the pressure of having to decide which old covenant laws believers are still under. The entire old covenant ended at the cross because Christ fulfilled the law on the cross.

One of the most common charges against this position is antinomianism—that is, a refusal to live under any law. The critique usually goes something like this: "If the Ten Commandments are not God's moral law, then we are freeing Christians to live anyway they please. We need clear guidelines on how to live our lives as Christians." Critics also point to certain positive statements about the old covenant in the New Testament (Mt 5:17-19; Rom 7:12; 1 Tim 1:8) as well as passages where Jesus and Paul repeated portions of the old covenant laws (see above) as evidence against this view.

In addition to these general criticisms, some have offered other critiques toward specific variations of this view. Before addressing these other weaknesses, I will outline a couple of subdivisions of this view. Although proponents of this view generally agree on the points outlined in the above overview, there are some significant differences between two key groups within this view.

The first subgroup within this view equates the old covenant with the Hebrew Bible and therefore argues that since Christians are no longer under the old covenant, much of the Hebrew Bible does not directly relate to Christians.[8] Proponents of this view usually argue that the only old covenant laws that apply to Christians are the laws that the New Testament authors repeat. Since the New Testament represents the new covenant, it determines which old covenant laws the Christian should follow. In other words, believers should not murder because the New Testament commands such behavior, not because this command is one of the Ten Commandments. Since the Hebrew Bible was written during the time when Israel lived under the old covenant, it was written for those who were under the old covenant, not those of us who are under the new covenant. Proponents argue that the Hebrew Bible does have continuing relevance to us as Christians, but a closer examination of how they use the Hebrew Bible reveals that this relevance is usually limited to the stories of Genesis 1–11 (typically called the Primeval History), moral lessons we can learn from the characters in the Hebrew Bible, and specific prophecies.[9] In the end, the Hebrew Bible equals the old covenant, stands subservient to the New Testament, and carries very little moral authority for modern believers.

The major weakness of the "old covenant = Hebrew Bible" view is its lack of respect for the Hebrew Bible as *Christian Scripture*. Many of the New Testament books (the best example is the book of Hebrews) make absolutely no sense if the ultimate message of the Hebrew Bible is "keep the law." The author of Hebrews argues for the superiority of Jesus and the new covenant by using the Hebrew Bible itself as his primary support (one only needs to

---

[8]This view is characteristic of classical dispensationalism. For example, C. I. Scofield (*The Scofield Reference Bible* [New York: Oxford University, 1945], 990), in his introduction to the Gospels, writes, "The Gospels do not unfold the doctrine of the Church. . . . The Gospels present a group of Jewish disciples, associated on earth with a Messiah in humiliation; the Epistles a Church which is the body of Christ in glory." For Scofield and other classic dispensationalists, the Old Testament and even the Gospels were indirectly related to the church whereas the Epistles were directly related to the church. Although few modern dispensationalists (Progressive Dispensationalists) would affirm Scofield's words, in my experience, their emphasis on the discontinuity of the various dispensations often results in some Christians—those unaware of the nuances of the position—viewing the Old Testament as synonymous with the old covenant. For an introduction to Dispensationalism, see Craig A. Blaising and Darrell L. Bock, *Progressive Dispensationalism* (Wheaton, IL: Victor, 1993).

[9]See John MacArthur's sermon archive (www.gty.org/resources/sermons) for an example of such imbalance toward the New Testament and selective use of the Old Testament. MacArthur, who refers to himself as a "leaky dispensationalist" (see www.gty.org/resources /questions/QA010/with-regard-to-dispensationalism-where-exactly-do-you-stand), has preached on every verse in the NT, but has only preached out of sixteen OT books. Of these sixteen OT books, he has preached fewer than five sermons from twelve of them.

count the number of citations from the Hebrew Bible in Hebrews). The New Testament writers saw great continuity between the message of the Hebrew Bible and that of the new covenant. To say that the Hebrew Bible is the same as the old covenant is to miss the ultimate hope (and dare I say, central message) of the Hebrew Bible, which centers on the hope of God's future restoration by means of his coming king, a topic we will return to later.

The second subgroup of No-Old-Law Christians consists of those who identify a dichotomy between law and gospel throughout the Bible.[10] Adherents of this position argue not only that the laws of the old covenant are antithetical to the gospel of grace and forgiveness in Jesus, but also that all laws, including those given in the four Gospels, are antithetical to the gospel of Jesus Christ. This position results in a negative view toward law in general; law exists simply for convicting sinners of their sin.

The major weakness of this group of No-Old-Law Christians is the perceived overreaction against all laws or commands in the Bible. When Jeremiah, Paul, and other biblical authors present a negative appraisal of the old covenant's ability to produce righteousness (Jer 31:32; Rom 3:20; 4:15; 7:5), they typically connect this inability to the Israelites and not the laws themselves. Furthermore, when Paul and other New Testament writers make negative assessments of the law, they are referring to a specific group of laws—that is, the old covenant (remember our discussion of the law's referents). Therefore, it is inappropriate for us to take Paul's negative appraisal of the old covenant laws and apply them to all biblical (and even extrabiblical) laws.

MY OWN APPROACH

Now that we have overviewed the major interpretive options, I should put my cards on the table. My approach falls under the category of No-Old-Law Christians, but I distance myself from both of the subdivisions I just outlined. Thus, I am presenting a third subdivision of No-Old-Law Christians.[11] The following overview of my position is brief; I will expand upon

---

[10]Some strands of Lutheran theology hold this position. Modern Lutheran scholars often debate over the application of the third use of the law in the lives of Christians. For a modern survey of this issue, see Scott R. Murray, *Law, Life, and the Living God: The Third Use of the Law in Modern American Lutheranism* (St. Louis, MO: Concordia, 2002).

[11]My position has strong affinities with two recently proposed theological systems: (1) New Covenant Theology and (2) Progressive Covenantalism. While differences exist between the

many of the below affirmations as well as respond to common objections in a more in-depth manner later in this book.

I affirm that the old covenant was a temporary covenant God made with the nation of Israel for the purpose of setting them apart and using them to bless the other nations as his "kingdom of priests" (Ex 19:6). If Israel obeyed Yahweh's commands, he would bless them and use them as his instrument to bless the nations. Unfortunately, Israel repeatedly broke their covenant with Yahweh. Therefore, the old covenant highlighted Israel's sinfulness and led to a greater display of God's wrath against them. Israel's sin and God's corresponding judgment demonstrated to the Israelites (and us, as later readers) that the old covenant could not produce righteousness in Israel and that God would have to do a greater work to produce this required righteousness in his people.

This greater work came in the ministry, death, and resurrection of Jesus Christ, who fulfilled and thereby ended the old covenant and inaugurated the new covenant, a covenant that the authors of the Hebrew Bible foretold on numerous occasions. Christ's followers therefore are not under the old covenant laws but under the law of Christ. Although there is some overlap between the ethical requirements of both laws, the motivation and ability to obey differ significantly between the law of Christ and the old covenant. Under the new covenant, God transforms his people's hearts, blesses them unconditionally, and empowers them to live holy lives through his Spirit.

I like to think of the old covenant as a racecar running through the pages of the Hebrew Bible. Because of the nature of the covenant, the car's success was contingent on Israel's actions. The old covenant begins its race at Mount Sinai and almost immediately breaks down when the Israelites build the golden calf. Yahweh repairs the car by renewing the covenant with his people, but unfortunately the car never runs at full speed because Israel constantly rebels against Yahweh. In fact, the engine loses cylinder after cylinder throughout the Hebrew Bible. Finally, when God uses the Babylonians to judge his people, the engine drops to one cylinder and sputters along through captivity. When God brings the Israelites back to the land

---

two systems, their positions on the law are very similar. For an introduction to the former, see Tom Wells and Fred Zaspel, *New Covenant Theology* (Frederick, MD: New Covenant Media, 2002). For an introduction to the latter, see Stephen J. Wellum and Brent E. Parker, *Progressive Covenantalism: Charting a Course Between Dispensational and Covenant Theologies* (Nashville: B&H, 2016).

after their captivity, Ezra and Nehemiah institute religious reforms and Israel lives under foreign rulers, thus demonstrating that the car still has major engine damage. Finally, by the time Christ arrives, the car's engine barely works and the car is running on fumes. Through his work on the cross, Christ puts an end to the old covenant car and provides his people with a perfect car in the form of the new covenant.

When it comes to the other two subdivisions of No-Old-Law Christians, I disagree with both views and agree with the key weaknesses for each view that I outlined above. I affirm that the Hebrew Bible is *Christian Scripture* and that its message stands in continuity with the message of the New Testament. I also affirm that the laws were a good thing that God graciously gave his people for their good and his glory, even though they were not sufficient for producing righteousness in the people's lives.

To return to my opening illustration, you, like me when I was purchasing a vehicle, may be overwhelmed by this overview of the different approaches. I hope that this brief overview has helped you see some of the key issues involved in the interpretation of the old covenant laws. If you disagree with my approach, I invite you to continue reading. The rest of the book is not simply a defense of my own position but contains numerous tips on how to properly interpret and read these laws within the context of the biblical story, especially the Hebrew Bible. It is to this context that we now turn.

THREE

"IN THE BEGINNING," NOT "THOU SHALT NOT"

Have you ever started watching in the middle of a movie only to realize that you missed so much essential information you could never understand what is happening? If you were smart, you'd quit watching the movie and then watch it at a time when you could start from the beginning. Alternatively, maybe you are the person who starts watching a movie late, aware that you have missed some important scenes, but you are determined that you can "catch up" with the plot if you continue watching. Even though you may be able to understand what's happening, you are not going to understand the film at the level you would have if you had begun from the beginning.

Most people understand the importance of watching the whole movie in order to grasp its message. Unfortunately, many Christians do not recognize that this principle also applies to the Bible. If you start reading in the middle of the Bible without any reference to the larger story, chances are high that you're going to miss something. To understand a passage in the Bible, you must take the context of that passage seriously. The context of the passage begins with the verses and chapters immediately surrounding it but includes much more than that. The context of a biblical passage also includes the context of the book in which it is located and its place in the entire Bible. In other words, to understand a passage of Scripture, you must interpret the passage in light of these various levels of context.

Because this is one of the most important rules of interpretation, it serves as a good starting point for our discussion of the old covenant. In many discussions of the old covenant laws and their role in modern Christians' lives, we begin with Exodus 20 and forget that God gives the old covenant to the Israelites as part of a larger story. We can properly apply it to our lives only as we comprehend its role in the larger story. This is why I titled this chapter "'In the Beginning,' Not 'Thou Shalt Not.'" Before Israel arrives at the foot of Mount Sinai, sixty-eight chapters of the biblical story have taken place. These sixty-eight chapters and the chapters that follow Israel's departure from Mount Sinai provide the context for the old covenant. We can learn many things about the old covenant from its context, but before we evaluate this context, we must define the parameters of the biblical book within which we find the old covenant.

THE PENTATEUCH

Have you ever noticed that later biblical books do not mention Genesis, Exodus, Leviticus, Numbers, or Deuteronomy by name? Perhaps you have noticed, but have you ever wondered why these later authors do not mention these books? It is not because later biblical authors do not quote or allude to these first five books of the Bible. In fact, later biblical books regularly refer back to the events recorded in these foundational books. For instance, the Prophets and the Psalms are loaded with allusions to these books. Additionally, Jesus and the New Testament authors quote from them on numerous occasions.[1]

Commenting on the New Testament quotations of these five books, Gary Schnittjer writes, "The Five Books of Moses were the writings most read, most studied, and most quoted by the New Testament writers, and any and every practicing Judaic person at the turn of the era."[2] The minds of later biblical authors were so saturated with these early books that their writings dripped with the thoughts, themes, and words of Genesis–Deuteronomy.

---

[1]Barbara Aland et al., eds., *The Greek New Testament*, 4th rev. ed. (Stuttgart: United Bible Society, 1998), 888-89. The editors of the *Greek New Testament* identify twenty-one quotations from these books in Matthew's Gospel and another twenty-one quotations in Romans, and these numbers do not include allusions or verbal parallels.
[2]Gary Edward Schnittjer, *The Torah Story* (Grand Rapids: Zondervan, 2006), 9.

So to return to our question: Why do later biblical authors not mention these first five books by name? The answer is simple. They do not refer to them by name because they did not recognize these books as distinct books but as parts of a larger book. In other words, Genesis was not a biblical book in and of itself, but was part of a larger book, a book that included Genesis, Exodus, Leviticus, Numbers, and Deuteronomy. Therefore, when later biblical authors quote or allude to these five books, they often refer to the title of the single five-part book, which I have chosen to designate the Pentateuch.

This may not seem immediately relevant, but it's very important when it comes to interpreting the laws. Whenever we interpret a book of the Bible, our main goal should be to discover the author's intended meaning, and we discover this meaning by examining the numerous clues left for us in the book, one of which is the plot of the story (beginning, end, conflict, conflict resolution, etc.). To discover the plot of the story, we must first identify the beginning and the end of the story. We are then in a position to interpret the individual passages in light of the book. It therefore makes a significant difference in meaning whether we treat Exodus as a book in itself or as one part of a much larger work.

To demonstrate how important it is to determine the boundaries of the biblical book we are studying, let's take Leviticus as an example. Many Christians treat Leviticus as an isolated book with little to no regard for its surrounding books. When read in such a manner, it can be confusing for several reasons. First, the book begins with the following words: "The LORD called Moses and spoke to him from the tent of meeting, saying . . ." (Lev 1:1). After this initial statement, one immediately encounters the laws for offerings. If Leviticus is taken as a single book, this opening does not exactly provide a detailed setting like many other books in the Hebrew Bible, nor does it give the information we would expect in a book's introduction. Second, with the exception of a few chapters (chaps. 8–10 and 26), the book is dominated by laws, many of which relate to the priesthood and their tasks. If we read Leviticus in isolation, we do not know why Yahweh is giving these laws nor why Aaron and his sons serve as priests. For this information, we have to read the book of Exodus.

Now let us assume that God never intended for people to read the book of Leviticus as a single book but as part of a larger book that begins in

Genesis 1 and ends with Deuteronomy 34. If so, we have a much larger context by which to interpret the author's purpose for the laws in Leviticus. A couple of examples will suffice. First, the mention of Yahweh speaking to Moses from the tabernacle provides a link to the last chapter of Exodus, where Moses and the people finished the work of the tabernacle. When they finished, the cloud of God's glory filled the tabernacle, thus explaining why God speaks to Moses from the tabernacle. Leviticus 1:1 thus serves as a transition verse from the construction of the tabernacle to the laws concerning the offerings. Second, reading Leviticus as a continuation of Exodus enables us to identify the purpose of the laws in Leviticus because Exodus 19:3-6 records Yahweh's initiation of the old covenant with Israel. These laws are part of a specific covenant that Yahweh made with Israel for carrying out his redemptive plan in the world. Third, on a more specific level, Exodus 29 gives the instructions for the ordination of priests, and Leviticus 8 records the ordination. Not only does Exodus provide the background for the ordination of the priests, but it also gives the foundation for Yahweh's appointment of Aaron and his sons as priests.

The above discussion of Leviticus does not provide indispensable proof that Leviticus is not an isolated book. However, later biblical authors' references to this book provide the strongest support for treating the Pentateuch as a unity. There is a strong tradition throughout the Hebrew Bible (Ezra 7:6, 10; Neh 8:1-5, 14, 18; 9:3), the New Testament (Mk 12:26; Jn 5:46; Rom 3:21; Gal 4:21), and history (Jewish and Christian) of reading the first five books of the Bible as a single book, which serves as the foundation for the rest of the Bible. Figure 3.1 represents this book and its five-part division.

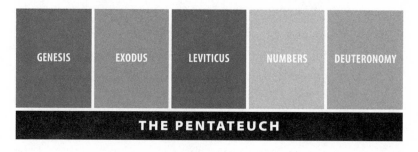

Figure 3.1. The Pentateuch's five-part division

In one regard, many of us are accustomed to thinking of books in this manner. A popular example is J. R. R. Tolkien's *The Lord of the Rings*. Although publishers and movie producers have tried to present this work as a trilogy, Tolkien's intention was to write one novel with six books grouped into three major parts: *The Fellowship of the Ring*, *The Two Towers*, and *The Return of the King*.[3] Tolkien himself regarded *The Lord of the Rings* as a single book and referred to it as "the sequel" to *The Hobbit*.[4] Just as people have treated Tolkien's three parts of *The Lord of the Rings* as separate books, Christians commonly treat the five books of the Pentateuch as independent books. Moses wrote his five books in the way that Tolkien wrote his six books: as a self-contained literary unit.

TITLES OF THE BOOK

Just as the old covenant has several titles, so also the Pentateuch has accumulated several titles. Like the old covenant's titles, each of these titles highlights a particular aspect of the book itself. The first title, "the Book of Moses," appears in 2 Chronicles 25:4, Ezra 6:18, Nehemiah 13:1, and Mark 12:26 and underscores the central figure in the book and the book's author.[5] On three occasions, Luke simply refers to the book as "Moses" (Lk 16:31; 24:27; Acts 15:21).

A second title is "the Book of the Law" (2 Kings 22:8, 11; Neh 8:3). Sometimes, a biblical author will add a prepositional phrase to the end of this title to emphasize the author. For example, 2 Kings 14:6 mentions "the Book of the Law of Moses" (emphasizing the human author; see also Neh 8:1), and 2 Chronicles 17:9 refers to the book as "the Book of the Law of LORD" (emphasizing the divine author; see also 2 Chron 34:14; Neh 8:18; 9:3).

PENTATEUCH

 A Greek term that means "fivefold book" and refers to the first five books of the Hebrew Bible.

---

[3]Douglas A. Anderson, "Note on the Text," in *The Lord of the Rings*, by J. R. R. Tolkien, 50th anniversary ed. (Boston: Houghton Mifflin, 2004), xi.

[4]Tolkien, "Foreword to the Second Edition," in *Lord of the Rings*, xxii-xxv.

[5]Since Moses is both the author of the book and a character within the book, readers should pay close attention to the context when I mention Moses.

A third title, the most common in academic circles, is the Pentateuch. This title, which does not appear in the Bible, was the name that the Valentinian Ptolemaeus gave to the book in AD 160.[6] The Greek word *pentateuchos* means "fivefold book" and emphasizes the unity of the five books. Since this is the standard designation for the book in academic circles, I have chosen to use it throughout this work. This title also alleviates some of the confusion that comes with the next title I will discuss.

A final title used for the book is the most common title used throughout the Bible: the Law (notice the capitalization). Since the Hebrew word for law is *torah*, many refer to the book as the Torah. As you will recall from chapter one, this word does not necessarily mean "law" in the strict sense of a commandment but sometimes refers to general instruction. When later biblical authors refer to the first book of the Bible as Torah, they have more in mind than the laws within the book; they are referring to the instruction of the book as a whole.

The situation becomes confusing when later biblical authors use "law" to refer to two different things. In such instances, my earlier discussion of referents (chapter one) becomes important because "law" has multiple referents in the Bible. The two most important referents of "law" for the purposes of this book are the old covenant and the Pentateuch. The New Testament authors, more so than the authors of the Hebrew Bible, commonly use "the law" (*nomos*) to designate the old covenant and the Pentateuch.[7] In order to help readers, I will distinguish between these two referents in this work. When I refer to "the law" (lowercase), I am speaking of the old covenant, but when I use "the Law" (uppercase), I am referring to the Pentateuch.[8] Therefore, when a biblical author uses the word *law*, we have to ask the question: To what is the author referring? The author could be referring to the old covenant, the Pentateuch, general

---

[6]John Sailhamer, *The Pentateuch as Narrative: A Biblical-Theological Commentary* (Grand Rapids: Zondervan, 1992), 1.

[7]Walter C. Kaiser Jr., "The Law as God's Gracious Guidance for the Promotion of Holiness," in *Five Views on Law and Gospel*, ed. Wayne G. Strickland (Grand Rapids: Zondervan, 1996), 192, identifies the Septuagint's translation of *torah* as *nomos* as "the root of all our problems of relating Law to Gospel."

[8]Brian S. Rosner, *Paul, Scripture and Ethics: A Study of 1 Corinthians 5–7* (Grand Rapids: Baker, 1999), 182, uses similar categories ("Law as Mosaic covenant" vs. "Law as Scripture"). In his most recent work, *Paul and the Law: Keeping the Commandments of God* (Downers Grove, IL: IVP Academic, 2013), 26-31, he uses different categories and notes several other scholars who hold a similar view.

instructions from the Lord, a principle, or even the entire Hebrew Bible (see Jn 10:34; 15:25; 1 Cor 14:21).[9]

THE LAW

 The law (lowercase) refers to the old covenant, while the Law (uppercase) refers to the Pentateuch.

For a good case study, let's evaluate Romans 3:21-22, a passage in which Paul refers to both "the law" and "the Law" in the same sentence. He writes, "But now the righteousness of God has been manifested apart from the law, although the Law and the Prophets bear witness to it—the righteousness of God through faith in Jesus Christ for all who believe. For there is no distinction." Notice how understanding the referents of the word *law* helps us interpret this passage. The first use of "the law" refers to the old covenant since it does not produce "the righteousness of God." However, the second use of "the Law" refers to the Pentateuch. We know this because Paul couples "the Law" with "the Prophets," a reference to the second major division of the Hebrew Bible. Paul also states that this "Law" (Pentateuch) bears witness to "the righteousness of God through faith in Jesus Christ." These verses not only highlight the different referents of the word *law*, but they also underscore the contrast between the ability of the old covenant to produce righteousness and the means of righteousness that the Pentateuch teaches, a key theme of the present book.

Fortunately, some translations help readers understand the distinction between the multiple referents of the word *law*. In Romans 3:21-22, both the ESV and the NKJV properly interpret these references for us by not capitalizing the first occurrence (old covenant) and capitalizing the second (Pentateuch). In contrast, the NASB capitalizes both occurrences of the word, thus leaving it up to the reader to interpret the proper referents.

Yet in some places the English translations do not make a distinction when there is a clear distinction. A case in point is Galatians 4:21. Here Paul writes, "Tell me, you who desire to be under the law, do you not listen to the law?" When read in the context of the whole book, Paul's

---

[9]Walter Bauer, Frederick W. Danker, William F. Arndt, and F. Wilbur Gingrich, *A Greek-English Lexicon of the New Testament and Other Early Christian Literature*, 3rd ed. (Chicago: University of Chicago Press, 2000), 677-78.

first mention of the law refers to "the law" (old covenant). Paul uses the phrase "under the law" to describe an obligation to obey the old covenant laws (see Gal 3:23-25; cf. Rom 3:19; 1 Cor 9:20-21; Gal 4:4-5; 5:1). In contrast, Paul's second mention of the law in Galatians 4:21 refers to "the Law" (Pentateuch) because he immediately lets his readers "listen to the law" and, in so doing, discusses Abraham, not the laws given at Mount Sinai. Once again, Paul uses "law" to refer to two different things in the same verse.

Interestingly, the same translations that interpret Romans 3:21-22 for their readers do not interpret this passage. This lack of consistency in the English translations means that readers of the Bible must be sensitive to how biblical authors use the word *law* in the context of each biblical book. Although somewhat confusing, understanding this difference between "the law" as old covenant and "the Law" as the Pentateuch is an important component of understanding the message of the Bible. Many discussions regarding Christians and the old covenant do not progress because Christians fail to make a distinction between the various referents of the word *law*. Unfortunately, such a lack of precision often occurs at high academic levels.[10] This distinction also helps us make sense of both the positive and the negative statements about the law in the New Testament. Generally speaking, when New Testament authors speak negatively regarding the law or teach that Christians are not under the law, they have "the law" (old covenant) in view. But when they speak about the promises of the Law, the patriarchs (Abraham, Isaac, and Jacob), the faith revealed in the Law, or the book as Scripture, they are referencing "the Law" (Pentateuch). I have illustrated this distinction in Figure 3.2.

---

[10]For example, Kaiser ("The Law as God's Gracious Guidance for the Promotion of Holiness," 178-79, 184, 186-87, 189), in arguing against Christians who do not make distinctions between the old covenant laws, writes: "For the same law of Moses that gave us the legal aspects of that revelation also contains the promise made to the patriarchs. Would this mean that it is impossible to separate out the promise since there is no internal principle noted in the text of the *tôrâ* that advises us how to do this?" (189). See also Mark F. Rooker, *Leviticus*, New American Commentary 3a (Nashville: B&H, 2000), 72.

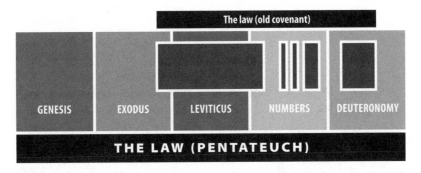

Figure 3.2. The "Law" and the "law"

THE STORYLINE OF THE PENTATEUCH

In the next two chapters, I discuss lessons we can learn when we interpret the old covenant in light of its literary context. My discussion centers on the parts of the Pentateuch that immediately precede and follow Israel's time at Mount Sinai. Understanding the old covenant involves more than just the immediate context of Sinai; a proper interpretation of it requires a knowledge of the broader context of the Pentateuch, so in this chapter's final section, I provide an overview of the storyline of the Pentateuch.

The Pentateuch, and consequently the entire Bible, begins with God's creation of the heavens and the earth (Gen 1:1). He blessed his creation and pronounced everything very good (Gen 1:31). He appointed human beings as his vice regents to rule over the rest of his creation, and he abundantly provided them a beautiful garden in which they were to worship him by cultivating the ground. He granted them the privilege of enjoying the fruit of all the trees in the garden except one, the tree of the knowledge of good and evil.

The idyllic conditions of Eden were short-lived because one day Adam and Eve succumbed to the temptation of the crafty serpent. They ate from the forbidden tree and brought punishment on themselves and a curse on the ground. God expelled them from the garden, the place of his presence, and guarded its entrance so they could not return.

Adam and Eve's rebellion against God did not stay with them; instead, it spread like a wildfire through subsequent generations. The early chapters of Genesis emphasize this rapid spread of sin and God's consequent response of judgment. In spite of humanity's unrelenting propensity toward rebellion, God provided grace and a solution to the problem through a man named Abram. God made a covenant with Abram, changing his name to Abraham and promising him a multitude of descendants, the land of Canaan, and blessings. These blessings were not Abraham's to hoard; no, God intended to use Abraham as a blessing to the nations.

Abraham eventually had a son named Isaac, and God passed the promises to him. Isaac transferred the promises to Jacob, whose name God changed to Israel. Jacob fathered twelve sons who served as the heads of twelve tribes of the nation. Jacob favored his son Joseph, and as a result, Joseph's brothers sold him into slavery. Joseph landed in the house of an important Egyptian leader, and eventually Joseph saved the Egyptians and his brothers from a terrible seven-year famine. Before his death, Jacob accompanied his family to Egypt.

The years passed, and Joseph's legacy faded. Another Pharaoh came to power who felt threatened by the Israelites, who were enjoying God's blessings in a foreign land. The Egyptian ruler attempted to slow the growth of the Israelites but ultimately failed because God's purposes prevailed. God raised up a mighty leader named Moses and commissioned him to deliver his people from Pharaoh's clutches. Pharaoh was unwilling to let the Israelites go, so God sent numerous plagues on his land. Finally, after Yahweh killed all the Egyptian firstborn males, Pharaoh released the Israelites.

After escaping their Egyptian captors, Israel journeyed across the wilderness to Mount Sinai. During their time at this mountain, Yahweh made a covenant with his people for the purposes of using them to restore his creation blessings to the world. Even while Yahweh was giving Israel the covenant stipulations, the people rebelled against him, thus casting doubt on Israel's ability to fulfill God's covenantal intentions for them.

Eventually, Israel left Mount Sinai and continued their trek toward the land God had promised to give Abraham's descendants. The journey was bumpy since Israel repeatedly rebelled and grumbled against Yahweh and his appointed leader, Moses. Yahweh judged the people on numerous occasions, but his most significant judgment fell upon the people at a place called Kadesh Barnea. Yahweh commanded the people to enter the Promised Land, but the people were afraid and consequently refused to enter the land God had promised to give them. As a result, God sentenced them to forty years of wilderness wandering, enough time for the rebellious generation to die.

At the end of the forty years, Moses brought the new generation to the edge of the Promised Land and gave them a series of speeches regarding their time in the land. These speeches are in the book of Deuteronomy and emphasize Israel's responsibility to demonstrate wholehearted allegiance to Yahweh and his covenant commands. He also emphasized that the people's prosperity and longevity in the land was contingent on their faithfulness to Yahweh. If they rebelled against Yahweh, they would encounter barrenness, defeat before enemies, and exile.

Sadly, Moses was very pessimistic about the people's future obedience and success in the land. Because of Israel's rebellious past and their present stubbornness, Moses predicted that the people would ultimately experience God's judgment and expulsion from the land. Thankfully, Moses did not leave the people without some hope. He prophesied that one day God would transform their hearts, return them to their land, and restore his blessings to them.

The Pentateuch ends with the death of Moses outside the Promised Land. Graciously, God allowed Moses to view the Promised Land from a mountain on the east side of the Jordan River. Before passing away, Moses appointed Joshua as the nation's next leader. The book ends with Moses' eulogy, which informs readers of his incomparable status as a prophet of Yahweh. Israel's first leader was gone, and the future looked both promising (God would give them the land) and bleak (Moses predicted their rebellion) for the nation.

FOUR

THE REST OF THE STORY (PART 1)

ISRAEL AT SINAI

My wife and I tell stories in completely different ways. If you were to ask us to tell you a story about any event in our lives, chances are very high that you would walk away wondering if we were talking about the same event. Our storytelling differences are particularly evident when we tell people how we met and fell in love. I usually give a bare-bones version of the story because several parts of the story embarrass me. My wife usually listens, laughing on the inside, and then tells "the rest of the story." Perhaps you have experienced this in your own life. You may have found yourself in a situation where you had to adjure the storyteller to tell "the rest of the story." Paul Harvey became an American icon by telling "The Rest of the Story" about countless historical events, institutions, and figures. Harvey frequently told unfamiliar or long-forgotten aspects of familiar stories. Such is our task in the next two chapters.

At the end of the previous chapter, I gave an overview of the storyline of the Pentateuch. In this and the next chapter, we are going to ask the following question: How does the storyline of the Pentateuch inform our understanding of the purpose and function of the old covenant? Too often, we base our understanding of the old covenant on the laws themselves, forgetting the larger story within which Yahweh gave this covenant. The larger story teaches us some important things about the old covenant, things that help us understand the old covenant laws. In this chapter I will discuss some things that took place while Israel was at Sinai. In chapter five I will zoom out further and discuss Israel's journey to and from Sinai.

ARRIVAL AT SINAI

When considering the old covenant's context, the best place to start is at a critical juncture in the story of the Pentateuch: Israel's arrival at Mount Sinai in Exodus 19. This chapter begins by updating us on the amount of time that had passed between Israel's deliverance from the Egyptians and their arrival at the base of the mountain: three months (Ex 19:1). During this three-month trek from the Red Sea to Mount Sinai, the Lord met the people's complaints with provision (Ex 15:22–17:7) and gave them victory over their attackers (Ex 17:8-16).

Once they arrive at Sinai, the people encamp at the base of the mountain, and Yahweh calls Moses up the mountain. Moses actually makes three trips up and down the mountain in chapter 19 (trip one: vv. 3-7; trip two: vv. 8-14; trip three: vv. 20-25) and one trip in chapter 20 (v. 21). Of these trips, Moses' first ascent is the most important for understanding the nature and function of the old covenant. As Moses makes his first trek up the mountain, Yahweh gives him a message for the people of Israel. Exodus 19:4-6a reads as follows: "You yourselves have seen what I did to the Egyptians, and how I bore you on eagles' wings and brought you to myself. Now therefore, if you will indeed obey my voice and keep my covenant, you shall be my treasured possession among all peoples, for all the earth is mine; and you shall be to me a kingdom of priests and a holy nation."

These verses provide several essential elements for understanding the role of the old covenant. First, Yahweh reminds the people of his gracious actions on their behalf using the analogy of an eagle carrying its young on its wings. Yahweh had brought Israel out of Egypt to the mountain just as he had promised Moses (Ex 3:12). Here Yahweh situates the giving of the old covenant within the larger story of the Pentateuch. Yahweh's reference to the exodus reminds us that God's relationship with Israel did not begin at Sinai. Furthermore, his reference to Israel as "the house of Jacob, and . . . the people of Israel" (Ex 19:3) reminds us of his covenant promises that were passed from Abraham to Isaac to Jacob. Second, the covenant that

Yahweh mentions in verse 5 refers to the covenant that he is about to make with the people of Israel. Thus, these three verses are an introduction to this covenant. Third, notice the "if-then" language in these verses. The Lord makes it clear to Israel that the wonderful benefits promised in verses 5b and 6a hinge on their obedience to the words of this covenant.

The making of this covenant with Israel reminds us of another important covenant Yahweh made earlier in Genesis: his covenant with Abraham (Gen 12, 15, 17).[1] God's covenant with Abraham has a key similarity with and a key difference from the Sinai covenant. The key similarity relates to Yahweh's choice of Israel as his people. In the Abrahamic covenant, God promised Abraham several things: blessing, land, and offspring. In a few key locations, God's promise of an offspring to Abraham is an individual descendant (Gen 15:4; 17:19; 18:10). However, in other places God promises Abraham that he would make his offspring like the stars of the sky and the dust of the earth (Gen 13:16; 15:5; 22:17). Israel's time in Egypt provides evidence that God fulfilled his promise to give Abraham numerous descendants. God's choice of Israel was the result of his faithfulness to his promises to Abraham, Isaac, and Jacob (Ex 2:24; 32:13; Deut 9:5).

In spite of this similarity, there is a major difference between these two covenants. Traditionally, scholars have underscored this difference by identifying the Abrahamic covenant as an unconditional (or unilateral) covenant and the old covenant as a conditional (or bilateral) covenant. However, some scholars have critiqued such distinctions.[2] Regardless of the language used to describe the covenants, the biblical text evidences several key differences between the Abrahamic covenant and the old covenant. The covenant ratification ceremonies associated with both covenants

---

[1] Some scholars (e.g., T. Desmond Alexander, *From Paradise to Promised Land: An Introduction to the Pentateuch*, 3rd ed. [Grand Rapids: Baker, 2012], 176-79; and Paul R. Williamson, *Sealed with an Oath: Covenants in God's Unfolding Purpose* [Downers Grove, IL: InterVarsity Press, 2012], 84-91) have proposed that Yahweh made two covenants with Abraham, an unconditional covenant in Genesis 15 and a conditional covenant in Genesis 17. The major weakness of such a proposal is the lack of evidence in later biblical texts, none of which refer to multiple covenants with Abraham (e.g., Ex 2:24; 6:3-4; Ps 105:9; Neh 9:8; Acts 3:25). For a critique of the two-covenant position, see Peter J. Gentry and Stephen J. Wellum, *Kingdom Through Covenant: A Biblical-Theological Understanding of the Covenants* (Wheaton, IL: Crossway, 2012), 263-80, and Jeffrey J. Niehaus, "God's Covenant with Abraham," *Journal of the Evangelical Theological Society* 56, no. 2 (2013): 249-71.

[2] Gentry and Wellum, *Kingdom Through Covenant*, 608-11, and Niehaus, "God's Covenant with Abraham," 260-71.

highlight the greatest distinction between them. When Yahweh ratified his covenant with Abraham (Gen 15:1-21), Yahweh made a "smoking fire pot and a flaming torch" pass between the animal pieces Abraham had laid out. These two objects represented Yahweh's presence, and Yahweh's passing through the animal pieces was a type of self-curse for covenant failure (cf. Jer 34:18-19). In other words, Yahweh promised to fulfill his promises to Abraham. In contrast, the people play an active role in the old covenant's ratification ceremony as they promise twice (Ex 24:3, 7; cf. Ex 19:8) that they will do all that Yahweh commanded. Moses sprinkles the people with blood as a reminder of their covenant obligations.[3] Thus, the fulfillment of the old covenant was contingent on the people's obedience to Yahweh's commands. The New Testament confirms this contrast by referring to the Abrahamic covenant as a promise that contrasts with the law (old covenant) (Rom 4:13-25; Eph 2:12-16; Heb 7:6; 8:7-8).

Since Israel's blessings were contingent on their obedience (Ex 19:5), what blessings would Israel receive if they obeyed? Verses 5b and 6a outline three things God would do for Israel if they obeyed the covenant he was about to make with them: (1) they would be a treasured possession to God, (2) they would be a kingdom of priests, and (3) they would be a holy nation.

Although Yahweh later (Ex 23:22-31; Lev 26; Deut 28) promises Israel physical blessings for covenant obedience, here the covenant blessings relate to who Israel would become before Yahweh and their role among the nations of the world. The first promise is that Israel would be his "treasured possession." The phrase "treasured possession" (*sǝgullâ*) refers to the possessions of a king (cf. 1 Chron 29:3). In some regard, Yahweh had already demonstrated that Israel was his treasured possession by judging the Egyptians and delivering them from bondage (v. 4). Yahweh, the ruler of the earth, had chosen Israel from all the nations of the world to be his prized possession. Yahweh's faithfulness to Israel throughout the Hebrew Bible despite their persistent rebellion reveals Yahweh's grace.

The next two descriptive phrases are closely related to each other and, unlike the first phrase, would only be realized when Israel fulfilled their covenant obligations. To become a kingdom of priests meant that Israel

---

[3] In spite of alternate interpretations of the blood-sprinkling ritual, Williamson (*Sealed with an Oath*, 100) concludes that "the twofold application of the blood (i.e., to the altar and the people) would appear to underline the bilateral nature of the covenant so ratified."

would be a nation made up of priests devoted to serving Yahweh. Later, Israel would receive laws related to the priesthood within their nation, but here God intended for the nation as a whole to serve in a priestly role. What would this look like?

The old covenant itself later gives instructions for priests, but two important priests appear in the biblical text before Israel arrives at Sinai. As readers of the Pentateuch, we should already have a basic understanding of priests from reading about these earlier priests. The first priest is Melchizedek, king of Salem and priest of the God Most High (Gen 14:18-21). Melchizedek brought Abram bread and wine after Abram's victory over Chedorlaomer and his allies. Melchizedek also blessed Abram on behalf of God, and in return Abram gave Melchizedek a tenth of his spoil. From this passage we can deduce that one function of a priest may have been to mediate God's blessings to others. Yahweh's later instructions regarding the priestly blessing in Numbers 6:22-27 confirm such a role (cf. Deut 21:5).

A second priest who appears in the biblical story before Yahweh gives Israel the old covenant is Moses' father-in-law, Jethro (Ex 18). Jethro brings Moses' wife and two sons to him in the wilderness. After Moses shares about Yahweh's great works in Egypt on behalf of his people, Jethro rejoices, blesses Yahweh, and acknowledges Yahweh's superiority over all gods. Then Jethro offers sacrifices to God and eats bread with the elders of Israel before God. Jethro's actions highlight another function of priests—that is, the offering of sacrifices. In like manner, the offering of sacrifices on behalf of the worshiping community becomes one of the primary functions of the Aaronic priesthood (cf. Lev 1–7). To approach Yahweh, the people had to go through a priest.

In summary, when Yahweh informed Israel that they would become a kingdom of priests if they obeyed him, they were to mediate between God and humanity. This raises another question: For whom would they mediate? They would mediate between Yahweh and the other nations of the world who belong to the king who says, "All the earth is mine" (Ex 19:5). Israel would mediate God's blessings to the nations and would lead the nations in the worship of Yahweh. Such a function reminds us of God's promise to Abraham in Genesis 12:3: "In you all the families of the earth shall be blessed." God therefore intended to use Israel to fulfill the Abrahamic covenant.

The last phrase Yahweh uses to describe Israel's potential identity is "a holy nation" (Ex 19:6). Just as Yahweh set the later Aaronic priests apart from the rest of Israel, so also Yahweh intended Israel to be set apart from the other nations. Israel's consecrated role would enable them to faithfully represent and mediate Yahweh's presence and blessings to the nations of the world. Yahweh would set his people apart by means of the old covenant laws. As they obeyed his covenant, they would look less like the nations around them and more like their king, thus imaging "God to the nations."[4] In one sense, Yahweh set Israel apart by entering into a covenant with them; however, throughout the laws, Yahweh commanded his people to reflect their identity in their national life. He required their conduct (practical holiness or righteousness) to line up with their identity (positional holiness).

Yahweh's election of Israel in order to bless the nations may seem a little counterintuitive to modern readers who value fairness and define it as equal opportunity and privilege. That is not the way Yahweh appears to work here with regard to Israel. We often see a similar pattern in sports. Coaches often set one player apart for a particular task for the benefit of the entire team. The best example is the quarterback. In football, the quarterback functions as an extension of the coach. For the most part, the quarterback coaches the team when he is on the field. Because of their importance, quarterbacks often receive privileges that other players do not.[5] For instance, quarterbacks rarely take hits in practice, and to ensure that they do not, they wear special jerseys so the other players know they are off limits. Now, the other players could get mad and cry foul, but they do not for good reason. The other players know that without a good quarterback their chances of winning suffer significantly. Like coaches do with their quarterbacks, Yahweh set Israel apart and gave them special privileges (and duties) for the benefit of the nations. The success of this game plan was contingent on the Israelites' faithfulness to the old covenant stipulations.

At this point, I want to relate this discussion to contemporary Christians. Exodus 19 teaches us that Yahweh made this covenant with the nation of

---

[4]Stephen G. Dempster, *Dominion and Dynasty* (Downers Grove, IL: InterVarsity Press, 2003), 101.

[5]Like all analogies, this analogy breaks down at some point. In this case, coaches often choose quarterbacks because of their skills, but Yahweh elects Israel on the basis of his sovereign grace.

Israel after he delivered them from the bondage of Egyptian slavery. Because Yahweh made this covenant with Israel, we should assume that the legal requirements therein were to govern Israel, not all nations (the Bible refers to the nations as Gentiles). Many believers fail to recognize this key aspect of the old covenant and therefore feel the need to choose which laws apply to them and which laws do not. Unless Yahweh applies these laws to other nations, we should assume that he intended the laws to fulfill his plan for Israel to be a kingdom of priests and a holy nation. Indeed, Psalm 147:19-20 explicitly states that the other nations were not under the jurisdiction of the old covenant: "He declares his word to Jacob, / his statutes and rules to Israel. / He has not dealt thus with any other nation; / they do not know his rules." Later in this book, I will take this one step further and argue that not only were Gentiles never under the old covenant laws but that after Christ's death and resurrection Jews were no longer under the old covenant laws.

When we study the New Testament in view of this same question, Paul supports such an interpretation of the old covenant. In Romans 2, Paul contrasts the Jews and Gentiles in relation to the law. He designates the former as those "under the law" (Rom 2:12) and the latter as those "who do not have the law" (Rom 2:14). Since God did not give the law to the nations, the nations are not under its jurisdiction. Furthermore, Paul implies that the Gentiles are not under the law in Romans 1 when he identifies God's revelation of himself in creation as the basis for the Gentiles' accountability and their standard of judgment (Rom 1:18-23).

REBELLIONS AT SINAI

Many movies, such as *Jaws*, *The Lord of the Rings*, and *Star Wars*, use musical themes to accompany certain characters or settings in the movie. Richard Wagner famously developed this practice of using musical themes—termed leitmotifs—to aid in the development of a story. We find a recent example of this technique in the *The Lord of the Rings*. The movie's composer, Howard Shore, employs different themes for characters, settings, and even the ring itself in the movie.[6] These musical themes can

---

[6]For an overview of Howard Shore's use of leitmotifs in *The Lord of the Rings*, see www.youtube.com/watch?v=e7BkmF8CJpQ.

cause the viewer to anticipate or reflect on certain characters or events as the movie unfolds, thus enriching the movie. By paying close attention to such melodic patterns, we as viewers can many times predict certain events in the movie.

When it comes to reading the Bible, we can draw an important lesson from the use of leitmotifs in film scores. Whenever we read a book of the Bible, we should look for patterns—not in terms of musical themes, but in terms of recurring events, themes, or key words. On many occasions, the author conveys his message by using such patterns. For example, the older sibling serving the younger is a pattern that appears frequently in the book of Genesis. In this section, we are going to look at a pattern within the laws in the Pentateuch. As Moses records Yahweh giving Israel the laws at Sinai, he also includes several key narratives within the laws. For example, we have already noted the narrative of Israel's construction of the tabernacle in Exodus 35–40, a narrative that emphasizes Israel's obedience to Yahweh's instructions. Another type of narrative embedded in the laws is what I call the rebellion narratives. In particular, three rebellion narratives appear in the midst of the laws, and their location creates a pattern that helps us understand Moses' purposes.

The golden calf (Ex 32–34). One of the greatest rebellions in the Bible is the golden calf incident in Exodus 32–34. The story is familiar to many readers, but its familiarity should not keep us from experiencing the shock of this event. While Moses was on the mountain receiving the instructions for the tabernacle (Ex 25–31) and the two tablets on which Yahweh wrote the Ten Commandments (Ex 32:15-16), the people grew weary of Moses' extended absence (forty days and forty nights [Ex 24:18]) and urged Aaron to make them "gods" who would "go before" them (Ex 32:1). In response, Aaron melted down the people's golden earrings and fashioned a golden calf to represent Yahweh, thus satisfying the people, who proclaimed, "These are your gods, O Israel, who brought you up out of the land of Egypt!" (Ex 32:4). Taking things a few steps further, Aaron then built an altar before the idol and proclaimed a feast to Yahweh, at which the people bowed down to the idol (Ex 32:8), presented offerings, shared a meal, and indulged in inappropriate revelry (Ex 32:5-6).[7]

---

[7]Many have identified the revelry (ESV: "play") of Ex 32:6 as inappropriate sexual behavior because the Hebrew word that describes this action sometimes appears in the context of

Wow! Had the Israelites so soon forgotten the great works God did for them in Egypt? Had they forgotten Yahweh's magnificent display of his glory when he appeared on Mount Sinai (Ex 19:16-18, 20:18-21, 24:17)? How could they? Why would they so quickly betray their God with whom they had just entered into covenant? For many the question is, did the people really think an idol they made delivered them from the Egyptians and led them through the wilderness? Indeed, we should be shocked!

A cursory review of this incident might tempt some people to regard the Israelites as less-than-intelligent since they were worshiping something they had just built with their own hands. However, when we look more closely, the Israelites appear less foolish, since they initially did not consider the golden calf a *replacement* of Yahweh but a *representation* of Yahweh. They were seeking a tangible symbol of Yahweh, much like the Egyptians and Canaanites fashioned idols to represent their gods (both cultures also used bulls to represent their gods). Such a motive explains why the people's pronouncement ("These are your gods, O Israel, who brought you up out of the land of Egypt!" [Ex 32:4]) mirrors Yahweh's introduction of himself in the prologue to the Ten Commandments ("I am the LORD your God, who brought you out of the land of Egypt" [Ex 20:2]) and why Aaron calls for a "feast to the LORD" (Ex 32:5). The Israelites were breaking the second commandment: "You shall not make for yourself a carved image, or any likeness of anything that is in heaven above, or that is in the earth beneath, or that is in the water under the earth. You shall not bow down to them or serve them" (Ex 20:4-5a). The image of a bull qualifies as something "that is in the earth beneath."

Yet there are indications in the text that Israel's sinfulness might have gone further than just breaking the second commandment. In their zealous worship of the golden calf, they probably moved past worshiping the calf as a *representative* of Yahweh and began worshiping it as a *rival* to Yahweh. Scholars have pondered the reason for the references to "gods" throughout Exodus 32 (see vv. 4, 8, 23, 31).[8] At some level, it seems that the people

---

sexual relations (Gen 26:8; 39:14, 17). See, e.g., Peter Enns, *Exodus*, NIV Application Commentary (Grand Rapids: Zondervan, 2000), 571; Walter C. Kaiser Jr., "Exodus," in Expositor's Bible Commentary 2 (Grand Rapids: Zondervan, 1990), 478; Umberto Moshe David Cassuto, *A Commentary on the Book of Exodus*, trans. Israel Abrahams (Skokie, IL: Varda, 2005), 414; Gary Edward Schnittjer, *The Torah Story* (Grand Rapids: Zondervan, 2006), 270.

[8]Cassuto, *Book of Exodus*, 413, argues that the people made the calf a partner with Yahweh. Enns, *Exodus*, 571, claims that the Israelites are creating a new system to rival the worship of Yahweh.

intended to worship another god (or gods) either alongside Yahweh or, even worse, instead of Yahweh. If such is the case, then the people also transgressed the first commandment. The tragic irony of this rebellion is that it occurs *while* Yahweh is giving Moses the two stone tablets with the Ten Commandments.

As expected, neither Moses nor Yahweh is pleased with Israel's actions. Moses shatters the stone tablets, grinds the calf into powder, and makes the people drink the water (Ex 32:19-20).[9] He also summons the willing Levites to take up their swords and kill everyone who continued to run crazy (Ex 32:25-28). The Levites killed three thousand men that day, but Yahweh wanted to go even further. He wanted to destroy the people and start over with Moses (Ex 32:10). During his dialogue with Moses on Mount Sinai, Yahweh gives his assessment of the people, calling them corrupt (Ex 32:7) and a "stiff-necked people" (Ex 32:9; 33:3, 5), a designation with which Moses agrees (Ex 34:9).

Thankfully for the people, Moses intercedes for them and pleads with God to withhold his intended destruction on the basis of his reputation (Ex 32:11-12) and his covenant promises to Abraham, Isaac, and Jacob (Ex 32:13). Yahweh relents of complete destruction but still sends a plague in their midst (Ex 32:35). Yahweh's forgiveness and restoration of the people reflects his compassion and mercy, qualities highlighted in his dialogue with Moses in chapters 33–34. In Exodus 34, Yahweh, at the request of Moses, passes before Moses on the mountain and reveals himself in the following manner:

> The Lord, the Lord, a God merciful and gracious, slow to anger, and abounding in steadfast love and faithfulness, keeping steadfast love for thousands, forgiving iniquity and transgression and sin, but who will by no means clear the guilty, visiting the iniquity of the fathers on the children and the children's children, to the third and the fourth generation. (Ex 34:6-7)

Yahweh's demonstration of his compassion and mercy at the time of Israel's great rebellion is one of many displays of mercy throughout Israel's history since Israel gives him numerous opportunities to show that he is "merciful

---

[9]For two interpretations of this action, compare Enns, *Exodus*, 574-75, and Douglas K. Stuart, *Exodus*, New American Commentary 2 (Nashville: B&H, 2006), 678.

and gracious, slow to anger, and abounding in steadfast love and faithfulness."[10]

Now let's turn our attention to the larger context of laws. At this point in the story, the Israelites have received the first two sections of laws: the Ten Commandments (God had spoken them from the mountain [Ex 20:1], but Moses had not received the stone tablets yet) and the Covenant Code. We have already highlighted the golden calf as a violation of the second commandment, but it is also significant that the prohibition against making idols is the first commandment Yahweh gives in the Covenant Code (Ex 20:22-23). The people therefore are not acting in ignorance when they build the golden calf; they are directly disobeying two clear commands they had received from God, and this transgression comes shortly after their agreement to obey "all the words that the LORD has spoken" (Ex 24:3, 7). How quickly they had forgotten their pledge! How quickly they had forgotten their God! Like a four-year-old boy who forgets his parent's instructions within three seconds, so Israel forgot their covenant commitment to Yahweh within forty days.

When Moses descends the mountain and witnesses the people worshiping the golden calf, he provides the Israelites (and us) with a dramatic presentation of the full implications of their rebellion by breaking the tablets (Ex 32:15-16). No sooner had the tablets touched Moses' fingers did Israel break the covenant represented on those tablets. When Moses throws the tablets on the ground in anger, there is a very real sense in which he is simply doing what the people had already done: broken their covenant with Yahweh. Therefore, when Yahweh renews the covenant, he states, "I am making a covenant" (Ex 34:10), and repeats (in Ex 34:11-26) several of the laws in the Ten Commandments and the Covenant Code.

As we have seen, the impetus for the golden calf was Moses' delay on the mountain. Moses was on the mountain for forty days and nights. What was he doing? Exodus 24 helps us understand what was taking place on Sinai. After Moses received the Covenant Code, he relayed the laws of that code to the people at the base of the mountain and ratified the covenant (Ex 24:3-8). Then Moses, Aaron, Aaron's sons, and seventy elders went up

---

[10]Moses quotes this verse when he intercedes for the people after they rebel against Yahweh again (Num 14:18). Later biblical authors often quote or allude to this verse. See Ps 86:15; 103:8; Jer 32:18; Joel 2:12-14; Jon 4:2; Mic 7:18; Nahum 1:3a.

the base of the mountain and shared a meal in Yahweh's presence (Ex 24:9-11). Thereafter, Yahweh summoned Moses to the top of the mountain to receive the stone tablets on which Yahweh had written the commandments (Ex 24:12). Additionally, Yahweh gave Moses the tabernacle instructions (Ex 25–31) during Moses' time on the mountain.

Although Moses had not given the people the tabernacle instructions before they built the golden calf, it is ironic that they were building the golden calf while Moses was receiving the tabernacle instructions, since these laws deal with where and how Israel should approach Yahweh as well as their leadership in this worship (i.e., Aaron and his sons). One might say that Israel was disobeying Yahweh while the words were still on his lips. The golden calf rebellion thus shows the people's immediate failure concerning two key aspects of worship. First, they failed to worship Yahweh in the proper way and in the proper place (bringing sacrifices to the tabernacle; see Ex 29:38-46). Second, the leader of this false worship was none other than Aaron himself (Ex 32:21, 25), the one whom the Lord had appointed to lead the people in proper worship at the proper place. Aaron's leadership in the golden calf rebellion might explain why Aaron did not participate in the tabernacle dedication (Ex 40).[11] Aaron's failure to lead the people in proper worship prepares us for the next major rebellion narrative.

The profane fire of Nadab and Abihu (Lev 10). After the golden calf rebellion, the remainder of Exodus records the construction of the tabernacle. Leviticus opens with seven chapters of laws regarding the different types of offerings Yahweh required the people to offer him. As expected, the priests play a central role in the administration of these offerings. It is no surprise, then, that the next two chapters in Leviticus record the consecration of Aaron and his sons for official service as priests in the tabernacle (chap. 8) and Aaron's first sacrifices as priest (chap. 9). Throughout these two chapters, the emphasis falls on Moses' (chap. 8) and Aaron's (chap. 9) obedience to the commands Yahweh had given Moses.[12] Aaron in particular is doing much better than he did in the golden calf incident.

---

[11]Gordon J. Wenham, *The Book of Leviticus*, New International Commentary on the Old Testament (Grand Rapids: Eerdmans, 1979), 131, makes this observation but moves in a different direction.

[12]Ibid., 134.

Now, if this were a fairy tale, we would read that Aaron and his sons faithfully served in the tabernacle all their days and the people lived happily ever after. But this is no fairy tale, so what happens next, although shocking, should not surprise us. Leviticus 9 ends with a great display of God's glory as a fire comes out from the presence of the Lord and consumes the offering Aaron had presented to him (Lev 9:22-24). Rightly so, this display left the people prostrate before the Lord. Moses had completed the consecration of the Aaronic priesthood according to Yahweh's instructions (Ex 29), and their service had officially begun!

Leviticus 10 begins with another display of the fire of God, but this time the fire does not consume an offering but the priests themselves, Nadab and Abihu. They were Aaron's two sons whom, along with their father, Yahweh had commissioned to serve as priests. The text informs us that as Nadab and Abihu approached the altar with incense, they "offered unauthorized fire before the LORD, which he had not commanded them" (Lev 10:1). Although we may not know precisely what they did wrong,[13] Yahweh's words to Aaron following this display of judgment show that Nadab and Abihu's action demonstrated a lack of concern for Yahweh's holiness and glory before the people: "Among those who are near me I will be sanctified, and before all the people I will be glorified" (Lev 10:3).

Just like the golden calf rebellion, Nadab and Abihu's profane fire appears at a key juncture in the laws. Coming after the consecration of the priesthood, the actions of Nadab and Abihu show once again the priests' inability to obey Yahweh's commands. In particular, Nadab and Abihu's action relates to the story that precedes it just like the golden calf rebellion related to the laws that preceded it. Such patterns help us understand the author's intentions for these stories. Gary Schnittjer recognizes a pattern involving many stories in the Pentateuch, in particular the golden calf and the death of Nadab and Abihu. This pattern appears at "the beginnings of new institutions in the Torah."[14] Accompanying the inception of these new institutions is "the almost immediate sinful failure of the human constituents in each case."[15] By using this pattern, Moses underscores what

---

[13]For a concise summary of the interpretive options, see Victor P. Hamilton, *Handbook on the Pentateuch*, 2nd ed. (Grand Rapids: Baker, 2005), 255-56.

[14]Schnittjer, *Torah Story*, 323. See p. 324 for a chart of these new-beginning failures.

[15]Ibid., 323.

becomes even clearer when we zoom out to an even larger context: the people's (and in particular the leaders') propensity to disobey Yahweh's commands. The golden calf showed the people's inability to obey the most important components of the old covenant, and the profane fire of Nadab and Abihu shows the inability of the priests to follow Yahweh's instructions for their institution.

The blaspheming son (Lev 24). A third and final rebellion that takes place while Israel is encamped at Sinai is the story of the blasphemer in Leviticus 24:10-23.[16] In this story, the son of an Israelite mother and an Egyptian father gets into a fight with an Israelite. During the fight, the son blasphemes the name of Yahweh, immediately drawing the ire of the people who subsequently bring him to Moses (Lev 24:11). The blasphemer is eventually stoned to death outside the camp for his transgression (Lev 24:23).

This rebellion narrative contains two similarities with the previous two rebellions. First, the son's blasphemy directly violates Yahweh's command at the end of Leviticus 22: "You shall not profane my holy name, that I may be sanctified among the people of Israel" (Lev 22:32). Although a chapter separates the command and the rebellion, the command still echoes in the blasphemer's story. Second, Schnittjer highlights the significance of this violation in relation to the golden calf incident. The people violated the first two commandments with the golden calf, and in this incident the blasphemer breaks the third commandment. Later, in Numbers 15:32-36, a man breaks the fourth commandment by gathering wood on the Sabbath. Schnittjer concludes that these four stories narrate the people's transgression of the first four commandments and set up the reader "to expect that God's chosen people will break all of his commands."[17] The presence and order of these stories highlight Moses' agenda in his writing.

However, there are two major differences between this rebellion narrative and the previous two. First, this story involves only one individual, who is moreover the son of an Israelite and an Egyptian, whereas the other two rebellion narratives involved the entire nation or their leaders. Second, this story underscores the people's obedience in carrying out Yahweh's prescribed punishment (Lev 24:23), whereas the previous two stories highlight

---

[16]Schnittjer (ibid., 322) points out that the only two narratives in the book of Leviticus narrate the deaths of rebels.

[17]Ibid., 354.

the people or their leaders' rebellion. These differences do seem to lessen this story's contribution to the paradigm of the rebellion narratives.

In spite of these differences, the story's context reveals a pattern that corresponds to the previous two rebellion narratives, a pattern that I have not yet mentioned. After the people put the blasphemer in custody (Lev 24:12), Yahweh instructs the people to stone him to death outside the camp (Lev 24:13-14). However, before dismissing Moses to carry out this punishment, Yahweh gives some additional laws (Lev 24:15-22), the first of which relates directly to the sin of blasphemy (Lev 24:15-16).

Significantly, this same phenomenon occurs after the other two rebellion narratives. Following the golden calf rebellion, Yahweh renews the covenant and gives the people more laws, the first few of which prohibit idolatry, especially when the Israelites enter the Promised Land (Ex 34:11-17). In a similar manner, Yahweh gives laws regarding the priests' service in the tabernacle after the death of Nadab and Abihu (Lev 10:8-11). Additionally, Moses prefaces Yahweh's instructions for the Day of Atonement (Lev 16) with a reference to the deaths of Nadab and Abihu (Lev 16:1). Moses' reference to the profane fire explains why Yahweh begins his instructions for the Day of Atonement with a death warning to Aaron about when (Lev 16:2) and how (Lev 16:3-19) he should enter Yahweh's presence.

This pattern also appears in connection with some of the laws Yahweh gives after Israel leaves Sinai. For example, the laws regarding the roles of the priests and Levites as well as their provisions (Num 18) come directly after the narratives of Numbers 16–17, which record the rebellion of Korah and his followers against Aaron as well as the budding of Aaron's rod as a symbol of God's election of him as his priest. After Moses displays Aaron's rod as a "sign for the rebels" (Num 17:10-11), the people cry out in fear of approaching the tabernacle (Num 17:12-13). In many ways, Numbers 18 stands as a response to their cry.

In each of these examples, Yahweh gives additional laws in response to a rebellion. The people's disobedience demonstrated a need for further clarity and guidance, thus prompting Yahweh to provide additional laws or to reiterate laws already given. Perhaps Paul had this pattern in mind when he wrote Galatians 3:19: "Why then the law? It was added because of transgressions, until the offspring should come to whom the promise had been made." Each rebellion produces more laws!

Adding laws in response to errant behavior is a universal phenomenon (cf. 1 Tim 1:8-11). Governments frequently add laws as people discover new ways to commit crimes or as technological developments provide new avenues for illegal actions. For example, the American government now requires prescriptions and additional monitoring for certain medications that once were over-the-counter medications because people were abusing these medications. Parents also add rules as their kids grow older or as their kids do things that their parents did not expect them to do. Children who lean toward compliance and obedience generally receive fewer rules than children who constantly walk the line of acceptable behavior. Parents of the latter children must constantly clarify and reinforce rules for right behavior. God's interaction with Israel is very similar to a parent's interaction with a rebellious child. Israel required constant clarification, restatement, and additions as they rebelled against God.

Moses did not have to include the three Sinai-rebellion stories in the Pentateuch. By choosing to include these stories and by creating patterns around them, he has helped us see Israel's propensity toward rebellion and Yahweh's subsequent adding of new laws or his clarification of current laws. Unfortunately, Moses does not limit his agenda to Israel's time at Sinai; he also highlights Israel's rebellious nature in the narratives that precede and follow Israel's time at Sinai. This larger context is the topic of the next chapter.

FIVE

THE REST OF THE STORY (PART 2)

BEFORE AND AFTER SINAI

Marketers can be extremely creative. Many advertising fads come and go, but one advertising fad has stood the test of time: before and after pictures. Whether it is for exercise equipment, diet pills, makeup, plastic surgery, or car cleaner, advertisers know the power of putting before and after pictures side by side on the television, computer screen, or magazine page. Showing the transformations of people, cars, and hairstyles sells products faster than simply talking about the products' abilities. People want to see that a product works before investing money into a purchase.

Now, if Moses was trying to sell the old covenant when he wrote the Pentateuch, he did a very poor job. Almost one year (Num 10:11) separates the before-Sinai and after-Sinai "pictures" of Israel, but the people appear to have regressed five years in their understanding of and obedience to Yahweh. These pictures help us see Sinai's impact on the people and draw some key lessons from the events that transpire on their journey.

One of the important things about before and after pictures is making sure that the same person is in both pictures. Imagine the marketing disaster if someone discovered that the person in the after picture was different from the person in the before picture. Regarding Israel in the

Pentateuch, we know that the same group of people arrive and leave Sinai. However, Moses has gone the extra mile to ensure that we compare Israel's journey to Sinai with Israel's journey from Sinai by including many parallel features in his descriptions of these journeys. Table 1 shows the numerous parallels between the two journeys.[1]

Table 1. Parallels between Israel's pre-Sinai and post-Sinai journeys

	Pre-Sinai (Ex 13–19)	Post-Sinai (Num 10–21)
Led by cloud	13:21	10:11 (cf. 9:15-23)
Victory song	15:1-18	10:35-36
Three-day journey	15:22	10:33
People complain	15:23-24	11:1
Moses prays	15:25	11:2
Manna and quail	16	11:4-35
Forty years	16:35	14:33-34
Water from rock	17:1-7	20:2-13
Enemies attack Israel	17:8-13	21:1
Destruction of enemies	17:13-14	21:2-3, 21-35

Although there are differences in the journeys (we will highlight some important ones in the next section), these similarities bind the two journeys together and invite comparison. So, what do we see when we take a closer look at both sections?

ISRAEL'S ACTIONS

Most of Israel's actions during their journeys to and from Sinai were negative. To be fair, Israel performed some positive actions on both sides of Sinai, but these positive actions consist almost entirely of military feats (Ex 17:8-16; Num 21:1-3, 21-35; 31:1-24).[2] In this section, we are going to compare Israel's sinful actions on both sides of Sinai in order to articulate the role of the old covenant. Table 2 outlines these actions.

---

[1] Adapted from Gary Edward Schnittjer, *The Torah Story* (Grand Rapids: Zondervan, 2006), 376, and John Sailhamer, *The Meaning of the Pentateuch: Revelation, Composition and Interpretation* (Downers Grove, IL: IVP Academic, 2009), 366.
[2] The only exception is the people's obedience in stoning the Sabbath breaker (Num 15:32-36).

Table 2. Israel before and after Sinai

Israel Before Sinai	Israel After Sinai
People complain about danger (Ex 14:10-12)*	People complain (Num 11:1)
People complain about water (Ex 15:24)	Some cry out for meat (Num 11:4-6)
People complain about food (Ex 16:2-3)	Miriam and Aaron speak against Moses (Num 12:1-2)
Some disobey and keep manna (Ex 16:20)	People refuse to enter land (Num 13–14)
People complain about water (Ex 17:3)	A man breaks Sabbath (Num 15:32-34)
	Korah, Dathan, and Abiram oppose Moses and Aaron (Num 16:1-3)
	People complain against Moses and Aaron (Num 16:41)
	People contend with Moses about water (Num 20:2-5)
	People speak against Moses and Yahweh (Num 21:4-5)
	Israelite men commit sexual immorality and idolatry with Moabite women (Num 25:1-3)

*Unlike the other complaint passages in Exodus 16–17, Exodus 14:10-12 does not explicitly designate Israel's words as a complaint. However, their questioning of Moses parallels their questioning in the other complaint passages.

Table 2 helps us clarify the old covenant's impact on the Israelite people. In spite of the continuity between Israel's actions, we may observe a couple of important differences in pre- and post-Sinai Israel.

First, Moses records twice as many sinful actions in Israel's post-Sinai journey as he does in their pre-Sinai journey. We may explain this phenomenon by noting that Israel's journey from Sinai to the plains of Moab (Num 10:11–36:13) was almost forty years longer than their journey from the Red Sea to Sinai (Ex 15:22–18:27). Such a time difference easily accounts for the larger quantity of sinful deeds. Yet we should be careful about dismissing this increase as the product of a longer journey because of the way biblical narratives work.

When biblical authors write narratives, they carefully select the stories they want to include. For instance, many biblical narratives fast-forward from the main character's birth to adulthood. We see this in the narratives of Jacob and Esau (Gen 25:24-28), Moses (Ex 2:1-11), Samson (Judg 13:24-25), and even Jesus (Mt 2:1–4:1). This selectivity is not limited to birth narratives but extends to every aspect of narratives. A quick comparison of the books of Kings and Chronicles demonstrates that the authors of both books leave out stories that appear in the other book. Authors include or exclude stories in accordance with their purpose or purposes (as we also see in the four Gospels). By including so many rebellion narratives in Numbers, Moses is not merely recording history. If he were simply recording history, the book of Numbers would be much longer! Moses has a theological agenda, and that theological agenda involves Israel's numerous instances of complaining, rebelling, and provoking Yahweh.

The differences between pre- and post-Sinai Israel relate not only to the quantity of their sins but also to the nature of their sins. The people's sins before Sinai consisted of them complaining and some of them keeping manna overnight. The people's sins after Sinai do include complaining about food and water, but they go much further.

First, the people's complaints in their post-Sinai journey are bolder. This is signaled by the first and last of the people's complaints in Numbers. Numbers 11:1 begins just like the complaint passages in Exodus (cf. Ex 15:24; 16:2; 17:3): "And the people complained." However, the passage adds a phrase to heighten the severity of their complaints: "in the hearing of the LORD," a phrase that indicates the people's complaints have more than Moses and Aaron (as in the Exodus passages) in their purview.[3] They have now boldly gone where they had not gone before with their complaints: before Yahweh. The last complaint passage in Numbers also demonstrates that the people aim their complaints at Yahweh. Numbers 21:5 reads, "And the people spoke against God and against Moses." As the only instance of the people speaking directly against Yahweh, Numbers 21 completes the Israelite's progression from bad to worse.[4] Their bold challenge of Yahweh's provision highlights their descent into the pit of ingratitude and unbelief.

Second, the rebellion narratives in Numbers demonstrate that the grumbling against Moses has moved beyond the populace to the leadership. The

---

[3]In Ex 16:6-8, Moses, in his rebuke of the people, interprets their complaints against himself and Aaron as complaints against Yahweh. Nonetheless, the original description of the Israelites' complaints directs them against Moses and Aaron. Thus, the people's target was Moses and Aaron, but Moses informed the people that a complaint against the leaders was a complaint against Yahweh. This distinction highlights the greater boldness in the people's post-Sinai complaints, wherein their target is Yahweh.

[4]R. Dennis Cole states that this verse marks one of the few instances where this verb is used "with the people as the subject instead of God or Moses." For Cole, this heightens the seriousness of their complaints. *Numbers*, New American Commentary 3b (Nashville: B&H, 2000), 346-47.

leadership's revolt against Moses begins with his own family and then moves to his tribe. Moses' own siblings, Miriam and Aaron, oppose him in Numbers 12, and then Korah, a member of Moses' tribe (the Levites), with the help of two Reubenites, gathers 250 important community leaders in a revolt against Moses and Aaron (Num 16). In both instances, Yahweh shows his support for Moses (and Aaron) by judging those who dared to oppose him.

Third, the people's rebellion even causes Moses and Aaron to sin against Yahweh. Numbers 20 records the people opposing Moses and Aaron at Kadesh because they could not find water. After consulting with Yahweh and receiving instructions from him, Moses, with Aaron by his side, strikes the rock twice, and Yahweh provides water for the people from the rock. But the story does not end here. Yahweh then tells Moses and Aaron, "Because you did not believe in me, to uphold me as holy in the eyes of the people of Israel, therefore you shall not bring this assembly into the land that I have given them" (Num 20:12). Although we do not know precisely what Moses and Aaron did wrong,[5] Yahweh's words make it clear they did not trust him and regard him as holy before the people, a statement that is eerily similar to the charge Yahweh leveled against Nadab and Abihu (Lev 10:3). Like the Israelites' unbelief (Num 14:11), Moses and Aaron's unbelief prevented them from entering the land.[6]

How do the people relate to Moses' rebellion? From his perspective, the people's complaints caused him to sin. On two occasions in Deuteronomy (Deut 1:37; 4:21), Moses attributes his punishment to the people's provocation. Psalm 106:32-33, a poetic reflection on this same event, confirms that Moses was not just playing the blame game like his original parents, Adam and Eve. The passage reads, "They angered him at the waters of Meribah, / and it went ill with Moses on their account, / for they made his spirit bitter, / and he spoke rashly with his lips." The people's murmuring even tainted the soul of their great leaders.

The fourth major difference in the nature of Israel's post-Sinai rebellion involves what I call "the greatest rebellion ever told": Israel's rebellion at Kadesh Barnea (Num 13–14). Yahweh had led the people to the edge of the Promised Land and commanded them to take possession of the land he was giving them. This should have been a day of celebration! Yahweh had kept

---

[5]For an overview of interpretive options, see Jacob Milgrom, *Numbers*, JPS Torah Commentary (Philadelphia: Jewish Publication Society, 1990), 448-56.
[6]Victor P. Hamilton, *Handbook on the Pentateuch*, 2nd ed. (Grand Rapids: Baker, 2005), 336.

his promises to Abraham, Isaac, and Jacob. Yahweh promised to fight for Israel. But somehow Israel forgot about the greatness of their God. They had forgotten how Yahweh had systematically dismantled Egypt, the most powerful nation in the world. Instead, they chose to focus on the size of the Canaanites and their cities (Num 13:26-29), and like grasshoppers (Num 13:33) they hopped away from their enemies in fear (Num 14:1-4). How could they? Why would they? After complaining about being in the wilderness, the people now refused to enter the "land flowing with milk and honey." This rebellion makes their complaining before Sinai look like child's play. Up to this point in the story, Israel's only bright spot was their obedience to Yahweh's instructions in battles (cf. Ex 17:8-16; Num 21:1-3, 21-35). Now they have come to the point where they rebel against Yahweh's marching orders.

The significance of this before and after comparison becomes greater when we reconsider one of Yahweh's purposes for the old covenant: to make Israel a holy nation. The Israel that leaves Sinai does not appear holy; in fact, they appear more sinful. It is like driving a car through a car wash and having it come out dirtier. The Israelites can do nothing right, and they are masters at doing evil in the eyes of the Lord. What happened? The most reasonable explanation is that the people, who were already quick to fall into temptation, became more sinful because of the laws they received at Mount Sinai. Stephen Dempster, who subtitles his discussion of Numbers "journey to hell and back," writes, "If Exodus and Leviticus were negative about the Israelite ability to fulfill the Sinai covenant, Numbers is downright pessimistic."[7] This does not mean that the laws were sinful or bad; it simply means the laws highlighted Israel's propensity to rebel against Yahweh. To put it another way, the old covenant provided the standard of conduct for the people, but it did not provide the people with the means to obey it.

Such an interpretation fits what the apostle Paul says about the old covenant in Romans 5:20: "Now the law came in to increase the trespass." When we look at Israel's journey from Sinai, we see that the trespass increased immediately. They are not a "holy nation." Israel acts like the hardheaded child whose parents dread telling him not to do something, because they know that instead of receiving it as instruction, the youth will change their prohibition into a great idea for fun.

---

[7]Stephen G. Dempster, *Dominion and Dynasty* (Downers Grove, IL: IVP Academic, 2003), 111.

Hebrews 8:7-8 also confirm this interpretation of the old covenant. In verse 7 the author of Hebrews writes, "For if that first covenant [old covenant] had been faultless, there would have been no occasion to look for a second [new covenant]." By "faultless," the author does not mean that the covenant contained evil laws; its fault lies in its inability to produce righteousness in God's people. Such is the author's point in verse 8 when he writes, "For he finds fault with them." The old covenant's major problem related to Israel's evil, not to the nature of the laws (cf. Rom 7:12).

YAHWEH'S REACTIONS TO ISRAEL'S SIN

The nation of Israel is not the main character of the Hebrew Bible. This designation belongs to the gracious God who created the universe and chose Israel for himself. Therefore, one of the primary questions in biblical interpretation is, what does this story teach us about God? The next step in our evaluation of the old covenant's context is to examine Yahweh's reactions to Israel's numerous sins. These reactions do teach us about his character, but they also give us more information about the old covenant. Table 3 provides a quick reference for one to see the key differences in Yahweh's responses.

Table 3. Yahweh's responses before and after Sinai

Yahweh's Responses Before Sinai	Yahweh's Responses After Sinai
Deliverance without punishment (Ex 14:13-31)	Fire from Yahweh burns some (Num 11:1)
Provision without punishment (Ex 15:22-26)	Provision with a plague (Num 11:31-34)
Provision without punishment (Ex 16:4-5)	Strikes Miriam with leprosy (Num 12:9-12)
Spoiled manna (Ex 16:20)	Plague and forty years of wilderness wanderings for the people (Num 14:26-38)
Provision without punishment (Ex 17:5-7)	Yahweh commands the assembly to stone the Sabbath breaker (Num 15:32-36)
	Earth swallows rebels and fire from Yahweh (Num 16:31-35)
	Plague from Yahweh kills 14,700 (Num 16:46-50)
	Provision with Yahweh forbidding Moses and Aaron from entering the land (Num 20:9-12)
	Venomous snakes kill many (Num 21:6)
	Plague from Yahweh kills 24,000 (Num 25:9)

As you probably noticed, there is a drastic difference in Yahweh's re-action to Israel's sin on either side of Sinai. In response to their complaining and testing before Mount Sinai, there is no record of punishment or even anger toward the people of Israel. If that were not enough, Yahweh, in a demonstration of his great mercy, simply provides for his grumbling people when they complain against him. But such mercy is not on display when Israel leaves the mountain. During Israel's post-Sinai journey, it seems that as soon as someone opens his or her mouth to speak against Yahweh or Moses, someone dies! Furthermore, on three occasions after Israel's post-Sinai rebellions, Yahweh expressed his desire to annihilate the people completely (Num 14:11-12; 16:20-21, 44-45). In Numbers 11–25, Yahweh's judgment is dis-played in some unusual ways: the ground swallows people, poisonous serpents attack, plagues strike people, Yahweh sends fire, and a woman becomes a leper. These deaths demonstrate something very important about the character of God, something that may not be popular in Western culture: not only is Yahweh a God of mercy, but he is also a God of wrath.

Why the drastic change in God's reaction to his people's sins? Did his character change while he was meeting with Moses on the mountain? Cer-tainly not! God's character had not changed. He is the same God who sent the flood, confused the languages of the world, destroyed Sodom and Go-morrah with fire from heaven, and judged the Egyptians with ten plagues (all pre-Sinai events). The Bible consistently records displays of Yahweh's judgment from the fall of Adam and Eve through the second coming of Christ. The major difference in the people's relationship with God was that they had entered into a covenant with him at Mount Sinai. They had agreed to do everything Yahweh commanded them (Ex 19:8; 24:3, 7). Therefore, this covenant increased God's wrath toward the people when they sinned against him. No longer could they claim that they did not know better. They did indeed know better, and because they knew better, the stakes were much higher.

In this regard, parenting serves as a good illustration. Parenting is one of the most difficult jobs in the world, especially when it comes to disci-plining one's children. As a parent, there is a constant tension between being too lenient and too strict. In trying to walk this tightrope, one of the key factors involved is the child's motives. Unfortunately, children are not always quick to tell us their motives (or the truth, for that matter), so parents often find themselves trying to discern whether a child's motive was ignorance or outright rebellion. Many parents try to remove some of this tension by clearly outlining their expectations and making sure their children understand both what they expect and what their children can expect if they fail to live up to their expectations. This is exactly what the old covenant did for Israel. Yahweh clarified his expectations for them so that when they did sin and ignite his holy wrath, they could not say, "But we didn't know."

Once again, such an interpretation aligns with Paul's explanation of the law in the book of Romans. In Romans 4:15 he writes, "For the law brings wrath, but where there is no law there is no transgression."[8] It only takes an attentive reading of the Pentateuch to see what Paul sees. Before Sinai, Israel complains and the Lord provides; after Sinai, Israel complains or rebels, and the Lord pours out his wrath!

THE NECESSITY OF RIGHTEOUSNESS

Before concluding our study of the old covenant's context, let's zoom out even further and connect our above conclusions to a prominent theme in the early chapters of the Pentateuch: the necessity of righteousness. Righteousness refers to living a life in proper relation to God and has some overlap with holiness because, as John Hartley notes, "Yahweh, the holy God, is righteous."[9] After reading of the fall of humanity and the spread of sin throughout the world (Gen 3–5), we encounter the first person the Bible describes as a righteous man: Noah. Even though Noah lived in the midst of an exceedingly wicked people, he was "a righteous man," "blameless in his generation," and one who "walked with God" (Gen 6:9).[10] What did Noah's righteousness get him? While God was pouring out his wrath on his

---

[8] A transgression is a violation of a specific command and is more specific than a sin. Although all have sinned, Paul is highlighting God's more severe judgment on Israel for directly violating specific commands. For a good discussion, see Douglas J. Moo, *The Epistle to the Romans*, New International Commentary on the New Testament (Grand Rapids: Eerdmans, 1996), 276-77.

[9] John E. Hartley, "Holy and Holiness, Clean and Unclean," in *Dictionary of the Old Testament: Pentateuch*, ed. T. Desmond Alexander and David W. Baker (Downers Grove, IL: InterVarsity Press, 2003), 420, clarifies the relationship between holiness and righteousness in the following manner: "Consequently, *holy* defines the character of biblical ethics. Nevertheless, we need to be aware that holiness encompasses far more than ethical behavior."

[10] Before we read of Noah's righteousness, Moses informs us that "Noah found favor in the eyes of the LORD" (Gen 6:8).

creation, Noah and his family were safe aboard the ark. In other words, Noah's righteousness delivered him from God's wrath.

This focus on the necessity of righteousness to escape God's wrath reappears in two other stories in Genesis. First, when God prepared to destroy Sodom and Gomorrah because of their sin, he revealed his plans to Abraham (Gen 18). Abraham immediately interceded on behalf of Sodom and Gomorrah, urging the Lord not to destroy the righteous with the wicked. Abraham did a countdown of sorts in an attempt to spare the (supposed) fifty, forty-five, forty, thirty, twenty, or ten righteous people in the city. One verse in particular gets at the heart of Abraham's request. In Genesis 18:25, Abraham said to Yahweh, "Far be it from you to do such a thing, to put the righteous to death with the wicked. . . . Shall not the Judge of all the earth do what is just?" Abraham understood the just character of God and thus appealed to God's justice in sparing the righteous from the destruction that was about to come upon the wicked cities. Once again, the text underscores the importance of righteousness in escaping the wrath of God.

A third example of this theme appears two chapters later when Abraham had another one of his call-my-wife-my-sister moments (Gen 20). After entering Gerar, Abimelech the king, who thought (because Abraham told him) that Sarah was Abraham's sister, took Sarah into his house. It didn't take long for Abimelech to discover that he had made a big mistake! God appeared to him in a dream and informed him that he was a dead man walking because of what he had done. What happened next is very significant. Abimelech responded by emphasizing his righteousness and innocence in the matter of Sarah. In fact, he said, "Lord, will You slay a righteous nation also?" (Gen 20:4 NKJV). Surprisingly, the Lord affirmed Abimelech's integrity (Gen 20:6) and instructed him to return Sarah to Abraham. Yet again, God spared a person from his wrath because of that person's righteousness.

Now, how does all of this relate to Israel's covenant at Sinai? As we have seen, Israel experienced God's wrath on numerous occasions after leaving the mountain, thus underscoring that Israel was an unrighteous nation and showing that the law could not (and did not) produce righteousness in their lives. Therefore, if they were going to be righteous, it would have to come by some means other than the old covenant.

Thankfully, the Pentateuch teaches us how a person becomes righteous through the example of Abraham. Genesis 15:6 reads, "And he believed the LORD, and he [Yahweh] counted it to him as righteousness." In contrast to Israel's continual lack of faith in Yahweh (Num 14:11), Abraham became righteous by trusting in Yahweh's promises and plans for his life (Gen 15:4-5). It should then come as no surprise that Paul uses Abraham to teach his readers about the righteousness that comes through faith in contrast to the works of the law (Rom 3:27–4:25; Gal 3). Abraham stands as the premier example of receiving righteousness through faith, and we become his sons and daughters when we follow his example of faith (Gal 3:7-8).

IS MOSES' HOPE IN THE OLD COVENANT?

We can summarize what we have discussed in the previous two chapters in the following manner. Moses spends much time in the Pentateuch focusing on the old covenant laws. As readers of the Pentateuch, we should not focus only on the fact that he spent so much time on the laws, but we must also focus on what he is trying to teach about these laws. In order to best articulate what he is trying to teach his readers about these laws, we must consider the context of the laws. Through such an evaluation, we have discovered that Moses emphasized the people's (and their leaders') constant violation of the Lord's commands. In other words, Moses placed as much emphasis on the rebellion of the people as he did on the laws themselves, thus underscoring the connection between the giving of the laws and the people's unrighteousness.

We may articulate one key objection some might have with this interpretation of the Pentateuch as follows: Does this mean that Moses did not write his book in order to instruct the people to keep the laws? My answer to this question is a small no and a big yes. I am arguing that Moses' *ultimate* hope for the people's blessing was not the old covenant laws but a future work of God. The positive aspect of Moses' message is the topic of a later chapter, so at this point I want to focus on the negative message of the Pentateuch and how that relates to the original readers.

Since we have already surveyed the books of Exodus through Numbers, we will look at the final book in the Pentateuch, Deuteronomy, to demonstrate Moses' negative appraisal of the old covenant's ability to produce righteousness in the people's lives. Deuteronomy, like Exodus–Numbers, emphasizes Israel's rebellion against the Lord. In reality, Deuteronomy contains some of the harshest assessments of Israel's rebellious nature. For example, Moses upbraids the people at one point by stating, "You have been rebellious against the LORD from the day that I knew you" (Deut 9:24). Moses did not leave any room for the people to think they were "good" people.

Probably the harshest assessment of the people comes at the end of the book when Moses and Yahweh tell the people what is going to happen in their future. Although Moses predicts the people's future rebellion in Deuteronomy 4 and 30, we are going to concentrate on Deuteronomy 31 in this discussion. In the second half of this chapter, there are three key predictions of Israel's rebellion. Yahweh makes the first prediction when he affirms twice that Israel would break the covenant he had just made with them (Deut 31:16-21). He bases this prediction on the evil inclination of the people (v. 21). Moses gives the next two predictions to the people, and in both instances he echoes Yahweh's words, informing the people that they would rebel once they entered the land (Deut 31:27-29). As if his predictions were not enough, Yahweh instructs Moses to write a song that would serve as a witness against the people when they rebelled against him (Deut 31:19-22). Yahweh's song for the people appears in Deuteronomy 32 and emphasizes the people's rebellion against their God.

The predictions of Israel's rebellion become even more astonishing when we consider Moses' emphasis on wholehearted devotion to Yahweh in the book of Deuteronomy. On countless occasions throughout the book, Moses exhorts the Israelites to devote themselves to the service of Yahweh. This devotion was not merely outward but involved their entire being ("with all your heart and with all your soul" [Deut 6:5; 10:12; 11:18]). Moses even emphasizes the blessings the people would experience if they obeyed Yahweh wholeheartedly. To demonstrate the contrast of these two themes (commands for obedience and predictions of rebellion), let's compare Moses' words to a war-time speech. One of history's finest leaders was Winston Churchill, the British prime minister during World War II. After the Dunkirk evacuation, Churchill stood before the British House of Commons and gave his famous "We Shall Fight on the Beaches" speech. Churchill concluded the speech with the following words:

Even though large tracts of Europe and many old and famous states have fallen or may fall into the grip of the Gestapo and all the odious apparatus of Nazi rule, we shall not flag or fail. We shall go on to the end, we shall fight in France, we shall fight on the seas and oceans, we shall fight with growing confidence and growing strength in the air, we shall defend our Island, whatever the cost may be, we shall fight on the beaches, we shall fight on the landing grounds, we shall fight in the fields and in the streets, we shall fight in the hills; we shall never surrender, and even if, which I do not for a moment believe, this Island or a large part of it were subjugated and starving, then our Empire beyond the seas, armed and guarded by the British Fleet, would carry on the struggle, until, in God's good time, the New World, with all its power and might, steps forth to the rescue and the liberation of the old.[11]

In Deuteronomy, Moses and the people are standing on the brink of the Promised Land, and Moses is motivating the people to enter the land, trust in Yahweh for victory, and live in wholehearted devotion to him. Now, imagine if instead of saying, "even if, which I do not for a moment believe, this Island or a large part of it were subjugated and starving," Churchill predicted that the British isles would fall to the Nazis. What would such a prediction do to the morale of the British soldiers? Yet this is exactly what Moses does to the people in Deuteronomy. He urges them to obey the Lord and receive the resultant blessings the Lord would pour out on them, but he immediately switches gears and informs the people that they would disobey and receive the curses that the Lord promised for disobedience, the chief of which was exile from their beloved land.

This lack of confidence in the people's obedience reveals that Moses and Yahweh never had any hope that the people would faithfully keep the covenant God was making with them. This does not mean that the laws were bad, but it does show that the people were unable to keep the old covenant because of their rebellious hearts. So, is the message of the Pentateuch to keep the laws of the old covenant? The answer is yes and no. For Moses' original audience in the land, it was yes. If they wanted to receive Yahweh's blessings in the land, they had to obey the stipulations of the old covenant;

---

[11]Winston Churchill, "We Shall Fight on the Beaches," June 4, 1940, www.winstonchurchill .org/resources/speeches/1940-the-finest-hour/128-we-shall-fight-on-the-beaches.

yet, as we have seen, they were disobedient from the beginning, and therefore no one had any confidence that they would actually obey in the future. Truly, the Pentateuch's vision goes far beyond Israel's life in the land. The ultimate message for the original audience in the land and for those of us who read the Pentateuch today is that righteousness, blessing, and life could not come through the old covenant because it increased rebellion and God's wrath toward sin. Righteousness, blessing, and life would have to come by some other means.

Some of you may still be struggling with how a book that gives so many laws can ultimately be negative toward those laws. Let me give you an example from Hollywood. The movie *The Magnificent Seven* is about seven gunslingers who are hired by a Mexican farm village to stop bandits from stealing their precious crops. Since the seven men do not know when the bandits are coming to town, they move into the town and live with the people. While there, the gunslingers spend time with the people and train the men of the village to defend themselves. Eventually, the raiders come back to the village and a great gunfight ensues. Several of the seven defend the village to death, inspiring many of the villagers to fight for their town.

If you are familiar with Westerns, then you'll know that one of the key themes of most Westerns is the adoration of the gunslinger who often brings justice and restores peace. Interestingly, *The Magnificent Seven* actually undermines this common theme. As the seven gunslingers live among the villagers, something begins to happen: the gunslingers begin to grow jealous of the villagers' work ethic and their love for family. In fact, they begin to question their profession and even talk about settling down after they have finished their task in the village.

For example, at one point in the movie, the bandits sneak into the village while the seven gunslingers are away. When the cowboys return, Calvera, the leader of the bandits, takes their guns and allows them to pack up before he sends them out of the village. When the cowboys leave to pack up their stuff, a conversation takes place between the two leading gunslingers, Chris and Vin. Walking up to Chris, Vin says, "You know the first time I took a job as a hired gun, fellow told me, 'Vin, you can't afford to care.'" After pausing briefly, he pointedly challenges Chris: "There's your problem."

Chris immediately replies, "One thing I don't need is somebody telling me my problem."

Vin, not backing down, continues, "Like I said before, that's your problem. You got involved in this village and the people in it."

Frustrated, Chris shoots back at Vin, "Do you ever get tired of hearing yourself talk?"

Vin then explains himself to Chris more fully by confessing his own problem: "The reason I understand your problem so well is that I walked in the same trap myself. Yeah, first day we got here, I started thinking: 'Maybe I could put my gun away, settle down, get a little land, raise some cattle. Things that these people know about me be to my credit—wouldn't work against me.' I just didn't want you to think you were the only sucker in town."

As soon as Chris and Vin finish their conversation, the scene shifts to another cowboy, O'Reilly, who is preparing to leave. Throughout the movie, three of the village boys had grown attached to O'Reilly. As O'Reilly sits on his bed, the boys come in and ask if they can go with them. When he tells them no, one of the boys says, "We're ashamed to live here. Our fathers are cowards." Angered, O'Reilly picks the boy up, puts him over his knee, and spanks him. He then stands the boy back up and lectures all three boys. He says,

> Don't you ever say that again about your fathers, because they are not cowards. You think I am brave because I carry a gun; well, your fathers are much braver because they carry responsibility . . . for you, your brothers, your sisters, and your mothers. And this responsibility is like a big rock that weighs a ton. It bends and it twists them until finally it buries them under the ground. And there's nobody says they have to do this. They do it because they love you and because they want to. I have never had this kind of courage. Running a farm, working like a mule every day with no guarantee anything will ever come of it . . . this is bravery. That's why I never even started anything like that . . . that's why I never will.

The movie ends by emphasizing this same theme. One of the seven men was actually not a professional gunslinger but a young man named Chico who followed the other six to the village after they had rejected him. Because of his persistence, they let him go to the village with them. Throughout the movie, Chico tries to prove himself to the gunslingers, whom he idolizes. However, he also falls in love with one of the village girls. In the final scene of the movie, Chris, Vin, and Chico ride their horses out of the village. As they are leaving, Chico sees the girl he loves working with some other women. At the village gate, the three men stop, and Chris turns to Chico and says, "Adios." Chico replies, "Adios," and rides back into the village toward the girl. As Chris and Vin watch him leave, Chris concludes, "The old man was right. Only the farmers won. We lost. We always lose."

Although the movie portrays gunslinging in a positive light (they save the village), the ultimate message of the movie is not "Be a gunslinger." The ultimate heroes of the movie are the villagers, who remind the gunslingers of the important things in life. The Pentateuch is similar. Although there are many laws in the book that the people are expected to keep, the primary message of the book is not "Keep these laws." Rather, the ultimate message relates to a future work of God that will solve the problem of the people's unrighteousness.

SUMMARY OF LESSONS FROM THE REST OF THE STORY

As the heart of this book, the previous two chapters provide important information regarding the old covenant. Because they are so important, I am going to conclude this chapter by summarizing the lessons we have learned from the larger context of the old covenant. These lessons help us understand the old covenant's purpose and function in the larger biblical story.

First, the old covenant was a conditional covenant between Yahweh and Israel intended to set apart Israel as a kingdom of priests. As his holy priests, they would bless the nations. Yet Yahweh placed the success of this plan in the people's hands. They had to obey his covenant stipulations in order to distinguish themselves from the other nations. Furthermore, as later readers, we must recognize that God did not make this covenant with all the nations (cf. Ps 147:19-20) and should therefore feel no obligation to transfer this covenant directly to a modern context.

Second, the people's journey from Sinai to the Promised Land demonstrates that because of the covenant, the people's sins increased. The covenant laws were good, but the people's hearts were evil. The covenant laws therefore gave the people more opportunities to transgress against Yahweh. Before judging the Israelites, we should recognize that we would have done the same thing as Israel had we been in their position. Israel, like Adam, serves as a prototype for all humankind. They not only show us what we would have done (cf. Rom 3:19), but they also serve as an example of what not to do (cf. 1 Cor 10:1-17).

Third, in parallel with the people's increased rebellion, Yahweh's wrath also increased because of the covenant. Because the people had committed to follow Yahweh and keep his covenant, Yahweh poured out his wrath on the people when they transgressed his word. Yahweh's displays of wrath further underscored the people's unrighteousness.

Finally, the people's inability to keep the covenant and Yahweh's corresponding judgment indicate that Yahweh had to intervene on behalf of the people. In other words, the people's failure points toward the need for a future work of God. The context of the laws has already demonstrated that if Yahweh does not step in, the story will end.

SIX

"THOU SHALT NOT REMOVE THEM"

WHAT ABOUT THE TEN COMMANDMENTS?

Many Christians give hearty approval to my argument that we are not required to keep the old covenant laws, but such approval usually comes with one major exception: the Ten Commandments. When I outlined the different approaches to the old covenant laws in chapter two, I titled one position "Ten Commandments Christians." In that chapter, I discussed the arguments for their position and noted that it is probably the most popular view among Christians today. Somewhere in most church buildings and Christian colleges, you will find the Ten Commandments posted in a prominent location. The Ten Commandments serve as a constant topic for Christian books.[1] Many Christians teach their children the Ten Commandments at a very young age, and numerous pastors preach sermon series on them each year. Many Western Christians, if asked, "What are the greatest commandments?" would summarize their duty to God with the Ten Commandments.

---

[1]Countless books have been written on the Ten Commandments. In recent years, the following books have appeared: J. I. Packer, *Keeping the Ten Commandments* (Wheaton, IL: Crossway, 2007); R. Albert Mohler Jr., *Words from the Fire: Hearing the Voice of God in the 10 Commandments* (Chicago: Moody Publishers, 2009); Patrick D. Miller, *The Ten Commandments* (Louisville, KY: Westminster John Knox, 2009); Philip Graham Ryken, *Written in Stone: The Ten Commandments and Today's Moral Crisis* (Phillipsburg, NJ: P&R, 2010); Mark F. Rooker, *The Ten Commandments: Ethics for the Twenty-First Century* (Nashville: B&H, 2010).

I experience this emphasis on the Ten Commandments regularly in my teaching. I teach two general education classes every semester on the Christian worldview. In my freshmen worldview class, I require my students to reflect on how our sins reflect Adam and Eve's original sin. Every semester, I get a handful of students who state God has given us the Ten Commandments as our guide, and just like Adam and Eve broke God's command not to eat from the tree in the garden, we willingly break the Ten Commandments. In my upper-level worldview class, when I ask my students to explain how we as Christians know what is right and wrong, they usually point to the Ten Commandments first. My students' answers demonstrate the pervasiveness of this teaching in the church, but many Christians do not limit the relevance of the Ten Commandments to Christians.

Some Christians are so convinced that the Ten Commandments have moral authority over all people that they proclaim or display them to unbelievers as God's ultimate standard for living. For example, some evangelism methods begin the gospel presentation with the Ten Commandments.[2] After using the Ten Commandments to show people their guilt as sinners, these evangelists move into the good news of grace and redemption. Some businesses proudly display the Ten Commandments in front of their business. "The Ten Commandments Judge," Roy Moore, was willing to lose his job as chief justice of the Alabama Supreme Court for the sake of keeping the Ten Commandments posted in front of the judicial building. Recently, I even saw a bumper sticker that simply read, "Keep the Ten Commandments."

Even though we live in an extremely secular and biblically illiterate society, one still finds allusions to the Ten Commandments in public discourse. For example, USA Today ran an article titled "The Ten Commandments of Winning 'American Idol.'"[3] This parody of the Ten Commandments contains ten rules for Idol contestants, each beginning with the phrase "Thou shalt (not)."[4] Such language demonstrates that our society has

---

[2]For example, see Ray Comfort and Kirk Cameron's approach at www.livingwaters.com.

[3]Brian Mansfield, "The Ten Commandments of Winning 'American Idol,'" USA Today, March 3, 2013, www.usatoday.com/story/idolchatter/2013/03/03/ten-commandments-of -winning-american-idol/1959421/.

[4]I find it interesting how entrenched the KJV translation of the Ten Commandments remains in our culture.

accepted a Judeo-Christian reading of the Ten Commandments as an encapsulation of the primary laws for living life. Thus, when the culture uses the phrase "Ten Commandments" to refer to ten important things in a particular activity, they are borrowing from Christians and their interpretation of Scripture.

Because of the emphasis on the Ten Commandments in churches and American discourse, many of my readers might be wondering, "How do the Ten Commandments fit into his understanding of the old covenant?" I just argued that Christians are not under the jurisdiction of the old covenant, so in this chapter I will proceed one step further by specifically addressing the issue of the Ten Commandments. Should Christians treat the Ten Commandments differently than the other old covenant laws? Should Christians view the Ten Commandments as their primary guide for living? Furthermore, should Christians proclaim the Ten Commandments as God's ultimate standard for right and wrong? To answer these questions, let's begin by evaluating the Ten Commandments' relationship to the other old covenant laws.

EXCURSUS: DIFFERENT ENUMERATIONS OF THE TEN COMMANDMENTS

The various Christian traditions number the Ten Commandments differently. Roman Catholics and Lutherans typically treat the commandment not to make idols as part of the commandment to have no other gods, whereas most other Christians—including Reformed, Anglican, and Eastern Orthodox—identify the ban on images as a separate command and thus regard it as the second commandment. Catholics and Lutherans subsequently divide the prohibition against coveting into two commands: do not covet your neighbor's wife and do not covet your neighbor's goods. For these Christians, the two commandments represent the ninth and tenth commandments, whereas other Christians regard them as a collective tenth commandment.

THE TEN COMMANDMENTS AND THE OLD COVENANT

The Ten Commandments appear as a group twice in the Pentateuch. We first encounter them at the beginning of the Sinai narrative in Exodus 20.

They were the first laws Yahweh gave the people after Moses ascended the mountain and led the people into a covenant with Yahweh. Then they appear a second time in Deuteronomy 5, a passage in which Moses recounts the nation's time at Sinai (Horeb) to the new generation of Israelites. These two presentations of the Ten Commandments contain two major differences.[5] First, the rationale for the Sabbath commandment differs. In Exodus, Yahweh grounds the Sabbath command in his rest on the seventh day of creation, whereas in Deuteronomy, Israel's slavery in Egypt serves as the basis for the Sabbath. Second, the reward for honoring one's parents differs slightly in the Deuteronomy version, where Yahweh's promise of long life in the land includes the additional phrase "that it may go well with you" (Deut 5:16).

In addition to Exodus 20 and Deuteronomy 5, Moses repeats nine of the Ten Commandments separately throughout the Pentateuch.[6] When Moses repeats the individual commandments, he often gives clarification, explanation, or the prescribed punishment for disobeying the commandments. Regarding the prescribed punishment, breaking many of the commandments resulted in death.[7]

The twofold repetition of the Ten Commandments as a group and the multiple repetitions of the individual commandments demonstrate the prominent role the Ten Commandments played within the old covenant. However, Moses gives additional indicators of their special role within this covenant. When Yahweh entered into the covenant with his people, the Ten Commandments were the first laws given to the people, the only laws that Yahweh spoke directly to the people, the only laws recorded on stone (with the finger of God), and the only laws placed in the ark of the covenant.

How then do we articulate their special role in the old covenant? Moses helps us do so in Deuteronomy 4. After reminding the people of God's appearance on the mountain with burning fire and thick darkness (Deut 4:11-12), Moses states, "And he declared to you his covenant, which

---

[5] Rooker, *Ten Commandments*, 6, notes that there are "at least 20 differences" between the two versions.
[6] The following passages repeat the commandments with identical or very similar wording: #1: Ex 22:20; 23:13, 24, 33; 34:14-16; Deut 6:14; #2: Ex 20:23; 34:17; Lev 19:4; 26:1; Deut 4:15-18; 27:15; #3: Lev 19:12; #4: Ex 23:12; 31:12-17; 34:21; 35:2-3; Lev 19:3, 30; 23:3; 26:2; #5: Ex 21:15, 17; Lev 19:3; 20:9; #6: Ex 21:12-14; #7: Lev 20:10; #8: Ex 22:1-4; Lev 19:11, 13; #9: Ex 23:1, 7; Lev 19:11.
[7] See Ex 21:12-17; 22:20; 31:14-15; 35:2; Lev 20:9; 24:15-17; Num 15:32-36; Deut 17:2-7.

he commanded you to perform, that is, the Ten Commandments, and he wrote them on two tablets of stone" (Deut 4:13; cf. Ex 34:28). In this verse, Moses places the Ten Commandments in apposition to Yahweh's covenant. In other words, he is not saying that the Ten Commandments are a mere part of the covenant; he is asserting that they are the essence of the covenant. Thus, if someone had asked Moses to summarize the old covenant, he would have simply directed them to the Ten Commandments. For this reason, biblical scholars generally argue that the other laws in the old covenant are explanations or expansions of the Ten Commandments.[8] Some scholars compare the Ten Commandments to the United States Constitution.[9] Just as the American government has enacted numerous specific laws based on the Constitution, so also the specific old covenant laws that follow the Ten Commandments are specific applications of the Ten Commandments.

The separation of the Ten Commandments from the rest of the old covenant laws would have been foreign to Moses. The old covenant was a unit. The other old covenant laws were integrally connected to the Ten Commandments, and Yahweh intended for the people of Israel to obey this body of laws in the Promised Land (see Deut 4:14; 5:31; 12:1). Therefore, as goes the old covenant, so go the Ten Commandments. If Christians are no longer under the old covenant, then they are no longer under the Ten Commandments. The absence of such divisions in Paul's discussions of the law supports such a conclusion. Paul regularly refers to "the law" without separating different components of the law.[10] Furthermore, Paul often states that believers are not "under the law" without any clarifying phrases (such as "with the exception of the Ten Commandments").

HISTORICAL ANCHORS OF THE TEN COMMANDMENTS

I am not a fisherman, but I have several friends who own boats and enjoy fishing. When I go fishing with my friends, we typically anchor the boat to avoid drifting. After ensuring the anchor has gripped the bottom of

---

[8]For example, see Miller, *Ten Commandments*, 4-6, and Rooker, *Ten Commandments*, 9.

[9]Douglas K. Stuart, *Exodus*, New American Commentary 2 (Nashville: B&H, 2006), 441; Miller, *Ten Commandments*, 6-7; and Rooker, *Ten Commandments*, 4.

[10]For a chart on Paul's references to the law as a whole, see Thomas R. Schreiner, *40 Questions About Christians and Biblical Law* (Grand Rapids: Kregel, 2010), 43.

the lake or river, we happily sit in one spot until we pull the anchor up. On a much larger and more impressive scale, large ships are able to anchor in much deeper waters. When anchored properly, the anchors hold these large ships firmly in place, even when the wind and waves push against the ship.

A close examination of the Ten Commandments indicates that they contain several historical anchors. Like anchors on a ship, these anchors hold the commandments in the context of Israel's covenant with Yahweh and their life in the Promised Land. The Ten Commandments contain three historical anchors. First, in both declarations of the commandments, the prologue is identical: "I am the LORD your God, who brought you out of the land of Egypt, out of the house of slavery" (Ex 20:2; Deut 5:6). This phrase describes the historical exodus in which God delivered the Israelites from the bondage of Pharaoh. Yahweh's deliverance served as a key salvific moment in God's plan for the nation and fulfilled his promise to Abraham (Gen 15:13-14). The prologue thus identifies the recipients of the Ten Commandments as the ancient Israelites who were standing at Sinai's base and entering into a covenant with Yahweh. Second and similarly, Deuteronomy's version of the Sabbath command grounds the commandment in Israel's Egyptian bondage. Like the prologue, this historical anchor limits the motivation to the nation of Israel. Third, the promise of long life (and prosperity in the Deuteronomy version) as a reward for honoring one's parents finds its fulfillment "in the land that the LORD your God is giving you" (Ex 20:12; Deut 5:16). In the context of the Pentateuch, the land has a specific referent—namely, the land of Canaan. If Israel's children honored their parents, they would enjoy a long and prosperous life in the Promised Land. These historical anchors show that Yahweh gave these commandments to a specific people at a specific time in a specific place for a specific purpose.

Since Yahweh's covenant with Israel serves as the historical anchor for these commandments, any argument for a broader application of these commandments must establish that Yahweh intended the Ten Commandments for a wider audience. Even though the New Testament authors do quote some of the commandments (a point to which I will return shortly), we can demonstrate that one command did not extend to all nations. More specifically, Paul identifies one commandment that has no authority over Christians: the Sabbath.

THE SABBATH

It happens every year around the month of June. My family and I are driving through town, and all of a sudden my kids get very excited. They see the firework tents! As a parent, my problem is that I cannot drive anywhere in town without seeing a firework tent, so inevitably, at some point before the Fourth of July, I take my kids to purchase some fireworks.

As we browse the inventory, I love watching them make their decision about which fireworks to purchase. I give each of them a budget, so they can only buy a few things. One of the best bargains at these tents is the firework package. Firework manufacturers prepackage a variety of fireworks and sell them cheaper than the same fireworks would be if one purchased them separately. Unfortunately, the smaller firework packages usually only contain one or two good fireworks and many cheap, small fireworks.

I have one daughter who loves the beauty of fireworks. She likes colors, multiple explosions, and a variety of unique features. Because of her taste in fireworks, she would rather buy two or three beautiful fireworks than a package full of so-so fireworks. Consequently, she walks away with fewer fireworks, but the fireworks that she buys are usually our family's favorites.

When a business sells multiple items in a package, the buyer receives everything in the package, even the items that she or he did not need or want. The Ten Commandments function in a similar manner. As I underscored in chapter two, those who argue that Christians (or all humans) are under the Ten Commandments typically argue that the commandments are a package that contains God's eternal, moral law. For them, the Ten Commandments have always been and will always be the perfect expression of God's will for all people. If such is the case, then we have to accept the whole package.

When I outlined the weaknesses of Ten Commandments Christians' position in chapter two, I noted how the New Testament does not treat the Ten Commandments as a package. In fact, if you recall, the New Testament authors do not even mention some of the Ten Commandments. In this section, I will demonstrate how Paul teaches that believers are no longer under the Sabbath commandment. If Paul releases Christians from the Sabbath, then he has dismantled the neat package of the Ten Commandments, and we cannot rightly say that Christians are under the Ten Commandments.

The Sabbath and the old covenant. Exodus 20:8 does not contain the first reference to the Sabbath in the Bible. The first mention of the Sabbath appears in Genesis 2 when God blessed and sanctified the seventh day because of his rest on that day (Gen 2:2-3). Moses does not explain the implications of this sanctification in Genesis 2:1-3. Later, however, when Yahweh gives Israel the Ten Commandments, Yahweh's seventh-day rest serves as the basis for Israel's Sabbath rest. Just as God rested from his work on the seventh day, so he required Israel to rest from their work on the seventh day.[11]

The Sabbath serves a unique function in the old covenant. Moses explains this unique function in Exodus 31:12-17 by giving two important clarifications. First, Yahweh identifies the Sabbath as the "sign" of the covenant between Yahweh and Israel. The sign of a covenant functioned as a tangible reminder of the covenant obligations and, in this case, Israel's God (Ex 31:13). Such a function sets the Sabbath apart from the rest of the Ten Commandments in a special manner. If Israel observed the Sabbath, it would remind them and future generations of Yahweh's purpose to set them apart through the covenant he made with them at Sinai (Ex 31:13). It therefore served as a reminder of their national identity as Yahweh's nation. The Sabbath served a similar function in Israel as the Fourth of July does for Americans. It was a national holiday (i.e., a holy day) on which the people celebrated their identity as Yahweh's chosen nation. Yahweh gives a second clarification of the Sabbath command in Exodus 31:12-17 by stating the penalty for Sabbath breaking: death (vv. 14-15; cf. Num 15:32-36). The severity of the punishment underscores the command's significance. Yahweh held Israel to a high standard of conduct and expected them to comply with his commands.

Several other passages in the Pentateuch provide additional details regarding the Sabbath in Israel's society. First, one of the questions an Israelite

---

[11]As he did with the Passover command (Ex 12), Yahweh actually gives Israel the Sabbath command before the official covenant ceremony at Sinai. The first Sabbath command for Israel appears in Ex 16:21-30.

might have is, What qualifies as work? Later rabbis gave very detailed definitions of work. For example, the Mishnah outlines thirty-nine prohibited Sabbath activities.[12] These prohibited activities included writing two letters (of the alphabet), baking, untying a knot, or sewing stitches. While not quite as detailed as the rabbinic laws, Yahweh provides an example in Exodus 35:3, when he commands the people not to kindle a fire in their residences on the Sabbath. Numbers 15:32-36 shows that Yahweh even prohibited the preparatory aspects of kindling a fire (i.e., gathering wood) on the Sabbath. Second, the laws permit, and even require, certain activities on the Sabbath. These activities include holy assemblies (Lev 23:3), the priests changing the showbread (Lev 24:8), and the priests offering additional sacrifices (Num 28:9-10). Finally, another important Sabbath passage is Leviticus 25, in which the Lord extends the Sabbath rest to the land. He instructs the people to give the land a Sabbath, not on the seventh day but in the seventh year (Lev 25:1-7). Leviticus 25 also gives instructions regarding the Year of Jubilee, which came about every seventh Sabbath year (i.e., once every forty-nine years) (Lev 25:8-55).

The above survey demonstrates the important role the Sabbath played in the people's obedience to the old covenant laws. Not only was it the sign of the covenant, but it set the basic pattern for the nation's life in the land. Second Chronicles 36:21 underscores the seriousness with which God took Sabbath disobedience in Israel by connecting Israel's seventy-year exile to their failure to give the land its Sabbath rests. Thus, part of the reason God expelled Israel from the land for seventy years was so that the land could experience its Sabbath rests (which the Israelites failed to practice during their possession of the land). Is it any wonder, then, that after their return to the land many of the Israelites (e.g., the Pharisees) took the Sabbath so seriously?

The Sabbath and the new covenant. When Jesus of Nazareth stepped on the stage of human history, the Hebrew Bible's ultimate hope was realized. Indeed, the Messiah had come, and he would do for the people what the old covenant was incapable of doing: produce righteousness in their lives. During his ministry, one of Jesus' regular activities was engaging with the Pharisees. Indeed, Jesus' attacks on these religious zealots led to his eventual

---

[12]Mishnah Tractate Shabbat 7:2.

death. If we examine Jesus' numerous encounters with the religious leaders of his day, Sabbath keeping was a constant source of tension. Jesus performed multiple healings on the Sabbath (Lk 13:10-17; 14:1-6), and his disciples even plucked grain on the Sabbath (Mk 2:23-28), each occasion drawing the ire of his opponents, especially the Pharisees. Jesus responded to their challenges in different ways, sometimes drawing out their hypocrisy (Lk 13:15-16; 14:5), sometimes proclaiming his lordship over the Sabbath (Mk 2:25-28), and sometimes highlighting the true intention of the Sabbath command (Mk 2:27; 3:4).

Even though Jesus pushed the limits of Sabbath keeping in the eyes of the Jewish religious leaders, he did not break the Sabbath. He directly attacked their oral traditions that had accumulated throughout the centuries, traditions that went far beyond the old covenant laws. As the Jewish Messiah who came to fulfill the law, Jesus lived under the law "to redeem those who were under the law" (Gal 4:4-5)—that is, to move Jews from slavery to the law to sonship in Christ (Gal 4:5-7).

No New Testament author teased out the implications of Jesus' work in relation to the old covenant laws more than Paul. I have mentioned Paul's teaching on the law several times throughout this book in order to support my interpretation of the Hebrew Bible. When it comes to Christians and the Sabbath, Paul gives us the clearest teaching on the Sabbath day's role for Christians. He deals with this topic in two key passages: Romans 14 and Colossians 2:16-17.[13]

Romans 14 is one of two Pauline passages, the other being 1 Corinthians 8, in which Paul deals with what modern believers call "gray areas."[14] More specifically, Paul deals with ethical issues over which early Christians disagreed with one another. Like many of the churches to whom Paul wrote letters, the church in Rome was composed of both Jews and Gentiles (see Rom 1:13-29; 11:11-36). Such a combination was sure to present problems when it came to living out the Christian faith in particular areas. We might compare it to a modern believer who had a strict, legalistic upbringing worshiping alongside a believer who had lived an ungodly life before conversion. As the apostle to the Gentiles, Paul was always living in this

---

[13]Some interpreters add Gal 4:8-11 to these passages.
[14]I define gray areas as actions that (1) Scripture, when rightly interpreted, does not explicitly forbid and (2) may be practiced by some believers in certain contexts.

conflict. Since God brought Jews and Gentiles together into one body (Eph 2:11-22), the early church had to work through several issues. The two issues Paul tackles in his letter to the Roman church are permissible foods and Sabbath keeping.

Paul outlines the problems in verses 2 and 5. Some believers eat anything, while others only eat vegetables (Rom 14:2). Likewise, some treat one day more importantly than the other days of the week, while other believers treat every day the same (Rom 14:5). Paul directs his instructions regarding these problems to both groups. To those who eat everything or treat every day the same (the stronger believers [Rom 14:1-2; 15:1]), Paul instructs them not to despise the weaker Christians or put an obstacle in their way (Rom 14:3, 10, 13). To those who only eat vegetables and observe a special day (the weaker believers), Paul commands them not to judge those with a stronger faith (Rom 14:3, 4, 10). He bases these commands on the reality that all believers will one day stand before Jesus to give an account for their actions (Rom 14:8-10). Furthermore, Paul urges the believers to "pursue what makes for peace and for mutual upbuilding" (Rom 14:19).

Since Paul does not specifically mention the Sabbath day in Romans 14, how do we know that Paul has Sabbath observance in view? Verse 5 reads, "One person esteems one day as better than another, while another esteems all days alike. Each one should be fully convinced in his own mind." Although Paul does not mention the Sabbath day specifically, a close examination of the passage indicates that at a minimum Paul intends the weekly Sabbath observance.[15] He may include festival days, but if he does, he does so *in addition* to the Sabbath, not *in contrast* to the Sabbath. Two pieces of evidence support this interpretation. First, in the context of a mixed audience in Rome (Jewish and Gentile), the weekly Sabbath is the most natural interpretation of Paul's "one day." The Jews highly valued the weekly Sabbath as the mark of covenant faithfulness, and this practice would have created tension with the Gentile Christians who were not accustomed to such an observance. Second, the Greek phrase translated "all days" by the ESV emphasizes each individual day. Paul could have written the phrase in

---

[15]For a good discussion of this passage as well as interaction with alternative interpretations, see Thomas R. Schreiner, *Romans*, Baker Exegetical Commentary on the New Testament (Grand Rapids: Baker, 1998), 714-16.

such a way to emphasize days in general, but he does not. The Greek phrase he uses emphasizes "each and every day." In fact, the ESV is one of the few modern English versions that does not translate the phrase "every day." Thus, even though Paul does not explicitly mention the weekly Sabbath, by affirming the stronger believers (among whom he puts himself; see Rom 15:1), Paul includes the weekly Sabbath in the days that may be treated like every other day.

Notice that Paul did not command those who regarded every day as the same to begin keeping a Sabbath day; no, he simply commanded them not to judge the weaker believers or cause them to stumble. If the Sabbath commandment is an eternal, moral law (as many Ten Commandments Christians argue), then Paul should have commanded the Christians who were not keeping any special days to begin walking in obedience to Christ immediately. Instead, Paul simply lumps Sabbath keeping in with other gray issues such as eating meat sacrificed to idols (cf. 1 Cor 8). Paul certainly does not maintain that Christians must keep the Sabbath day, much less every human being.

The second passage in which Paul addresses the Sabbath confirms our conclusions regarding Christians and the Sabbath day. In the second half of Colossians 2, Paul teases out the implications of Christ's work with a view toward the false teachers in Colossae. These false teachers were pushing the Colossians toward a strict legalism that was contrary to the gospel of Christ. Drawing attention to the Sabbath, Paul writes, "Therefore let no one pass judgment on you in questions of food and drink, or with regard to a festival or a new moon or a Sabbath. These are a shadow of the things to come, but the substance belongs to Christ" (Col 2:16-17). Paul commands the Colossians not to let the legalists judge them in several areas, arguing that dietary laws, festivals, and Sabbath days were shadows.[16]

Paul's comparison of the dietary laws, festivals, and the Sabbath to a shadow is not the only part of this passage that confirms my proposal regarding the Christian's relationship to the law. You may have noticed that verse 16 begins with "therefore," which shows that Paul is connecting

---

[16]Paul's reference to "a festival or a new moon or a Sabbath" echoes a common expression in the Hebrew Bible that referred to Israel's holy days (see 1 Chron 23:31; 2 Chron 2:4; 31:3). The word *Sabbath* is plural in the Greek ("sabbaths"); however, this does not affect the meaning of the passage. Like Rom 14, this passage most certainly includes the weekly Sabbath observance.

his command "let no one pass judgment on you" to the verses that precede it (Col 2:11-15). These verses focus on the implications of the death and resurrection of Christ. For example, verse 14 states that Christ cancelled "the record of debt that stood against us with its legal demands. This he set aside, nailing it to the cross." The shadow ("the record of debt that stood against us with its legal demands") ended at the cross. On the cross, Christ officially ended the old covenant, and the sign of the old covenant found its completion. It is because of Christ's removal of these requirements that Paul commands the Colossian believers not to allow the false teachers to judge them about these former requirements. Once again, Paul makes it clear that the Sabbath day has not carried over in new covenant ethics.

Paul's teaching on the Sabbath demonstrates that Christians are not required to keep the Sabbath, but Paul does not address God's Sabbath rest on the seventh day of creation. Some Christian Sabbath-keepers use God's Sabbath rest to argue that Christians are still under the Sabbath. They identify the Sabbath as a creation ordinance since the Sabbath day was part of God's good creation. As I underscored earlier, Genesis 2:1-3 does set the seventh day apart, but the passage does not give an explicit command for humankind to rest. So, what do believers do with this passage in light of Paul's teaching? The answer lies in the book of Hebrews. The author of Hebrews underscores the reality of a Sabbath rest (not day) for Christians in Hebrews 3:16–4:10. After affirming this rest in Hebrews 4:3 ("For we who have believed enter that rest"), the author explains what this rest looks like in Hebrews 4:9-10: "So then, there remains a Sabbath rest for the people of God, for whoever has entered God's rest has also rested from his works as God did from his" (cf. Rev 14:13). Interestingly, the author of Hebrews bases the Christian's Sabbath rest on God's Sabbath rest after creation. Just as Moses applies God's Sabbath rest to Israel's Sabbath day (under the old covenant), so the author of Hebrews applies God's Sabbath rest to believers' future rest in God's new creation.

Before going further, I want to make an important clarification. My affirmation that Christians are not obligated to observe the Sabbath day does not mean that Christians should not rest physically. As stewards of our bodies in a frantic, fast-paced world, we certainly need rest, and most of us could learn a few lessons about what it means to rest well. Physical rest reminds us that we are created beings and that our work is not our life. Yet because of the freedom Christ has given us, this rest does not have to be on a particular day. Throughout church history, believers have chosen the first day of the week as their day of gathering for corporate worship. Many believers have also chosen the Lord's Day as a day of rest and family time. Does this mean that Sunday has become the Christian Sabbath? In order to answer this question, let's take a brief look at the relationship between the two days.

The Sabbath and the Lord's Day. The New Testament (see Acts 20:7; 1 Cor 16:2; Rev 1:10) and the writings of the early Christians provide ample evidence that the church designated Sunday as its day of gathering corporately in order to celebrate the resurrection of Jesus Christ, which took place on Sunday, the first day of the week (see Mt 28:1; Mk 16:9; Lk 24:1; Jn 20:1).[17] For this reason, the early church designated this day "the Lord's day" (Rev 1:10). This shift away from the Sabbath raises a couple of questions. First, did the shift away from the Sabbath include a shift away from a day of rest? Second, how does this shift relate to those who call the Sabbath a creation ordinance?

Early Christian references to the Lord's Day do not emphasize the Lord's Day as a day of rest but as a day of worship. The idea of a Sabbath rest on Sunday is not only absent from the New Testament, but it also does not appear in second-century Christian writings. Regarding the postapostolic church's understanding of the Lord's Day, New Testament scholar Richard Bauckham writes:

> There is no second-century evidence that Sunday was regarded as a day of rest. We do not know how much of the day was taken up by Christian corporate activities, but both persecution and economic circumstances must often have kept many Christians at work during the working hours of the day. As we have seen, the Sabbath commandment was never applied to the Christian Sunday, despite many occasions on which second-century writers must have spoken of such an application if they had held it.[18]

---

[17]Ralph P. Martin, *Worship in the Early Church*, rev. ed. (Grand Rapids: Eerdmans, 1974), 79, quotes Ignatius and the Didache as examples from the early church.

[18]Richard J. Bauckham, "Sabbath and Sunday in the Post-Apostolic Church," in *From Sabbath to Lord's Day*, ed. D. A. Carson (Eugene, OR: Wipf and Stock, 1999), 274.

The parallels between the Jewish Sabbath and the Christian Lord's Day only apply to corporate worship; they do not extend to the primary component of the Jewish Sabbath, rest from labor.[19]

The shift from Sabbath to Lord's Day also presents a problem for those Christians who identify the Sabbath day as a creation ordinance, meaning that God instituted the Sabbath as part of his original creation.[20] If one labels the Sabbath a creation ordinance because God sanctified the seventh day during his creation of the world, then one cannot move the Sabbath to a different day based on Christ's work of redemption. If one grounds the Sabbath in creation, then at minimum one would need an explicit command that moves the Sabbath day from the last to the first day of the week. The New Testament contains no such command. Therefore, to hold this view consistently, one would have to reject the tradition of the early church (which is permissible, since the New Testament does not command Sunday worship or rest) and rest on Saturday. Although some modern Christians practice Saturday rest, most Ten Commandments Christians do not, thus presenting another inconsistency between belief and practice.

THE TEN COMMANDMENTS, THE SABBATH, AND CHRISTIAN WITNESS

Having spent my entire life in America's Bible Belt, I have encountered my fair share of Ten Commandments Christians. I have also witnessed several ways Christians can bring harm on the witness of the gospel when they hold up the Ten Commandments as their standard for living. In what follows, I will discuss three areas in which Christians can harm their witness by upholding the Ten Commandments as the moral guide for modern Christians. Since these areas relate to the Sabbath command, these critiques would not apply to those who argue that Christians are only under nine commandments, a position which also has problems when we consider the packaged treatment of the Ten Commandments in the Hebrew Bible.

---

[19] The Jews gathered in synagogues for corporate worship on the Sabbath day (e.g., Lk 4:16; Acts 13:14).

[20] Thomas R. Schreiner, "Good-Bye and Hello," in *Progressive Covenantalism*, edited by Stephen J. Wellum and Brent E. Parker (Nashville: B&H, 2016), 168-70, gives four additional arguments against viewing Sabbath observance as a creation ordinance.

The first potential way Christians can bring harm to the message of the gospel is through their hypocrisy regarding the Sabbath. Imagine that you are an unchurched person who has little to no biblical knowledge, and you casually stroll into a local church one Sunday morning. As you walk into the foyer of the church, you notice a large plaque with the title "The Ten Commandments." As you begin to read the actual commandments, the first words strike you as odd, and you wonder who God brought out of Egypt. Nevertheless, you keep reading. You can understand the message of most of the commandments, but you begin to think about the command to keep the Sabbath day holy.

As you contemplate this command, you see a gentleman who looks like he might know how to solve your dilemma, so you approach the man and ask him, "What does it mean to keep the Sabbath day holy?" The man smiles and replies, "It means that we do not work on Sunday." Immediately, more thoughts go through your mind as you think about all the Christians you know who do various yard work and house chores on Sunday. What about the Christians who have to work on Sunday? What about the preacher? What qualifies as work? Does it mean an official job? It seems that if these commandments are our primary responsibilities before God, then something is amiss. Many of the people who identify these commands as their standard for living do not take the Sabbath seriously.

Although the above situation is hypothetical, most Christians do *not* keep the Sabbath in any way close to its original intention. In fact, most Christians have never stopped to think about the original command, its later explanations (e.g., do not make a fire on the Sabbath), and the penalty for noncompliance (i.e., death). In my view, these Christians do not sin by breaking the Sabbath; they cause problems by holding up the Ten Commandments as the standard by which all people should live. Even if a Christian chooses to keep the Sabbath, she must be careful not to proclaim it as a universal law, since so many Christians treat "all days alike" (Rom 14:5).

The second potential way Christians can harm the witness of the church in the world is through modeling bad biblical interpretation. Since most Christians can give no reasonable answer for how the Sabbath is still applicable, why it has moved to Sunday, why the death penalty no longer applies, and why Paul treats it as a nonessential command, the world sees a pattern of biblical interpretation that is at best ignorant and at worst disingenuous. For example, if someone were simply to read the rest of the old covenant, he might wonder why he does not have to build an earthen altar to God (Ex 20:22-26) or why Christians do not enforce the later penalties for breaking the Ten Commandments. Unfortunately, few Christians have answers for these types of questions.

The third potential way Christians can damage the church's witness is by modeling a lack of love toward other believers. Paul concludes his discussion of the weaker and stronger Christians in Romans 14 by emphasizing that all believers will stand before God's judgment seat (Rom 14:10). He then writes, "Therefore let us not pass judgment on one another any longer, but rather decide never to put a stumbling block or hindrance in the way of a brother" (Rom 14:13). What is sad about the application of this passage today is that many Christians who falsely believe that we are under the Ten Commandments are willing to pass judgment on their fellow believers in order to uphold a command we are no longer under (i.e., the Sabbath). In the same way, Christians who do not keep the Sabbath must be careful not to cause another brother to stumble when they enjoy their freedom.

As I stated regarding the other old covenant laws, I affirm that the Ten Commandments are good laws. They are not evil in any way. But upholding them as the rule of life for modern Christians presents several issues that could ultimately end up hurting the witness of the church in the eyes of a watching world. We thus need greater clarity and precision regarding these issues. The Ten Commandments served as a summary of the old covenant; Christ has given those of us under the new covenant another summary, which we will discuss in the next chapter.

THE TEN COMMANDMENTS IN THE NEW TESTAMENT

Many Ten Commandments Christians reply to the above argument with something like the following statement: "But since the New Testament authors repeats nine of the ten, then do they not imply that we are still under the Ten Commandments?" My next chapter will address this question in a more general manner, but before we move to that chapter, I will make three points about the New Testament's repetition of the Ten Commandments.

First, the assertion that the New Testament repeats nine of the Ten Commandments rests on an overgeneralization. The New Testament teaches ethical principles that nine of the commandments reflect, but no New Testament author quotes the first four commandments verbatim. That the New Testament authors teach the concepts reflected in the first three commandments (the fourth commandment is the Sabbath command) without directly appealing to the Ten Commandments demonstrates that the Ten Commandments do not provide the primary motivation for Christians to worship God alone (commandments one and two) and use his name reverently (commandment three). In other words, the New Testament authors do not tell their readers to worship God alone because it is part of the Ten Commandments. The lack of such a basis prepares us for a different motive for obedience under the new covenant. Ephesians 4:25-28 provides an example of Paul prohibiting the same actions as the Ten Commandments (commandments eight and nine) without appealing to the Ten Commandments themselves. We will discuss this motive in the next chapter.

Second, when the New Testament authors do quote the Ten Commandments, we must be responsible interpreters and interpret them in their context. Not only should we notice that the New Testament authors quote the Ten Commandments, we must also ask what they teach about them. Space does not permit an extensive survey of these passages, so I will make a few remarks about the New Testament teaching on the final six commandments.

Three individuals directly quote multiple commandments from the Ten Commandments in the New Testament: Jesus, Paul, and James. Jesus quotes some of the Ten Commandments on two occasions.[21] On both occasions, he is speaking within the context of a Jewish audience and demonstrates that mere adherence to the Ten Commandments is insufficient for a righteous life. Paul makes a similar point in Romans 13:9-10[22] when he argues that some of the Ten Commandments and "and any other commandment" (v. 9) can be summarized by the second-greatest commandment ("You shall love your neighbor as yourself"). He thus concludes, "Love is the fulfilling of the law" (v. 10). James comes to the same conclusion as Paul (even though he wrote his epistle before Paul wrote Romans). James

---

[21]Mt 5:21-30 and 19:16-22 (cf. Mk 10:17-22; Lk 18:18-23).

[22]In Rom 2:21-22, Paul alludes to commandments two, seven, and eight when highlighting the hypocrisy of the Jews. He also quotes the tenth commandment when demonstrating how the law showed him his sin (Rom 7:7-8).

refers to the second-greatest commandment as the "royal law" (Jas 2:8) in his argument against favoritism. He also underscores the unity of the law when he writes, "For whoever keeps the whole law but fails in one point has become guilty of all of it" (Jas 2:10). To illustrate his point, James quotes the sixth and seventh commandments.

Jesus, Paul, and James do assume that many of the ethical requirements reflected in the Ten Commandments apply to believers; however, their comments demonstrate that the second-greatest commandment functions as an adequate summary for the last six of the Ten Commandments as well as all other commandments. Thus, the New Testament moves beyond the requirements of the Ten Commandments in some significant ways. Not only do the New Testament authors not treat the Ten Commandments as a unified package, but they also prescribe more and different ethical requirements.

Finally, Paul does quote the fifth commandment as a direct command for the children in Ephesus (Eph 6:2). However, Paul's use of this command does not necessarily mean believers are under the Ten Commandments. Rather, it demonstrates the similar ethical requirements of the old and new covenants. He quotes and reapplies it to believers because it expresses the very ethical requirements he expects from his readers. A somewhat analogous situation is Paul's use of non-Christian writings to make a point with his hearers in Acts 17:28 and Titus 1:12. Although not inspired Scripture, these other sources provide an apt expression of Paul's point, so he uses them. I would apply the same to the Ten Commandments. Paul's use does not mean Christians are under the jurisdiction of the Ten Commandments; however, some of them provide a good example of proper behavior under the new covenant.

The above survey of the Ten Commandments in the New Testament highlights the ethical continuity of the old and new covenants. However, if we are not directly under the jurisdiction of the Ten Commandments, then what should Christians use as their ethical guidelines? Is there a simple summary of God's desire for Christians? Let's turn our attention to the law under which Christians live.

SEVEN

DOES THIS MEAN I CAN DO WHATEVER I WANT?

Grandparents are one of God's greatest gifts to families. As a kid, I lived a short walk from my grandparents' house and would always take advantage of this close proximity. Regularly, I would stop by their house to have a glass of my grandmother's southern iced tea and to watch *The Price Is Right* with my grandfather. I learned many life lessons by watching my grandparents live life to the fullest. My grandmother was a cheerful woman who had an extremely loud laugh. My grandfather taught me what it means to work hard as I watched him summer after summer grow enough vegetables in his gardens to feed multiple families.

For many grandchildren, the greatest thing about grandparents is the spoiling. Many grandparents have adopted the "spoil 'em and leave 'em" attitude. They see their primary role as buying their grandkids anything they ask for while at the same time rarely disciplining them. As fun as this is for grandparents, it does have an impact on the grandchildren and their understanding of life. In biblical terms, we might call this attitude "much grace, no law."

As I have argued that Christians are not under the authority of the old covenant, and therefore the Ten Commandments, you may have been thinking to yourself that I have made God into a soft grandfather who gives his grandchildren everything with little care for their ultimate behavior. If so, you are not alone, because opponents of No-Old-Law Christians commonly use such an argument. The official title of this "grandpa" view is antinomianism (meaning "against the law"). On a more basic level, people typically express the objection in this manner: "Does this mean I can murder? Commit adultery? Steal? Does this mean that I can do whatever I want?" These questions are questions that get to the heart of what we call Christian ethics. How do we as Christians know what is right and wrong? If we do not have the old covenant or the Ten Commandments to guide our actions, what do we have? The purpose of this chapter is to answer these questions. In short, the law (notice the lowercase) of Moses is not the guide for the Christian; the guide for the Christian is the law of Christ.

THE LAW OF CHRIST

On two occasions in his epistles, Paul mentions the "law of Christ." His first reference to Christ's law appears in 1 Corinthians 9:21 in the context of explaining how he becomes "all things to all people, that by all means [he] might save some" (1 Cor 9:22). He emphasizes that he became "as one under the law" in his Jewish ministry with the hope of winning them to Christ, even though he was "not . . . under the law" (1 Cor 9:20). On the flip side, he states that he became "as one outside the law" (1 Cor 9:21) to Gentiles. In order to protect himself from the charge of antinomianism, he clarifies that he is "under the law of Christ" (1 Cor 9:21). Like many other New Testament passages, 1 Corinthians 9 reaffirms my proposal regarding the old covenant laws. Paul explicitly states that he is not under the law (again, notice the lowercase), even as a Jew, but proudly identifies himself with the law of Christ. Unfortunately, he does not delineate the specific requirements of this law to the Corinthians, so this passage leaves us wondering about the contents of Christ's law.

In Galatians 6:2, the second passage in which Paul mentions the "law of Christ," he writes to the Galatian Christians, "Bear one another's burdens, and so fulfill the law of Christ." Here again, Paul does not explicitly identify the law of Christ; he simply informs the Galatians that their action of bearing each other's burdens fulfills Christ's law. This fulfillment gives us a hint, but it does not explicitly clarify the law. So, what is the law of Christ?

The most logical place to begin our search for Christ's law is the Gospels. Indeed, two important Gospel passages help us answer this question. First, one of the few areas in which Jesus agreed with the scribes was the question of the most important commandment in the Hebrew Bible (Mk 12:28-34; Lk 10:25-28). Jesus and the scribes identified the Shema as the greatest commandment: "Hear, O Israel: The Lord our God, the Lord is one. And you shall love the Lord your God with all your heart and with all your soul and with all your mind and with all your strength" (Mk 12:29-30; quoted from Deut 6:4-5). Yet Jesus never quoted this commandment alone; he always added what he called "the second": "You shall love your neighbor as yourself" (Mk 12:31; quoted from Lev 19:18). Jesus' identification of these laws as the greatest commandments indicates what Christ's law might be. In fact, Paul echoes Jesus' teaching in Galatians 5:14, when he writes, "For the whole law is fulfilled in one word: 'You shall love your neighbor as yourself.'" At its most basic level, the law of Christ is the law of love, love of God and love of neighbor. Such an interpretation fits well with Galatians 6:2, where Paul tells the Galatians that they fulfill the law of Christ when they carry each other's burdens. Sacrificial love for another believer demonstrates one's love for neighbor and God.

A second passage that helps us identify the law of Christ comes at an important juncture in the Gospel of John. Throughout the first twelve chapters of John, Jesus demonstrates and proclaims his identity to all of Judea, Galilee, and Samaria. His ministry shifts significantly in John 13, a chapter that begins with Jesus washing his disciples' feet and dismissing Judas to carry out his intended betrayal. With his betrayer gone, Jesus speaks to his remaining disciples about his coming departure, reassuring them and comforting them with news of a coming Helper, the Holy Spirit (Jn 14:16).

After informing his disciples of his coming departure, he gives them what he titles "a new commandment": "A new commandment I give to you, that you love one another: just as I have loved you, you also are to love one another. By this all people will know that you are my disciples, if you have love for one another" (Jn 13:34-35).[1] What makes this commandment "new"? Didn't we just discuss Jesus' quotation of the second-greatest commandment? Has love not always been central to the will of God? It is not the command to love that is new, but the manner of love. Christ commands his disciples

---

[1]Martin Luther, *A Commentary on the Epistle to the Galatians* (1535), trans. Theodore Graebner, Accordance electronic ed. (Grand Rapids: Zondervan, 1949), n.p., also identifies Jn 13:35 as the law of Christ.

to love one another just as he loved them. How did Christ love his disciples? Well, he explains his love toward the disciples in John 15:12-13: "This is my commandment, that you love one another as I have loved you. Greater love has no one than this, that someone lay down his life for his friends." Such a great, sacrificial love should characterize all Christ followers. Christ's love was not a love that did to his neighbors only as he did for himself. No, Christ's love was a love that did for his neighbors what they could never do for him in return. His death for his friends was the greatest personal sacrifice of all time. Such is the model and call for those who choose to follow the one who has given the greatest example of the greatest love!

Yet there is more. Jesus continues in verse 35 by identifying this great love as the badge of discipleship. In other words, the disciples' love for one another is what identified them to the world as Christ followers. As Christ's disciples loved each other to the point of laying down their lives for one another, the watching world would associate such great love with their master's great love.

Furthermore, Christ's new commandment gives primacy to those who are fellow disciples.[2] Three times in the span of these two verses (Jn 13:34-35) Jesus says, "Love one another." This one-anotherness of the new commandment underscores the new community that Jesus formed, that continued through the disciples, and that includes all subsequent Christ followers (cf. Jn 17:6-26). The new commandment places the primacy of the disciples' love on the community of Christ followers. This primacy does not negate Christ followers' obligation to love those outside the community. In fact, Jesus prayed to the Father for all believers in the following manner: "That they may all be one, just as you, Father, are in me, and I in you, that they also may be in us, so that the world may believe that you have sent me" (Jn 17:21). Believers can only attain this oneness as they submit themselves to Christ's new commandment, thus exalting him in the eyes of the world. This passage therefore demonstrates that the great love believers should have for one another does not exclude the world but is for God's glory in the world.

Once again, Galatians 6 helps us understand this interpretation of the new commandment. Paul writes, "So then, as we have opportunity, let

---

[2]For support, see D. A. Carson, *The Gospel According to John*, Pillar New Testament Commentary (Leicester: Apollos, 1991), 485-86.

us do good to everyone, and especially to those who are of the household of faith" (Gal 6:10). Like Christ, Paul places the primacy of love (i.e., "do good") within the community of faith, but this primacy is not a license to neglect the love of outsiders, since he also commands the Galatians to do good to all.

In summary, the law of Christ is not simply the law of love; it is a particular type of love.[3] First, the law of Christ is a love that reflects the great love Jesus demonstrated when he gave his life for others on the cross. Hence, Christ's law is not based on a law code but on Christ's example. Second, the law of Christ is a love that emphasizes Christ's faithful covenant community as the primary arena in which this love is performed. As outsiders witness this love within the believing community, they will understand more fully Christ's love for the world.

Before moving to the next section, one final characteristic of the law of Christ merits our attention. Just as the laws that Moses gave to the Israelites were part of a covenant, so the law of Christ is also part of a covenant, the new covenant. Jesus instituted this covenant at his death. When Jesus took the cup after the Last Supper, he said, "This cup that is poured out for you is the new covenant in my blood" (Lk 22:20). Therefore, just as the Ten Commandments serve as the summary of the old covenant's ethical requirements, so also the law of Christ serves as the summary of the new covenant's ethical requirements. One could obey all ten of the Ten Commandments and never come close to the sacrificial love demanded in the law of Christ. In this sense, the law of Christ requires a higher commitment and a greater sacrifice than the Ten Commandments.

THE OVERLAP OF THE COVENANTS: ETHICS

As I was surveying the two Great Commandments in the previous section, you may have correctly noticed that Yahweh gave those two commandments to Israel as part of the old covenant. Does this not imply that everyone is under the old covenant in some way? Since Christ said these were the two most important commands in the old covenant, surely he would expect

---

[3]F. F. Bruce, *The Epistle to the Galatians*, New International Greek Testament Commentary (Grand Rapids: Eerdmans, 1982), 261, identifies the law of Christ as "the whole tradition of Jesus' ethical teaching, confirmed by his character and conduct . . . and reproduced within his people by the power of the Spirit."

his followers to obey them. If they obeyed them, would they not be living under the authority of the old covenant? These questions represent a dilemma with which many believers struggle. Throughout the years, this same struggle has caused me to study and reflect on the continuity and discontinuity of the old and new covenants. Articulating these similarities and differences will occupy our attention for the rest of this chapter. Ultimately, the old covenant and new covenant have too many differences to represent the same strand of covenant relations, but before we discuss their differences, let us turn our attention to an area of overlap between the covenants: ethics.

Many of us have a hard time releasing some of the old covenant laws because they accord with what God requires under the new covenant. Such is the case with the Ten Commandments in particular. In many respects, parts of the old covenant overlap with how all humans know they should live, even if they reject Christ. Very few unbelievers believe that murder, kidnapping, and child abuse are good things. Where then do unbelievers get these standards of morality? Unbelievers might give a variety of reasons for their morality. Some might attribute it to a pursuit of the common good of all humanity. Others might attribute it to their genetic makeup. Others might attribute it to their upbringing. As Christians, we know where this standard of morality comes from. For starters, we affirm that God created human beings in his own image (Gen 1:26-27), and although scholars have dialogued for years regarding what the image of God is, many attribute our moral nature to this image. Even after Adam and Eve rebelled against their Creator, humans have retained God's image and therefore have an innate understanding of right and wrong. Some theologians and philosophers refer to this innate, universal knowledge of right and wrong as natural law.[4]

NATURAL LAW

God's eternal, universal law that he built into the created order and, more specifically, human hearts.

Paul writes about this universal awareness of right and wrong in Romans 1–2. In Romans 1, he argues that all who practice unrighteousness

---

[4]For a good introduction to natural law, see J. Budziszewski, *Written on the Heart: The Case for Natural Law* (Downers Grove, IL: InterVarsity Press, 1997), and *The Line Through the Heart: Natural Law as Fact, Theory, and Sign of Contradiction* (Wilmington, DE: ISI Books, 2009).

are "without excuse" because God has revealed himself in his created world (Rom 1:18-20). He ends the chapter with the following description of these unrighteous rebels: "Though they know God's righteous decree that those who practice such things deserve to die, they not only do them but give approval to those who practice them" (Rom 1:32). So how do Gentiles, who are primarily in view in 1:18-32, know "God's righteous decree"? Paul explains how in Romans 2.

After discussing "the day of wrath when God's righteous judgment will be revealed" (Rom 2:5), Paul explains God's justice as it applies to both Jews and Gentiles. While explicating God's standard of judgment (Rom 2:7-11), he introduces the issue of the law (of Moses) (Rom 2:12-16). He contrasts the position of these two groups toward the law in verse 12, writing, "For all who have sinned without the law will also perish without the law, and all who have sinned under the law will be judged by the law." Paul's description of Gentiles as those "without the law" leads him to discuss the Gentiles' knowledge of their requirements before God. He writes, "For when Gentiles, who do not have the law, by nature do what the law requires, they are a law to themselves, even though they do not have the law. They show that the work of the law is written on their hearts, while their conscience also bears witness, and their conflicting thoughts accuse or even excuse them" (Rom 2:14-15). Paul states twice in verse 14 that the Gentiles "do not have the law." The Gentiles' lack of a written code contrasts with the Jews who had received the law and its instruction (Rom 2:17-20; 9:4). However, the Gentiles are not off the hook, because Paul states that they do have a law, a law that in some ways reflects the law Yahweh gave to the Jews. This law is an internal law, as evidenced by Paul's references to their hearts, conscience, and thoughts. This natural law (notice Paul's use of the phrase "by nature") provides the standard by which God will judge the Gentiles "on that day when, according to my gospel, God judges the secrets of men by Christ Jesus" (Rom 2:16).

The Hebrew Bible contains three pieces of evidence that support Paul's teaching regarding Gentiles, the old covenant, and the natural law. First, Yahweh required strangers who dwelt among the Israelites to obey most of the covenant stipulations (Ex 12:48; Lev 17:10-12; 18:26; 20:2; 24:15-22; Num 35:15). When a stranger entered Israel's land and chose to live among the Israelites, he was thereby submitting himself to the covenant regulations.[5] If the old covenant laws were for all the nations, there would be no need to distinguish the stranger who lived in Israel's land from the rest of the nations. The Hebrew Bible itself therefore does not expect the nations (i.e., Gentiles) to live under the old covenant (cf. Ps 147:19-20).

Second, Deuteronomy 14:21 forbids the Israelites from eating anything that dies naturally but permits strangers who dwell in Israel and foreigners to eat it. Such a distinction indicates that Yahweh had different standards for Israel than he did for the other nations, thus highlighting the unique function of Israel's covenant and the Gentiles' position as those "not under the law."

Third, Isaiah, Jeremiah, Ezekiel, and several of the Minor Prophets prophesy against other nations. In their indictments of these nations, the prophets condemn them for numerous sins. Preeminent among these sins are the nations' mistreatment of Israel, pride, and idolatry.[6] The prophets also condemn their unjust war practices, lies, theft, oppression, trust in wealth, covetousness, violence, wickedness, and terrorizing of the earth.[7] Yet these prophetic indictments never mention the nations breaking Yahweh's covenant. In contrast to the nations, the prophets regularly highlight Israel's breach of the covenant as the reason for Yahweh's judgment.[8] The prophetic oracles against the nations thereby confirm that although the nations were not under the old covenant, Yahweh held them accountable for their sins. The old covenant laws prohibited many of the sins identified by the prophets (e.g., idolatry, lying, and covetousness), but the prophets never called the nations back to the old covenant. They expected the nations to know their actions were wrong. On what basis did they expect this? The simplest and most persuasive answer is the natural law that God has built into his created order.[9]

---

[5]I owe this insight to my colleague Mark Rapinchuk.

[6]Mistreatment of Israel: Jer 48:27; 50:11, 33; 51:24, 34-35; Ezek 25:3, 6, 8, 12, 15; 26:2; Amos 1:11; Obad 10-14; Zeph 2:8, 10. Pride: Is 13:11; 14:12-15; 16:6; 23:9; Jer 48:26, 29, 42; 49:16; 50:29, 32; Ezek 27:3; 28:2-6, 17; 29:3; 30:6, 18; Obad 3; Hab 2:5; Zeph 2:10, 15. Idolatry: Is 19:1-3; 21:9; Jer 48:35; 50:2, 38; 51:44, 47, 52; Ezek 30:13; Nahum 1:14; Hab 1:11; 2:18-19.

[7]Unjust war practices: Amos 1:3–2:3; Nahum 3:1; Hab 2:8. Lies: Nahum 3:1, 4. Oppression: Is 14:4-6. Trust in wealth: Jer 48:7; 49:4. Covetousness: Jer 51:13; Hab 2:6, 9. Violence: Ezek 28:16; Nahum 3:1; Hab 2:8, 12, 17. Wickedness: Ezek 31:11; Jon 1:2. Terrorizing the earth: Ezek 32:23-27, 30.

[8]Is 5:24; 42:24; Jer 11:2-10; 16:10-13; 22:9; 31:32; Ezek 2:3; 16:59; 20:10-13; Amos 2:4; etc.

[9]For a good discussion of natural law in the Prophets, see John Barton, *Understanding Old Testament Ethics: Approaches and Explorations* (Louisville, KY: Westminster John Knox, 2003). In particular, see Barton's second chapter, "Natural Law and Poetic Justice in the Old Testament."

God's natural law helps us understand the ethical overlap between the old and new covenants. When the ethical demands of the new covenant overlap with those of the old covenant, Christians should not conclude that we are still under the old covenant; rather, we should attribute the overlap to both covenants reflecting God's universal standards of right and wrong. In other words, *some* of the old covenant laws are *expressions* of God's universal moral law, but the old covenant laws themselves are not the moral law given to all people for all time. In particular, the Ten Commandments have a high degree of overlap with God's natural law, yet they are not identical. The old covenant laws that reflect God's universal natural law are historical and covenantal expressions of God's natural law.

This ethical overlap explains why the New Testament authors quote some of the old covenant laws and apply them to their readers. As I argued at the end of the previous chapter, the New Testament authors' use of the laws does not mean we are under the old covenant. They simply reused these laws because they expressed the ethical imperative they wanted to convey to their readers. The way modern businesses create policy and procedure manuals provides a helpful illustration. Whenever a new business begins, the owners typically write a policy and procedures manual. However, many companies do not start from scratch; instead, they often take other companies' policy and procedure manuals and use some of these policies in their own manual. In other words, they take the policy and use it in the context of their own company (recontextualization).[10] Likewise, when the New Testament authors quote old covenant laws for their hearers, they take the laws and recontextualize them in the new covenant. Instead of saying Christians are under some of the old covenant laws, we should say some of the old covenant laws correspond to new covenant ethics or that the New Testament authors have reappropriated the old covenant laws in their context.[11]

Natural law also explains the ethical overlap between many of the world's major religions. Buddhism, Islam, Christianity, and other religions contain many identical ethical requirements because God has engraved his (natural) law upon the hearts of all people. Natural law also explains the

---

[10]Jeanine Brown, *Scripture as Communication: Introducing Biblical Hermeneutics* (Grand Rapids: Baker, 2007), 232-67, uses the term *recontextualization* instead of *application*.

[11]Brian S. Rosner, *Paul and the Law: Keeping the Commandments of God* (Downers Grove, IL: IVP Academic, 2013), 159-205, uses the term *reappropriation* to describe the New Testament's use of the laws.

overlap between some old covenant laws and other ancient Near Eastern laws.[12] At some level, humans know what is right and wrong because God has built his standards of right and wrong into his created order and, more specifically, the hearts of all people.

As an example of how natural law works, let's look at murder. The sixth commandment reads, "You shall not murder" (Ex 20:13). On the basis of the law of Christ, we affirm that Christians should not murder. I am unaware of any believer who would argue that murdering someone is a form of love. Since the Ten Commandments prohibit murder, some Christians look at this commandment and say, "See, we are still under the Ten Commandments." There are two flaws in this way of thinking. First, Exodus 20 does not contain the first mention or prohibition of murder in the Bible. The first recorded murder is Cain's murder of his brother Abel. A quick perusal of this story in Genesis 4 makes it abundantly clear that Cain knew murder was wrong. How did he know? One may argue that he knew because God had told him so, though God chose not to include this conversation in the Bible. While such a conclusion is possible, natural law is probably already at work here. Therefore, because of natural law provided by God, Cain knew that it was wrong to murder before God gave the explicit command not to murder.

The first official prohibition of murder appears several chapters after Cain's murder of his brother. After Noah unloads the ark, Yahweh commands him not to eat the blood of animals and then gives an indirect prohibition against murder when he states, "From his fellow man I will require a reckoning for the life of man. 'Whoever sheds the blood of man, by man shall his blood be shed, for God made man in his own image'" (Gen 9:5c-6). Yahweh did not give this command because of humanity's ignorance of right and wrong. We can safely assume that humans already knew that murder was wrong not just because of Cain and Abel but also because Yahweh connects his judgment of humankind in the flood to their violence (see Gen 6:11-13), which certainly included murder.

The second flaw in the belief that we are under the old covenant (or parts of it) because of similar commands is that it fails to distinguish between

---

[12]For example, Mark F. Rooker, *The Ten Commandments: Ethics for the Twenty-First Century* (Nashville: B&H, 2010), 18-19, highlights the overlap between the fifth through tenth commandments and other ANE law codes.

the stipulations of a covenant and the covenant itself. The old covenant is much broader than the laws (stipulations) contained within it. The covenant includes a prologue, benefits for keeping the covenant stipulations, consequences for failing to keep the stipulations, a ratification ceremony, and more. Just because some of the covenant stipulations are similar does not mean that the covenants are the same.

Perhaps the illustration of differences between national laws will help to explain the overlap between the old and new covenants. In the United States, we have numerous laws against various activities. As a citizen, I am responsible to know and obey these laws. These laws affect most of my actions on a daily basis. I may travel to a different country and discover many different laws in that country. For example, if I travel to the UK, I had better obey their law of driving on the left side of the road even though I am accustomed to driving on the right side of the road in America. I cannot drive on the right side of the road in the UK and tell them, "In my country, the law states we must drive on the right side of the road." While I am in a foreign country, I am obliged to obey their laws, not those of my home country.

Yet, on the flip side, I might also discover that the foreign country has many of the same laws as the United States. Most countries have similar laws pertaining to murder, theft, property rights, and other matters. I was recently driving in Israel and had to obey their speed limits. This overlap in the laws of two countries parallels the overlap between the old covenant laws and the law of Christ. In this regard, we can say that the "what" of both the old and new covenants overlaps. However, when I am in a foreign country, I do not obey its laws because I am an American; I obey the laws because I am under that country's jurisdiction. Although my action is the same, my motive is different. The same holds true for the old and new covenants, which brings us to the differences between these covenants.

THE DIFFERENCES BETWEEN THE COVENANTS

A cursory comparison of the old and new covenants reveals some obvious differences. First, Yahweh made the old covenant with the nation of Israel. Israel was a geopolitical entity, and therefore numerous old covenant laws relate to the administration of justice in their society. On the other hand, the church does not comprise a geopolitical entity but consists of "sojourners and exiles" (1 Pet 2:11) spread among the nations who, like many of the faithful Old Testament saints, "desire a better country, that is, a heavenly one" (Heb 11:16).

A second difference relates to the punishment for sins. The old covenant outlined specific punishments for various offenses and even designated the persons responsible for administering justice in Israelite society. Under the new covenant, God does not outline specific punishments for sins. In fact, the new covenant emphasizes that because of Christ's atoning work, believers are not condemned (Rom 8:1). God does discipline new covenant believers (Heb 12:3-11), and Christ will require an account for their actions at his judgment (2 Cor 5:10), but God's actions under the new covenant contrast significantly with the punishments under the old covenant.

Two additional areas of difference between the old and new covenants should be mentioned to underscore my assertion that the differences between these two covenants far outweigh the similarities between them: motivations for and means of covenant obedience.

The motivations for covenant obedience. To return to our illustration about the laws of different nations, even though a law may be identical in two countries, there still could be differences related to the law. For instance, the United States will punish stealing by sending you to jail for a short time, whereas stealing in some countries will cost you a finger or even a hand. The latter provides a more significant motivation for obedience than the former. Many people are willing to risk some jail time to satisfy their hunger, but few people are willing to risk their hand for food.

Whereas the previous example relates more to degrees of motivation, the "why" of obedience under the old and new covenants is not one of degree but one of contrast. To explore this contrast, let's think about Israel's motivations for obeying the old covenant. Yahweh's initiation of the covenant with Israel in Exodus 19 provides two motivations. First, Yahweh's first words from Sinai read, "Thus you shall say to the house of Jacob, and tell the people of Israel: 'You yourselves have seen what I did to the Egyptians, and how I bore you on eagles' wings and brought you to myself'" (Ex 19:3b-4). Yahweh's gracious acts on Israel's behalf served as a key impetus for their obedience to him. Because Yahweh had judged the Egyptians and cared for his people, their appropriate response should have been faithfulness to him and the covenant. This motivation for obedience becomes a recurring theme throughout the Pentateuch and the rest of the Hebrew Bible. In the prologue to the Ten Commandments, Yahweh states, "I am the LORD your God, who brought you out of the land of Egypt, out of the house of slavery" (Ex 20:2). In Deuteronomy, Moses recounts the exodus (Deut 4:20, 34-38; 6:20-23; 10:19-22; 11:2-4; 29:2-3), Yahweh's provision in the wilderness (Deut 2:7; 8:2-5, 14-16; 29:5-6), Yahweh's military support (Deut 2–3; 29:7-8), and even Yahweh's gift of the old covenant (Deut 4:8; 33) as evidences of Yahweh's care for Israel, thus providing motivation for the people to follow their God faithfully.

Second, as I discussed in a previous chapter, Israel's special status before Yahweh and their unique task among the nations was contingent on their obedience. If they obeyed Yahweh and kept his covenant, he would make them a "holy nation," a "kingdom of priests," and his "special treasure" (Ex 19:5-6 NKJV). Even though Yahweh had graciously provided for the people, the old covenant's ultimate success rested on Israel's shoulders. The remainder of the Hebrew Bible highlights Israel's failure in this respect, but it also highlights God's grace and mercy as he continued to treat Israel as his "special treasure" despite their failure to live as a holy nation before him.

The blessings and curses that Yahweh outlines for Israel serve as a third incentive for Israel's obedience under the old covenant. Mentioned in several places (Lev 26; Deut 11:26-32; 28; 30:15-20), these blessings and curses receive their most extensive treatments in Leviticus 26 and Deuteronomy 28.[13] Deuteronomy 11:26-28 encapsulates the purpose of the blessings and curses the most succinctly: "See, I am setting before you today a blessing and a curse: the blessing, if you obey the commandments of the LORD your God, which I command you today, and the curse, if you do not obey the commandments of the LORD your God, but turn aside from the way that I am commanding you today, to go after other gods that you have not known."

Leviticus 26 and Deuteronomy 28 outline the specifics of these blessings and curses. The blessings Yahweh would give Israel if they obeyed his covenant relate to their prosperity in the Promised Land. Yahweh would increase their harvests, herds, and children. Furthermore, he would give

---

[13]Lev 26 does not use the words *blessings* and *curses*, but a simple reading of the passage and a comparison of Lev 26 to Deut 28 demonstrate that these chapters address the same topic.

them victory over their enemies and make them "the head" of the nations (Deut 28:13). Conversely, if Israel did not obey the laws, they would inherit the curses, which receive much more attention in Leviticus 26 and Deuteronomy 28, indicating "an expectation of covenant violation."[14] Instead of prosperity in the land, Israel would encounter plagues, diseases, drought, famine, attacks from wild beasts, and numerous other calamities. Far worse for Israel, Yahweh would grant their enemies victory over them and exile them to a foreign land where they would serve as slaves. In Deuteronomy 30:15, Moses uses the phrase "life and good, death and evil" instead of "blessings and curses." Life and death are apt descriptions of the two options for the nation of Israel. They could either have a prosperous life in the land or experience a national death (exile). The choice was theirs, and unfortunately they chose the latter.

These two options, life/blessings and death/curses, go back to the Garden of Eden, wherein Yahweh gave Adam and Eve the choice between life and death. Because of Adam and Eve's disobedience, Yahweh cursed the ground, expelled Adam and Eve from the garden, and brought death into the world. Thus, Adam and Eve's time in the garden prefigured Israel's future in the land. Just as Yahweh exiled Adam and Eve from his presence in the garden, so Yahweh also exiled Israel from his presence in the land. The ultimate symbol of Yahweh's removal of Israel from his presence is the Babylonian destruction of the temple. Although Yahweh's presence had "left the building" before the destruction (see Ezek 10), the temple ruins provided a tangible symbol of his departure.

Having evaluated Israel's motivations for old covenant obedience, let us now turn our attention to the "why" of our obedience to the new covenant. As in the old covenant, Christians obey Christ's law because of Yahweh's gracious election of us as his people. Just as Yahweh brought Israel out of the land of slavery, so also he has freed us from the slavery of sin through Christ's death for sin and resurrection from the dead (Rom 6:1-10). His salvific initiative in our lives serves as the primary motivation for holy living. God's gracious initiative is the only motivator for obedience that the old and new covenants have in common. Let's take a look at two major differences.

---

[14]Stephen G. Dempster, *Dominion and Dynasty* (Downers Grove, IL: IVP Academic, 2003), 110.

Perhaps the best contrast between the old covenant and the new covenant appears in 1 Peter 2:9, which reads, "But you are a chosen race, a royal priesthood, a holy nation, a people for his own possession, that you may proclaim the excellencies of him who called you out of darkness into his marvelous light." In this verse, Peter uses key phrases from Exodus 19:4-6, the passage that outlines the old covenant conditions. Peter, speaking to believers in Asia Minor, removes the conditional elements of Exodus 19 and applies Israel's roles to the church. Rather than having to obey a covenant in order to be "a royal priesthood, a holy nation, a people for his own possession,"[15] Peter asserts that believers are each of these things. In other words, Peter has reversed the motivations from result (Israel) to basis (the church). As Christians, we do not obey *in order to become* a holy nation and royal priesthood; we obey *because* we *are* a holy nation and royal priesthood. God makes us a holy nation and a royal priesthood by giving us a new birth "through the resurrection of Jesus Christ from the dead" (1 Pet 1:3). Because of our position before God in Christ, we "proclaim the excellencies" of our God who called us "out of darkness into his marvelous light" (1 Pet 2:9).

The second major contrast between the motivations for obedience concerns the old covenant blessings and curses. Since the two ways (blessings vs. curses) are operative from creation, we may safely conclude that these two ways represent Yahweh's normal operating procedure with humanity. If such a conclusion is true, then what does this look like under the new covenant? In Galatians 3:13-14, Paul explains how Christ's work changed the outworking of the blessings and curses: "Christ redeemed us from the curse of the law by becoming a curse for us—for it is written, 'Cursed is everyone who is hanged on a tree'—so that in Christ Jesus the blessing of Abraham might come to the Gentiles, so that we might receive the promised Spirit through faith." Once again, Christ's work takes center stage in understanding the differences between the old and new covenants. Christ's death as "a curse for us" results in Gentiles (and Jews; notice Paul's use of "we" at the end of v. 14) receiving "the blessing of Abraham." How freeing and how marvelous! Jesus took the curse so that we might freely receive the blessings. Like 1 Peter 2:9, this passage teaches that our reception of these blessings

---

[15]Peter's use of "royal priesthood" instead of "kingdom of priests" results from his use of the Septuagint (Greek) version of Ex 19:5.

does not depend on our obedience; it depends completely on Christ's work as the object of God's cursing.

Paul expresses similar sentiments in two other passages. In the first, 2 Corinthians 5:21, he writes, "For our sake he made him to be sin who knew no sin, so that in him we might become the righteousness of God." As in Galatians 3:13-14, Paul here underscores the great exchange that took place on the cross, substituting "sin" for "curse" and "righteousness" for "blessing." Israel failed to demonstrate righteousness under the jurisdiction of the old covenant, but in Jesus we gain righteousness. Paul focuses exclusively on our benefits in the second passage, Ephesians 1:3, when he teaches that God "has blessed us in Christ with every spiritual blessing in the heavenly places." Unlike Israel under the old covenant, our journey begins with blessing, and we live out of the spiritual blessings that Christ has given us. Our obedience does not result in additional spiritual blessings, since "in Christ" we already have "every spiritual blessing." Our faithfulness to Christ might affect our enjoyment of the spiritual blessings, but it does not change our possession of the spiritual blessings. Conversely, our disobedience does not result in God removing his presence from our lives in judgment (i.e., curses).[16]

The emphasis on spiritual blessing in Ephesians 1:3 naturally raises the question of physical blessings for believers, especially when we consider the emphasis on physical blessings under the old covenant. Although spiritual blessings were certainly a part of the old covenant, the Hebrew Bible emphasizes Israel's (potential) physical blessings in the land.[17] In contrast, the New Testament emphasizes the spiritual blessings that believers enjoy in the present age. Yet the New Testament also underscores future physical blessings for believers, thus explaining its emphasis on our future resurrection and the restoration of all things (new heaven and new earth). We "wait eagerly for adoption as sons, the redemption of our bodies" (Rom 8:23), and we will one day rule over the nations with Christ (1 Cor 6:2; Rev 2:26-27; 3:21; 5:10). As believers, we live in the reality of every spiritual blessing and in the hope of every

---

[16]Believers do not experience God's judgment (Rom 8:1), but believers can experience God's loving discipline (Heb 12:3-11). Furthermore, a believer's possession of God's spiritual blessings does not preclude sin's natural consequences (Gal 6:7-9).

[17]In fact, proponents of the prosperity gospel, who teach that Christians should be healthy and wealthy, erroneously apply these old covenant blessings to modern Christians.

physical blessing because of Christ's work on our behalf. We truly have victory in Jesus (1 Cor 15:57)!

The means of covenant obedience. Let's return to our illustration of national laws one more time. When two countries have the same law, not only is my motive for obeying the law in another country different, but the means by which I obey the law may be different. If I am driving in the UK or in America, I should honor the posted speed limit. Even though the law and the speed limit itself may be the same, the way I do this will be significantly different in both countries. In America, I sit on the left side of the car (unless I work for the United States Postal Service) and drive on the right side of the road. However, if I am driving in the UK, I sit on the right side of the car and drive on the left side of the road. Although I am moving the same speed in both instances, the means by which I drive the car is different in each case.

This illustration leads us to the final and greatest difference between the old and new covenants: the "how" of obedience. I emphasized in chapter five that Israel's post-Sinai actions demonstrated their lack of righteousness and thus their rightful receipt of God's wrath. To find the solution to this problem, we do not have to wait until the New Testament. As we will discuss more fully in a later chapter, the Hebrew Bible, beginning in the Pentateuch itself, gives numerous prophecies about God's restorative work in his people's hearts. Jeremiah, prophesying about the new covenant, states that God will write his law on his people's hearts and forgive their sins so that everyone will know him (Jer 31:31-34). Ezekiel states that Yahweh will give his people a new heart and that he will put his Spirit in them so that they will walk in his statutes and judgments (Ezek 36:24-27). This new work of God's Spirit stands in contrast to the rebellious, sinful hearts of the Israelites throughout the Hebrew Bible. The people were destined to failure unless God changed their hearts (cf. Deut 29:4; 30:1-6).

God fulfills these prophesies in the new covenant as the Spirit produces obedience and righteousness in his people. In the New Testament, and Paul's letters in particular, the law (again, notice the lowercase) contrasts with four key items: faith (Rom 3:21-31), promise (Rom 4:13-17), grace (Rom 6:14), and the Spirit (2 Cor 3:4-8). As believers place their faith in God's promise of salvation, which extends back to the garden,

God graciously sends his Spirit into their hearts to adopt them as his children (Rom 8:15-17) and to empower them to live holy lives (Gal 5:16). The Spirit's role in believers' lives stresses most clearly the key difference between the "how" of obedience to the two covenants. Unlike Israel under the old covenant, new covenant believers obey God from the inside out.[18] This explains why Paul consistently urges believers to be "led by the Spirit," to "walk by the Spirit," and to be "filled with the Spirit" (Rom 8:4-14; Gal 5:16; Eph 5:18). Indeed, the phrase "living by the Spirit" is an apt summary of the Christian life. As believers submit to the work of the Spirit in their hearts, the Spirit produces in them the fruits of righteousness. Thus Paul is able to say, after listing the fruit of the Spirit, "Against such things there is no law" (Gal 5:23). Christians who consistently live by the Spirit naturally stay away from the prover-bially cliff of lawlessness. While there were many faithful followers of God in the Hebrew Bible (1 Kings 19:18), the people of Israel corporately did not obey the old covenant laws, because they were unable to obey the laws. Every Christ follower on the other hand can obey the law of Christ, because God has given every Christ follower a new heart and the Spirit, who produces God's righteousness in our lives.

Such an emphasis on the Spirit's role does not mean that believers can do whatever they want (antinomianism). God has so changed us that our Spirit-led desires fall in line with the law of Christ, which we have seen is the law of sacrificial love. This truth also accords with Paul's questions in Romans 6. He begins the chapter by asking, "Are we to continue in sin that grace may abound?" (Rom 6:1) and then several verses later asks, "Are we to sin because we are not under law but under grace?" (Rom 6:15). In both cases, he answers his own question with a hearty "By no means!" (Rom 6:2, 15). For Paul, a believer living under the jurisdiction of grace instead of the law was not dangerous. Instead, as believers understand their identity as God's slaves (Rom 6:22), they live according to their Spirit-led desires (Rom 8:5-11).

To illustrate my argument in this chapter, I have included figure 7.1, which demonstrates the similarities and differences between the covenants.

---

[18]God's Spirit was active in the lives of his faithful servants in the Hebrew Bible. For example, 1 Samuel 16:13 notes, "The Spirit of the Lord rushed upon David from that day forward." Under the new covenant, all covenant members receive the Holy Spirit, not just a few.

Figure 7.1. Similarities and differences between the covenants

When it comes to the differences between the old and new covenants, these two covenants are oceans apart (to return to our illustration of the laws in different countries for the last time). Although some of the laws overlap, when we consider the covenantal context of the laws, the differences between the covenants become very prominent. Remember that this does not mean the Hebrew Bible and the New Testament are oceans apart. In fact, the messages of the Hebrew Bible and the New Testament are very similar. Both underscore the old covenant's failure to produce righteousness in the lives of God's people, and both show that God's work through the Messiah is the only answer for his people. Does this mean that Christians should mentally remove the old covenant laws from the Hebrew Bible? We will address this question in the next chapter.

EIGHT

WHY SHOULD WE READ THE LAWS?

At this point in the book, you are probably either mad or glad. If you come from a tradition that places significant weight on the applicability of the old covenant laws in the lives of Christians, then you may be somewhat frustrated. However, if you struggle with the laws and their role in the believer's life, then you may feel a sense of relief. Since you struggle to read the laws, you may have felt your guilty conscience ease. Although I have emphasized that Christians are no longer under the old covenant laws, I am going to change directions in this chapter and argue that Christians have a responsibility to read, know, and apply the old covenant laws. To put it another way, my goal in this chapter is to convince you to climb the mountain of laws in the Pentateuch. Just because we are not under these laws does not give us the right to dismiss them as worthless, especially considering the significant role they play in the biblical story. Indeed, our ability as Christians to understand the biblical story and to interpret later biblical books relates directly to our knowledge and interpretation of the old covenant laws.

One of my seminary professors once told an illustration that helps articulate the old covenant's function in the biblical story. The story of Noah and the flood is one of the more popular stories in the Bible. Most of us know the story well, but we often fail to think about how we read this story. When God decides to destroy the earth by means of a flood, he gives Noah instructions on how to build the ark and specifies the animals Noah should bring on the ark. Most Christians, after reading this story, are not tempted to build an ark in their backyard. Why? We clearly understand that God gave these instructions to Noah in a particular place at a particular time for a particular reason.

While we are not tempted to obey the specific instructions given to Noah regarding the ark, we usually draw some lessons from the story that help us understand the text, and from these lessons we derive principles to apply to our lives. For example, we have already seen the pattern, which finds expression in this story, of the necessity of righteousness in order to escape God's wrath. Noah escaped God's wrath in the flood because of his righteousness (Gen 6:9). This lesson helps us read later biblical stories and reminds us of Christ's great work in our own lives, whereby he "who knew no sin" became sin for us "so that in him we might become the righteousness of God" (2 Cor 5:21). We should praise the one who gave us his righteousness in order to spare us from the wrath God pours out on "all ungodliness and unrighteousness of men" (Rom 1:18).

Our approach to the old covenant laws should parallel the typical approach to Noah's story. Like his instructions to Noah, God gave the old covenant laws to a particular people at a particular time for a particular purpose, thus displaying his righteousness in an ancient Near Eastern context. We should therefore feel no obligation to appropriate these laws directly to our twenty-first-century context. Also, like the Noah story, when we read these laws in their context, we can draw some lessons from them that help us understand the overall biblical story, and then we can derive applications for our lives. In fact, if we do not read these laws in this manner, we severely handicap our understanding of the biblical story and miss its relevance for our lives.

Most of us do this on a regular basis with movies. When we watch a movie, we look for themes and then recontextualize these themes in our lives. We do not stop the movie after every scene and ask, "How does this scene apply to my life?" To do so would ruin the movie and cause us to miss the bigger picture of the storyline. Likewise, when we read the laws, we do not have to apply every law; instead, we must always keep the big picture of Israel's story in view. In previous chapters, I discussed the old covenant's function in the Pentateuch's storyline. Now let's turn our attention to some lessons that will aid us in understanding the larger biblical story.

LESSONS FROM THE LAWS OF EXODUS AND LEVITICUS

A detailed analysis of the 613 laws in the Pentateuch would take about three books and a decade of my life. In order to avoid such an experience, I am going to draw lessons from some larger sections of laws in Exodus–Numbers and selected laws in the book of Deuteronomy.

The tabernacle. After Israel arrives at Mount Sinai, the bulk of the material in the second half of Exodus relates to the tabernacle. Exodus 25–31 contains the tabernacle instructions, and Exodus 35–40 narrates the construction and dedication of the tabernacle. Yahweh instructed Israel to build a sanctuary according to the pattern he showed Moses so that Yahweh could dwell in their midst (Ex 25:8-9). The tabernacle had two sections, the Holy of Holies (the Most Holy Place) and the Holy Place, which were separated by a veil (Ex 26:33). The Holy of Holies contained the ark of the covenant, the locus of God's presence with the people (Ex 25:10-22). Three pieces of furniture were in the Holy Place: the table for the showbread (Ex 25:23-30), the lampstand (Ex 25:31-40), and the altar of incense (Ex 30:1-10). The entrance of the tabernacle faced the east, which is also where the entrance to the tabernacle court (Ex 27:9-19) was located. The altar of burnt offering (Ex 27:1-8) and the bronze basin (Ex 30:17-21) were in the tabernacle court. The materials (e.g., gold and fine linen) and the colors (blue, purple, and scarlet) used in the construction of the tabernacle (Ex 25:3-7) underscore its role as the royal residence of Yahweh.

While reading the detailed instructions and the meticulous account of the tabernacle's construction, one can easily lose sight of the big picture. The climactic moment in the narrative of the tabernacle's construction helps us understand the tabernacle's significance in the biblical story. After the people erected the tabernacle, "the cloud covered the tent of meeting, and the glory of the LORD filled the tabernacle" (Ex 40:34). Yahweh's glory was so overbearing that "Moses was not able to enter the tent of meeting" (Ex 40:35). Such a spectacular event highlights the tabernacle's ultimate purpose and explains why Moses devotes so much attention to it. The tabernacle was Yahweh's dwelling place among his people (Ex 25:8; 29:45). Israel's king dwelt in their midst and thus required his people to take the appropriate steps in constructing his dwelling place.

Yahweh's glory filling the tabernacle directs our attention backward and forward in the biblical story. The story takes us back to the Garden of Eden, wherein God dwelt with Adam and Eve. Even though the narrative only mentions Yahweh's presence in the garden immediately after their sin (Gen 3:8), we can safely assume that God regularly dwelt in the garden before sin entered the world. Adam and Eve enjoyed unhindered fellowship with Yahweh before their sin. God resided in their midst, and the garden served as his divine sanctuary.[1] Adam and Eve's sin changed their relationship with God in significant ways. Upon hearing Yahweh in the garden, Adam and Eve voluntarily fled from his presence (Gen 3:8), thus underscoring the shamefulness of sin before a holy God. Furthermore, when Yahweh exiled Adam and Eve from the garden, he not only prevented them from accessing the tree of life (Gen 3:24), but he also removed them from his dwelling place.

The tabernacle represented God's initiative in creating himself a dwelling place among his people again. Although Yahweh dwelt in their midst, the tabernacle served as a constant visible reminder that sin separated Israel from Yahweh. Instead of uninhibited fellowship with Yahweh, the people approached him by means of priests who offered sacrifices on their behalf. Yahweh even restricted the priests from his presence, only permitting the high priest to enter the Holy of Holies once a year on the Day of Atonement.

The tabernacle also prepares us for Solomon's temple. For many years, Yahweh dwelt among the people in the tabernacle. Eventually, David expressed a desire to build Yahweh a permanent dwelling place (2 Sam 7:2). Yahweh did not permit David to build him a temple but told David that his son would (2 Sam 7:13). After Solomon completed the temple and the priests brought the ark into the Holy of Holies, Yahweh's glory filled the temple. First Kings 8:10-11 reads, "And when the priests came out of the Holy Place, a cloud filled the house of the LORD, so that the priests could not stand to minister because of the cloud, for the glory of the LORD filled the house of the LORD." Perhaps you noticed the similarities with Exodus 40. Once again, the cloud of Yahweh's glory prevented anyone from entering his Holy Place. Solomon's temple in Jerusalem now served as Yahweh's dwelling place on earth.

---

[1]For a list of parallels between the Garden of Eden and Israel's later sanctuaries, see Gordon J. Wenham, "Sanctuary Symbolism in the Garden of Eden Story," *Proceedings of the World Congress of Jewish Studies* 9 (1986): 19-25.

The focus on God dwelling with his people in the tabernacle and temple takes a different turn in the book of Ezekiel. The book begins with a strange vision of God's chariot throne. Ezekiel identifies this as "the appearance of the likeness of the glory of the LORD" (Ezek 1:28). Later, in chapter 10, Ezekiel once again sees this chariot throne; however, this time Yahweh's glory does the opposite of what we saw in Exodus 40 and 1 Kings 8. Shockingly, Yahweh's glory *leaves* the temple and, eventually, the city (Ezek 10:15-20; 11:22-23), indicating that God has forsaken his people to their enemies and exiled them because of their obstinate rebellion. Just as Yahweh's exile of Adam and Eve represented their removal from his presence, so also Yahweh's forsaking the temple and the Babylonian's subsequent destruction of the temple represented Yahweh's removal of his people from his presence.

Like most of the prophets, Ezekiel did not leave the people without hope. Although God's glory had departed, Ezekiel concludes his book with a vision of a new temple (Ezek 40–48), which, like Solomon's temple, Yahweh fills with his glory (Ezek 43:1-5). Israel's great hope was that God would once again reside in his people's midst.

Such a day came when "the Word became flesh" (Jn 1:14) in a manger just outside the city of Bethlehem. In describing Jesus' incarnation, John actually uses tabernacle language. John 1:14 reads, "And the Word became flesh and dwelt among us, and we have seen his glory, glory as of the only Son from the Father, full of grace and truth." We could translate the phrase "dwelt among us" as "tabernacled among us." In other words, Jesus, as the divine Son of Man, dwelt among the people just as God dwelt among his people in the tabernacle and temple. Moreover, those who saw Jesus saw God's glory just like the ancient Israelites witnessed God's glory when his cloud filled the tabernacle and temple.

The theme of Jesus as the new and true tabernacle/temple extends beyond John's description of Jesus' incarnation; it served as a key component of Jesus' teaching and ministry. Jesus demonstrated his authority over the temple when he scattered the sellers and money changers from the temple courts (Mt 21:12-13), but he did not stop here. He also claimed to be the temple when he informed the Jewish religious leaders that he would raise the temple (his body) in three days (Jn 2:19). Such bold and shocking claims highlighted Jesus as God's dwelling place on earth and eventually led to his death, at which point God gave us another indication of a shift in the temple's role. After narrating Jesus' death, Matthew states, "The curtain of the temple was torn in two, from top to bottom" (Mt 27:51). Yahweh's presence was no longer limited to the high priest on the Day of Atonement. The tearing of the temple veil visualized the newfound access to God's presence that his people would enjoy because of Jesus' death (cf. Heb 10:19-20). Jesus had taken care of the sin that separated God's people from his presence for so long.

Not only did Jesus replace the tabernacle/temple, but he also replaced the Aaronic priesthood. The author of Hebrews repeatedly emphasizes that Jesus has become our great high priest. As our perfect and eternal high priest (Heb 7:26-28), Jesus leads us "into the inner place behind the curtain, where Jesus has gone as a forerunner on our behalf" (Heb 6:19-20). Since our high priest "has been tempted as we are," we can approach God with confidence (Heb 4:15).

Since Jesus serves as our high priest at the Father's right hand, where is the true temple today? Did the Jerusalem temple resume its function as Yahweh's dwelling place after Jesus' ascension? Are we waiting for another temple? Several passages in the New Testament Epistles answer these questions for us. The first of these passages, Ephesians 2:19-22, states:

> So then you are no longer strangers and aliens, but you are fellow citizens with the saints and members of the household of God, built on the foundation of the apostles and prophets, Christ Jesus himself being the cornerstone, in whom the whole structure, being joined together, grows into a holy temple in the Lord. In him you also are being built together into a dwelling place for God by the Spirit.

Paul uses the imagery of a building to describe the church, but he does not describe just any building; he describes the "holy temple." In this passage, Paul addresses Gentiles who were once far removed from God's people and promises (Eph 2:11-12, 19) but have now been brought near and made one with Jewish believers in the church (Eph 2:13-19). In describing this new "household of God," which includes Jews and Gentiles, Paul outlines the different parts of the building: the apostles and prophets serve as the foundation, Christ is the cornerstone, and the church is the building under construction. As a holy temple, the church is now God's dwelling place

(Eph 2:21-22). God's temple, his dwelling place, is no longer a stone building, but his temple is now his people, the church. He dwells in our midst through his Spirit (1 Cor 3:16).

Peter also identifies the church as God's temple. In 1 Peter 2:4-5, he compares the church to two of the tabernacle/temple's key components: the building itself and the priests. The passage reads, "As you come to him, a living stone rejected by men but in the sight of God chosen and precious, you yourselves like living stones are being built up as a spiritual house, to be a holy priesthood, to offer spiritual sacrifices acceptable to God through Jesus Christ." Peter refers to believers as "living stones" who "are being built up as a spiritual house." Like Paul, Peter compares believers to the walls of the building itself. Although Peter does not specifically refer to this building as a temple, the context contains so many temple allusions (priests and sacrifices in v. 5; Jesus as the cornerstone in vv. 6-7) that we should identify this "spiritual house" as the temple of the living God. As God's people, we are God's house in this world.

Quickly shifting the metaphor, Peter then describes the church as "a holy priesthood." God has set his church apart (the meaning of holy) as his priests, and just like the priests under the old covenant, the church offers sacrifices, not the sacrifices of bulls and goats, but spiritual sacrifices that are acceptable because we offer them through our great high priest, Jesus Christ. Because of Christ's victory over sin, God's people now enjoy uninhibited fellowship with him as his Spirit lives within them, and consequently, his people now serve as priests who offer sacrifices to him.

The final chapters of Revelation are particularly important as we complete our survey of the biblical teaching on the tabernacle and temple. After describing God's creation of the new heaven and new earth in one simple verse (Rev 21:1), John spends the next thirty-one verses describing the new Jerusalem that came down from heaven (Rev 21:2–22:5). Upon seeing the new Jerusalem, John hears a voice saying, "Behold, the dwelling place of God is with man. He will dwell with them, and they will be his people, and God himself will be with them as their God." (Rev 21:3). With the arrival of the new Jerusalem on the new earth, the story is complete. God fully restores the intimacy between himself and humanity, the same intimacy Adam and Even experienced in the garden. No longer does God need a building (physical or spiritual) to dwell with humans; he himself will permanently tabernacle in their midst. Such is made explicit in Revelation 21:22 when John writes, "And I saw no temple in the city, for its temple is the Lord God the Almighty and the Lamb."

In summary, our survey of the biblical teaching on God's dwelling among his people has demonstrated the significance of the tabernacle in the development of this theme. To reiterate my point, although none of us should be tempted to construct a tabernacle in our church parking lots, this does not mean that the tabernacle instructions and the narration of its construction in Exodus are irrelevant to us today. Understanding the tabernacle in light of the larger biblical story helps us understand the church's role more clearly. As members of the church, we are God's tabernacle on this earth. In other words, God's dwelling place with humanity is through his Spirit in his spiritual house. Such a reality cannot help but motivate us to live holy lives built on our chief cornerstone, Jesus Christ.

The sacrificial system. Immediately following the completion of the tabernacle and the overwhelming display of God's glory in Exodus, Yahweh gave laws regarding one of the primary activities at the tabernacle: the offerings. These offerings provided the means by which the people were to approach Yahweh's holy presence. Leviticus 1–7 contains regulations for five different offerings, three of which involve a sacrifice for the atonement of sin (burnt [Lev 1:4; 5:10], sin [Lev 4:20, 26, 31, 35; 5:6, 13], and guilt [Lev 5:16, 18; 6:7]). Additionally, Yahweh, in Leviticus 16, gives instructions regarding the Day of Atonement, a sacred day on which the high priest made atonement for the Holy of Holies, the tabernacle, the altar, the priests, and all the assembly (Lev 16:33) by means of several sacrifices.

Israel's sacrificial system underscores four important concepts related to how sinful people approach a holy God. First, the sacrifices teach us about the need for atonement. For a sinful people to maintain communion with Yahweh, they needed Yahweh to forgive their sins and thereby purify them for fellowship. The sacrifices provided this purification for the people. The word *atonement* refers to the removal of sin and its associated consequences.[2] When the people sacrificed an animal to Yahweh, Yahweh

---

[2] The exact meaning of the Hebrew word for "atonement" (Hebrew root: *kpr*) is uncertain. Both Mark F. Rooker, *Leviticus*, New American Commentary 3a (Nashville: B&H, 2000), 51-53, and Gordon J. Wenham, *The Book of Leviticus*, New International Commentary on the Old Testament (Grand Rapids: Eerdmans, 1979), 28, propose a dual meaning for the word depending on the context. The meaning "cleanse" or "wipe" applies to "those contexts where

removed their sin and guilt. The atonement Israel experienced through animal sacrifice was not salvific; instead, the atoning sacrifices functioned as a means for Israel to maintain ritual purity before Yahweh (see Heb 9:8-14; 10:1-10). Yahweh had already chosen them as his people; the sacrifices provided the necessary means for Israel to approach their God.

A second prominent concept in Leviticus's sacrificial legislation is that of substitution. In the laws for three sacrifices, Yahweh required the worshiper to "lay his hand" on the animal's head before the sacrifice (Lev 1:4; 3:2, 8, 13; 4:4, 15, 24, 29, 33). The early chapters of Leviticus do not explain this practice, but Yahweh prescribed a similar practice on the Day of Atonement. Before sending the scapegoat away, Aaron laid both hands on the goat's head and confessed the people's sins (Lev 16:21). This action symbolized the goat carrying Israel's sins out of the camp (Lev 16:22). Although the worshiper's hand laying before sacrifices differed somewhat from the high priest's hand laying on the Day of Atonement, some scholars interpret the worshiper's hand laying as a symbol of transfer from the worshiper to the sacrifice.[3] The act could symbolize the worshiper's acknowledgment that the animal was dying in his or her place or that the animal was bearing the sins of the worshiper. Either option underscores the animal's death as a substitute for the worshiper. Without the animal sacrifice, the worshiper bore his or her sin and guilt.

A third important component of sacrifice was the role of blood. Being a priest in Israel was a bloody job. After the worshipers slaughtered their sacrifice, the priests sprinkled the blood on the altar or, in the case of the sin offering, other places in the tabernacle. On the Day of Atonement, the priest sprinkled blood on the ark of the covenant in the Holy of Holies (Lev 16:11-17). The shedding and sprinkling of blood was a crucial component of the atonement process. Leviticus 17:11 aptly summarizes the importance of blood: "For the life of the flesh is in the blood, and I have given it for you on the altar to make atonement for your souls, for it is the blood that makes atonement by the life." The mention of the blood's atoning role makes this verse unique. The blood of animals played a sacred role in atoning for the people's sins.

---

the altar or the sanctuary is the direct object of the verb," but the meaning "to pay a ransom" fits with "most of the passages that speak of sacrifice 'making atonement' for someone" (Wenham, *Book of Leviticus*, 28).

[3]For example, Rooker, *Leviticus*, 87, and Wenham, *Book of Leviticus*, 62.

A final and closely related sacrificial concept concerns the type of animal sacrificed. Throughout the early chapters of Leviticus, the phrase "without blemish" echoes through the sacrificial laws. Leviticus 22:17-25 supplements these early chapters by specifying the unacceptable blemishes. Yahweh's stringent sacrificial requirements stressed his sacredness and the high price of atonement. The offering of an unblemished sacrifice required the worshiper to offer his or her best to Yahweh. To fail to do so was an abomination before Yahweh (cf. Deut 17:1). Malachi 1:6-14 helps us better understand the significance of an unblemished sacrifice. While rebuking his people for offering blemished sacrifices, Yahweh reminds his people that their governor would not even accept their sacrifices (Mal 1:8) and that he (Yahweh) is a great king whose "name will be feared among the nations" (Mal 1:14). The type of sacrifice indicated the worthiness of the one to whom the worshiper offered it. Since there is no one more worthy than Yahweh, his sacrifices were to be without blemish.

Like the tabernacle, Israel's sacrificial system forms one strand in a tightly woven cord that traverses the biblical story. This cord begins in the early chapters of Genesis, where we find the first offerings in the Bible. Genesis 4 informs us that Cain and Abel both brought offerings to the Lord, Cain "an offering of the fruit of the ground" (Gen 4:3) and Abel an offering "of the firstborn of his flock and of their fat portions" (Gen 4:4). To our amazement as readers, we quickly discover that the Lord "had no regard" for "Cain and his offering" (Gen 4:5). Commentators have long discussed why the Lord accepted one offering and not the other.[4] While many of the proposals are intriguing, the text does not simply say the Lord respected Abel's offering and did not respect Cain's. In both instances, the focus is on the offering *and* the giver. In fact, the acceptance or rejection of the giver precedes any mention of their offering, demonstrating that the offering's acceptability did not depend solely on the offering itself but also on the giver.

A second important offering in the early chapters of Genesis was the burnt offering Noah presented to Yahweh shortly after he disembarked from the ark. Before his equilibrium even had time to balance after such a

---

[4]For a review of the proposals, see Gordon J. Wenham, *Genesis 1–15*, Word Biblical Commentary 1 (Waco, TX: Word, 1987), 104.

long sea journey, Noah built an altar and offered burnt offerings. Yahweh's response to Noah's offerings teaches us something important about sacrifice. Genesis 8:21 reads, "And when the LORD smelled the pleasing aroma, the LORD said in his heart, 'I will never again curse the ground because of man, for the intention of man's heart is evil from his youth. Neither will I ever again strike down every living creature as I have done.'" Those familiar with the Noah narrative should recognize the parallels between this verse and Yahweh's pre-flood assessment of humanity: "The LORD saw that the wickedness of man was great in the earth, and that every intention of the thoughts of his heart was only evil continually" (Gen 6:5). Both verses emphasize the evil of human hearts, but God's response to human evil is completely different in the two passages. Why is Yahweh's response so different? As far as humans are concerned, Genesis 8:21 shows that there has been no change. So, what changed? We find the answer in Noah's burnt offerings, the aroma of which pleased God and thus prompted his promise not to destroy all creatures again. Noah's priestly sacrifices give us the first glimpse of an important theme: the necessity of sacrifice for appeasing God's wrath against sin.

The above examples are not the only pre-Sinai instances of Yahweh worshipers bringing an offering before his presence (e.g., Gen 22:13; 35:14). All of these earlier sacrifices foreshadow the sacrificial laws and provide the seedbed for an understanding of the role of sacrifice in the worship of Yahweh. In fact, the themes gleaned from these stories glide along through the biblical story like a zip line. For example, the truth that God regards both the worshiper *and* the sacrifice connects with the necessity of confession in the sacrificial laws (Lev 5:5) but finds its loudest echoes in the Prophets. Several prophets inform the people that their sacrifices are unacceptable to God (Is 1:10-17; Jer 6:19-20; Mal 1:6-14). Why did God reject their sacrifices? The people were not caring for the weak and oppressed in their society (Is 1:15-17), they rejected his words (Jer 6:19), and they offered blemished sacrifices (Mal 1:6-14). Notice that only one of these passages focuses on the offering itself. Isaiah and Jeremiah both focus on the people's actions as the reason for Yahweh's rejection of their sacrifices. Isaiah criticizes them for failing to love others, and Jeremiah rebukes them for failing to love God. God was not impressed with their rituals; he desired the totality of the worshiper's allegiance.

The sacrificial imagery of the Hebrew Bible ultimately prepares us for Christ's work. The Gospel writers emphasize Jesus' role in forgiving sin (Mt 1:21), but John gives the clearest indication that the blood of bulls and goats is not the ultimate sacrifice for sin. In John 1:29, John the Baptist, upon seeing Jesus, exclaimed, "Behold, the Lamb of God, who takes away the sin of the world!" By calling Jesus the "Lamb of God," John the Baptist emphasized Jesus' role as a sacrifice for sins, yet unlike the sacrifices of the old covenant, this sacrifice was able to "take away the sin of the world."

The Gospels also teach Jesus' fulfillment of another sacrifice, the sacrifice of the Passover lamb. By instituting the Lord's Supper at the Passover meal and emphasizing his coming death (Mt 26:17-30), Jesus highlighted his fulfillment of this significant festival. John makes another connection to the Passover lamb when he identifies the nonbreaking of Jesus' legs as a fulfillment of the command for Israel not to break the legs of the Passover lamb (Jn 19:31-37).

In addition to the Passover lamb, Jesus also demonstrated his fulfillment of two key old covenant components when he instituted the Lord's Supper. When he mentioned the "blood of the covenant" (Mt 26:28), Jesus drew his hearer's attention to the blood of the old covenant, which Moses sprinkled on the people at Mount Sinai. After sprinkling the blood on the people, Moses said, "Behold the blood of the covenant that the LORD has made with you in accordance with all these words" (Ex 24:8). Jesus did not ratify the new covenant with the blood of bulls but with his own blood. Second, by stating that his blood was "poured out for many for the forgiveness of sins," Jesus alluded to the old covenant atoning sacrifices. Clearly, we need to understand the old covenant and its practices if we are going to perceive the significance of Christ's sacrificial death.

The Epistles also identify the death of Jesus as the sacrifice for sins (Rom 3:25; 8:3; 1 Cor 5:7; 2 Cor 5:21; Eph 1:7; 5:2; 1 Pet 1:19; 2:22-25; 1 Jn 2:2), yet within the Epistles, the book of Hebrews gives the most extensive treatment of this topic. In particular, Hebrews 9:1–10:18 shows how the once-for-all sacrifice of Christ for sin provides perfect cleansing and permanent redemption for those who follow him. If we think in light of the four key sacrificial components listed above, Hebrews teaches that Jesus was the perfect sacrifice (Heb 4:15; 7:26-28; 9:14), who shed his blood (Heb 9:11-14, 22; 10:4; 12:24) as a substitutionary sacrifice (Heb 7:27; 9:28;

10:10-14) to atone for our sins (Heb 7:27; 9:11-15, 26-28; 10:10-14). Jesus fulfills every aspect of the old covenant sacrificial system. The author of Hebrews says it best when he writes, "Where there is forgiveness of these, there is no longer any offering for sin" (Heb 10:18).

Even though the New Testament emphasizes Jesus as the perfect and final sacrifice for sin, the New Testament authors often use sacrificial imagery to describe the Christian life before God. Paul sometimes compared his suffering to a drink offering (Phil 2:17; 2 Tim 4:6) and once described the Gentiles he led to Christ as "the offering of the Gentiles" (Rom 15:16). He characterized the Philippians' faith as a sacrifice (Phil 2:17) and their monetary support as "a fragrant offering, a sacrifice acceptable and pleasing to God" (Phil 4:18). In Romans 12:1, Paul commanded the Roman believers to offer their bodies as a sacrifice to God. He describes this "living sacrifice" as "holy and acceptable to God, which is your spiritual worship." In contrast to the dead animals the priests presented to God under the old covenant, believers offer their bodies as a living sacrifice.

Outside of Paul, two other New Testament books describe the Christian life with sacrificial imagery. The author of Hebrews commands his readers to offer God "a sacrifice of praise" (Heb 13:15) and identifies sharing with others as a sacrifice that pleases God (Heb 13:16). Peter describes believers as a "holy priesthood" that offers "spiritual sacrifices acceptable to God through Jesus Christ" (1 Pet 2:5).

Notice three things about these New Testament passages that use sacrificial imagery to describe a believer's life. First, conspicuously absent from these passages is any focus on the atoning aspect. The New Testament authors understood Christ's atoning sacrifice as the be-all and end-all sacrifice for sin. Second, several of these passages highlight the acceptability of the Christian's sacrifice before God. In Romans 12:1 and Hebrews 13:16, the acceptability of the sacrifice before God serves as the motivation for performing the sacrifice. Peter goes further and identifies the reason why the believer's sacrifice is acceptable; God accepts it because it is "through Jesus Christ" (1 Pet 2:5). Although not explicitly mentioned in every passage, this reason stands in the backdrop of every passage. God accepts our sacrifices only because of Jesus' sacrifice. Finally, the imagery in several of these passages (Phil 2:17; 4:18; 2 Tim 4:6; Rom 12:1) stresses the sacrifice's costliness for the worshiper.

Holiness. One of the primary themes of Leviticus is holiness. Words related to holiness appear over 150 times in Leviticus, thus distinguishing Leviticus as the biblical book with the highest concentration of "holy" words.[5] The phrase "Be holy, because I am holy" serves as a constant refrain throughout Leviticus, providing unity to the book and reminding us of God's intention for Israel to be a "holy nation" (Ex 19:5-6). Holiness carries connotations of both purity and separation. In reality, we cannot separate these two concepts. Purity of conduct serves as the means by which one is "set apart" to Yahweh. Leviticus 20:26 provides an example of the interconnectedness of these two ideas: "You shall be holy to me, for I the LORD am holy and have separated you from the peoples, that you should be mine." Yahweh's act of separating his people from the rest of the world serves as the basis for the people's holy conduct.

Since Yahweh's intent was to separate Israel from the other nations by means of their conduct, many of the laws God gave the Israelites in Leviticus relate directly to the practices of the nations around them. This truth accentuates the unique cultural function of the law. Ultimately, many of the laws only make sense when we understand them in view of their ancient Near Eastern context.[6] For example, laws concerning parapets on roofs (Deut 22:8), boundary stones (Deut 19:14), gleaning practices (Lev 19:9-10), and many other practices of the ancient Near East do not transfer directly to a twenty-first-century context.

Instead of obeying these laws and thereby living distinctly from other nations, Israel chose to live like the other nations. They did not live as God's holy people but like the nations around them. Many books in the Hebrew Bible underscore this theme, but the book of Judges gives it the most emphasis. Daniel Block identifies the theme of Judges as "the Canaanization of Israel."[7] Throughout the cycles of rebellion-judgment-petition-deliverance in the book, Israel evidences a propensity to adopt the gods and practices of their neighbors. However, the last few chapters of Judges push the reader even further. In particular, Judges 19 recounts the gut-wrenching, horrific account of the Levite's concubine, whom the men of Gibeah raped

---

[5]Rooker, *Leviticus*, 46.
[6]For an extensive list of the cultural differences, see David A. Dorsey, "The Law of Moses and the Christian: A Compromise," *Journal of the Evangelical Theological Society* 34 (1991): 325-28.
[7]Daniel I. Block, *Judges, Ruth*, New American Commentary 6 (Nashville: B&H, 1999), 58.

and left dead at the door. If you read this story, you should immediately recognize its parallels to the story of the angels visiting Sodom and Gomorrah (Gen 19). These similarities demonstrate just how unholy the nation of Israel had become during the period of the judges. Their wickedness goes beyond that of the Canaanites. Israel had become as wicked as the most wicked of cities, Sodom and Gomorrah. Unfortunately, Israel had succeeded in moving as far away from God's plan as they possibly could.

Israel's lack of holiness eventually led to their exile from the land. In time, Yahweh brought his people back to their land under the leadership of Zerubbabel, Ezra, and Nehemiah. Sadly, the people once again failed to live distinctly from the nations around them. Ezra and Nehemiah both had to institute reforms among the people. In particular, Ezra rebuked the people for intermarrying with the nations around them (Ezra 9–10). Several years later, Nehemiah had to correct the same issue as well as several others (Neh 13). Although the people were in the land, they still had a major sin problem and were therefore still in exile spiritually.[8]

This sin problem did not find a solution until Israel's Messiah arrived. Christ's death provided the permanent solution for sins and granted believers a righteous and holy standing before God (2 Cor 5:21). Additionally, as we discussed in the previous chapter, God has given us new hearts and his Spirit, who enables us to live holy lives before him. Paul often stresses his readers' holy standing before God by designating believers as "saints" (Rom 1:7; Eph 1:1; Phil 1:1), a word that means "holy ones." God has set us, his people, apart to himself. Just like Israel, we bear a responsibility to live lives that reflect our position as God's people.

The New Testament authors teach believers' responsibility to walk in purity and holiness before God and a watching world. Indeed, in many of his letters (e.g., Romans and Ephesians), Paul begins by focusing on Christ's work and our consequential right and privileged standing before God. Yet he doesn't stop there; he exhorts his readers to walk in a manner worthy of Christ's work (Eph 4:1). He gives numerous specific commands, painting a picture of what a holy life looks like.

Peter also explains the implications of Christ's work in the life of the believer. In fact, Peter quotes Leviticus in his first letter: "But as he who

---

[8]Stephen G. Dempster, *Dominion and Dynasty* (Downers Grove, IL: IVP Academic, 2003), 224.

called you is holy, you also be holy in all your conduct, since it is written, 'You shall be holy, for I am holy'" (1 Pet 1:15-16). To be certain, Peter was not urging believers to follow the laws in Leviticus; however, he was showing that just as Israel was to be set apart from the nations, so believers are to be set apart from the world in which they live. First Peter 1:14 provides evidence for such an interpretation. This verse, which precedes Peter's command for the church to have holy conduct, focuses on the other side of the coin. It reads, "As obedient children, do not be conformed to the passions of your former ignorance." Peter's mention of "the former passions" finds a parallel in 1 Peter 4:2-3, where Peter expounds on the lifestyle of the Gentiles (and the past lifestyle of the Christians to whom he is writing): "living in sensuality, passions, drunkenness, orgies, drinking parties, and lawless idolatry" (1 Pet 4:3). Just as Israel's obedience to the numerous old covenant laws should have set them apart from the other nations, so believers, when their conduct differs from that of the nations, stand out to the point that the world thinks it is strange that the church does not chase after the same things they do (1 Pet 4:4).

Using the laws for ethical guidance. Peter's quotation of Leviticus's command for holiness provides a good opportunity to address an important issue. Earlier in this chapter, I mentioned how we can derive principles from the laws to apply to our lives. As I have tried to demonstrate in the previous section, we need to derive principles from larger sections of laws or larger themes in the laws, and we *must* ground these principles in the work of Christ and his fulfillment of the old covenant. We should be very cautious about trying to derive a principle from every old covenant law.[9] Such an approach can become extremely subjective and miss the big picture of the Pentateuch's message.

To prevent overly subjective applications of the laws, we must anchor the principles we derive in the larger biblical story. For example, many of

---

[9]For an example of this approach, see Joe Sprinkle, *Biblical Law and Its Relevance: A Christian Understanding and Ethical Application for Today of the Mosaic Regulations* (Lanham, MD: University Press of America, 2005), 20-25. Christopher J. H. Wright, *Old Testament Ethics for the People of God* (Downers Grove, IL: InterVarsity Press, 2004), esp. 62-74, proposes a paradigmatic approach for applying the Hebrew Bible to modern Christians. Wright's approach deals with broader themes in the Hebrew Bible and therefore provides a better means of applying the laws (and the Hebrew Bible) to modern believers.

the old covenant laws highlight Yahweh's desire for Israel to care for the helpless in their society. This larger theme finds repeated emphasis throughout the entire Bible. In particular, the Prophets constantly rebuke Israel for their failure to care for the helpless. Although we are not under the old covenant laws, we can read them as a reminder that God desires that we care for the helpless in our own cultural context.

I believe this is why Peter quoted Leviticus's holiness command for his own readers. Holiness is the explicitly stated principle that lies behind all the old covenant laws. Therefore, the question for every generation of God's people is: How can we reflect our "set apartness" to God in how we live our lives? While many behaviors will remain constant throughout time (because of God's eternal law), some behaviors will differ from generation to generation and location to location. These differences do not mean that God's moral standards have changed; they reflect the cultural differences of each generation and each location.

Finally, some scholars have highlighted the wisdom nature of the old covenant laws.[10] In the Bible, wisdom relates closely to creation. Since God created an ordered world (both ethically and scientifically), we can observe the way God's world works and gain a sense of God's moral order. Throughout this book, I have called this moral order God's natural law. Even though Christians are not under the old covenant laws, by reading the laws we can gain wisdom for living.

Since many of the laws are casuistic in form, they reflect God's will in particular circumstances. Our circumstances may differ from Israel's, but as we continually read of God's "just decisions" for Israel in their particular context, we gain a sense of justice and righteousness.[11] John Sailhamer puts it this way:

> The Pentateuch therefore is a book much like Proverbs. One can read it and find there a healthy sense of what is right and good as well as what is not good. Justice is imprinted on the heart by reading and meditating on its words. This is illustrated in the admonitions of Joshua 1:8 and

---

[10]Brian S. Rosner, *Paul and the Law: Keeping the Commandments of God* (Downers Grove, IL: IVP Academic, 2013), 159-205. John Walton, *Ancient Near Eastern Thought and the Old Testament: Introducing the Conceptual World of the Hebrew Bible* (Grand Rapids: Baker, 2006), 287-311.

[11]John Sailhamer, *The Meaning of the Pentateuch: Revelation, Composition and Interpretation* (Downers Grove, IL: IVP Academic, 2009), 561-62.

Psalm 1:2. The source of wisdom is meditation on the Scriptures, which includes its laws.[12]

Such an understanding of the laws further underscores their value as part of Scripture without having to view them as laws that govern the church.

SELECTED LAWS FROM DEUTERONOMY
AND THEIR ROLE IN THE BIBLICAL STORY

As I grow older, I become more aware that I lived a sheltered life in many areas. No, I did not grow up in an ultrastrict Christian home. My parents gave me a great deal of freedom, especially in my choice of movies and television shows, which is why I am always surprised when my peers discuss popular movies that I did not see growing up. My ignorance of movies became shockingly clear while I was watching the 2013 Super Bowl. During the game, Honda ran a commercial for its CR-V. The commercial began with a sick man talking to his boss on the phone. After his boss tells him to take the day off and get some rest, the man jumps out of bed, jumps into his CR-V, and heads out for a day full of adventure. He rides a roller coaster, tosses rings at a carnival, visits a museum, goes to the beach, attends a horse race, and participates in a parade. In the course of his excursions, he narrowly escapes being spotted by his boss on two occasions. The commercial ends with him dropping his CR-V off with a valet driver, who speeds off in the vehicle.

The commercial made sense to me. In my mind, Honda was appealing to the average American's love for fun and adventure. They portrayed their CR-V as a means by which one can attain such an ideal. Even the man's final words—"Life moves pretty fast. If you don't stop and look around once in a while, you miss it"—fit well with the rest of the commercial, especially since he said them as the valet driver sped off in the CR-V.

Even though I was able to make some sense of the commercial, I had missed the whole point. Sadder still, I did not realize that I had missed the whole point of the commercial until I overheard some of my students discussing the movie that provided the background for the commercial, *Ferris Bueller's Day Off*. Numerous features of the movie resurface in the commercial. First, Matthew Broderick plays Ferris in the movie and stars

---

[12]Sailhamer, *Meaning of the Pentateuch*, 562.

in the commercial. Second, instead of narrowly escaping close encounters with his boss (as in the commercial), in the movie Ferris narrowly escapes his high school principal, who is aware of Ferris's antics. Third, the valet attendants who drive off with the CR-V at the end of the commercial parallel the attendants who drove around town in the Ferrari that Ferris and his friends had dropped off in the movie. Finally, the last line of the commercial is a key quote from Ferris's opening monologue in the movie.

Honda had created a commercial based on the movie, expecting their viewers to know the movie and therefore recognize the allusions. The commercial did not begin with the following statement: "Please watch *Ferris Bueller's Day Off* in order to understand this commercial." No, they assumed that enough of their target audience would understand the parallels and thereby "get it." Unfortunately, I did not meet that minimum requirement.

The biblical authors frequently do the same thing that the producers of the commercial did. They quote from or allude to earlier biblical books without informing their readers that they are doing so. English translations often help us identify New Testament quotations of the Hebrew Bible by putting quotation marks around the text and by identifying the passage from which the quote comes. Yet English translations do not identify every allusion to the Hebrew Bible.[13] Many times, the reader must identify these allusions, and without a knowledge of the Hebrew Bible, many readers simply miss the point of the passage. To make matters worse, many Christian interpreters do not realize that later books in the Hebrew Bible quote and allude to earlier books. For instance, almost every book from Joshua to Malachi contains multiple allusions to the Pentateuch. Ignorance of the Pentateuch's contents severely cripples one's ability to understand these later books. Is it any wonder that so many Christians struggle with understanding the Hebrew Bible?

I could fill a whole book with examples of this phenomenon, but since the Hebrew Bible's use of the Hebrew Bible is not the topic of my book, I have chosen to give two examples from the book of Kings to illustrate my point. In both examples, I will show how the anonymous author of Kings writes his story with several of Deuteronomy's laws in the background. The author expects his reader to know these laws and to understand how they

---

[13]An allusion is an intentional reference to a passage without directly quoting the passage. An allusion may consist of a key word or phrase.

relate to the message of his book. Like my ignorance of *Ferris Bueller's Day Off*, an ignorance of these laws results in an inability to understand fully the message of Kings.

The central sanctuary. Deuteronomy 12 begins the Deuteronomic Code with the law of a central sanctuary. In this chapter, Moses commands the people to destroy all the Canaanite worship sites so that they would not worship Yahweh as the Canaanites worshiped their gods (vv. 1-4). Furthermore, Moses instructs the Israelites to worship at the place where the Lord chooses to dwell (v. 5). They were to bring all their sacrifices, offerings, and tithes to this central location (vv. 6-14) in the presence of Yahweh (v. 7).

After they entered the land, the Israelites had several central sanctuaries through the years (Shiloh [1 Sam 3:21], Gilgal [1 Sam 11:14-15], and Hebron [2 Sam 2:1-4]), but God ultimately finalized this command when he appointed Solomon to build the temple. Solomon noted this fulfillment when he dedicated the temple in 1 Kings 8. In verse 29 of that chapter, he referred to the temple as the place of which the Lord said, "My name shall be there." This phrase echoes the law of the central sanctuary in Deuteronomy 12 and highlights the temple as the key connecting point between heaven and earth.

Solomon's dedication of the temple marked a short-lived high point in Israel's history. Indeed, Solomon himself, with his entourage of idol-worshiping foreign women, began the downward spiral (1 Kings 11). The downfall of Solomon's kingdom culminated in its division, which took place during the reign of Solomon's son Rehoboam (1 Kings 12). Shortly after Rehoboam came to the throne, Jeroboam led the ten northern tribes in a revolt, thus establishing another kingdom in the north. From that point forward, the designation "Israel" no longer referred to all twelve tribes; it referred to the ten northern tribes. "Judah" became the designation of the Southern Kingdom, with Jerusalem as its capital city.

With Jerusalem, the kingdom of Judah controlled the temple, the place where God chose to dwell. As one might imagine, this created a predicament for Jeroboam and his newly founded kingdom. If his people obeyed God's law, they would go to Jerusalem to offer sacrifices and offerings to Yahweh. So, what did Jeroboam do? He did the wrong thing! He built two worship centers in his territory and placed a golden calf at each location, one in the northernmost city of Dan and the other in the southern city of Bethel. He even appointed priests (who were not Levites), instituted a festival, and offered sacrifices—all direct violations of the old covenant laws. Although he maintained his people's loyalty, he risked incurring Yahweh's wrath. The parallels between Jeroboam's golden calves and the nation's golden calf at Sinai are astonishing. Was Jeroboam ignorant of Israel's history, or was he mimicking Israel's history? His pronouncement to the people in 1 Kings 12:28 points to the latter. He announced, "Behold your gods, O Israel, who brought you up out of the land of Egypt."

Jeroboam's golden calves clearly violated the second commandment (do not make a graven image), but they were also a direct violation of the law of the central sanctuary in Deuteronomy 12. Jeroboam willingly led his people away from the temple in Jerusalem, and even worse, he led them into gross idolatry. Jeroboam's golden calves were not a good start for the Northern Kingdom and became representative of their continual disregard for Yahweh throughout their short history. When the author of Kings gives his assessment of these northern kings, he often writes something like this: "He walked in all the way of Jeroboam the son of Nebat, and in the sins that he made Israel to sin" (1 Kings 16:26). Jeroboam's golden calves became the yardstick by which Yahweh measured the kings of Israel, and unfortunately, none of them measured up. As readers, we know the evil of Jeroboam's golden calves, but with a knowledge of Deuteronomy 12, Jeroboam's actions look even worse.

Yet the author of Kings does not limit his use of Deuteronomy 12 to the kings of Israel; he also evaluates the (Davidic) kings of Judah with the law of the central sanctuary by mentioning the high places in his summary statement for each Judean king.[14] While there are more good kings in the Southern Kingdom than there were in the Northern Kingdom, very few of the southern kings removed the high places. Although Solomon reigned before the Divided Kingdom, the author's assessment of Solomon provides an example of how he evaluated the Davidic kings: "Solomon loved the LORD, walking in the statutes of David his father, only he sacrificed and made offerings at the high places" (1 Kings 3:3). The author's reference to Solomon's worship at the high places serves as an asterisk on his positive comments. We find similar assessments for many of the kings of Judah (1 Kings 15:11-15; 22:41-44; 2 Kings 12:1-3; 14:1-4; 15:1-4, 32-35), all of whom

---

[14]Tremper Longman III and Raymond B. Dillard, *An Introduction to the Old Testament*, 2nd ed. (Grand Rapid: Zondervan, 2006), 182-84.

were loyal to Yahweh except for their worship at the high places. The high places thus served as a major weakness of the Judean kings. In the end, only two Davidic kings removed the high places: Hezekiah and Josiah (2 Kings 18:3-4; 23:1-25). Thus, Hezekiah's and Josiah's removal of the high places distinguished them from the rest of the good kings in Judah. By highlighting Hezekiah's and Josiah's faithfulness to Yahweh, even to the point of removing the high places, the author of Kings demonstrates that these two kings are in a league of their own.

Can we understand the message of Kings without knowing the law of the central sanctuary? Yes, we can still understand the primary message of the book, and we can still grow spiritually by reading it. But as I have demonstrated, we miss a key component of the message of the book of Kings since the author uses this law as an important part of his evaluations of the kings. Both the construction of alternate worship sites and worship at the high places directly violated Yahweh's command for his people to worship him at the place where he chose to dwell, and as Solomon emphasized in his dedication of the temple, this place was Yahweh's house in Jerusalem.

The laws for kings. Deuteronomy 17:14-20 outlines important responsibilities for the kings who would rule Israel once they entered the Promised Land. These laws are as follows:

1. The king should be an Israelite, not a foreigner.

2. The king should not multiply horses (especially from Egypt).

3. The king should not have many wives.

4. The king should not multiply silver and gold.

5. The king should write a copy of the law in a book.

6. The king should read and obey the law.

These laws provided boundaries for the kings so that they would remain faithful to Yahweh and lead the nation to demonstrate the same faithfulness. The prohibition against horses and riches protected the king from relying on military might (cf. Ps 20:7; Is 31:1) and wealth (cf. Ps 62:10b) instead of Yahweh. The prohibition against many wives protected the king's heart from straying. These three negative prohibitions served as one side of the coin, while the fifth and sixth laws served as the other side of the coin. Yahweh commanded the king to make a copy of the law for the purpose of obedience (Deut 17:19-20). As the king read and observed the law, Yahweh would cause him to "continue long in his kingdom" (Deut 17:20).

As with the law of the central sanctuary, the author of Kings does not explicitly refer to the laws for kings, but he assumes the reader's knowledge of these laws. The laws thus provide criteria to evaluate the various kings in the book of Kings. In particular, the author uses these laws as his backdrop for the story of one important king, Solomon.

Christians typically interpret the narrative of Solomon's reign (1 Kings 1–11) in the following manner: Solomon was a very good king until the end of his reign, when his numerous wives turned his heart from Yahweh to their gods. Without a knowledge of the laws for the kings in Deuteronomy 17, this standard interpretation appears accurate because the author emphasizes Solomon's apostasy at the end of the Solomonic narrative (1 Kings 11). However, if we read the Solomonic narrative in light of Deuteronomy 17, such an interpretation has some problems. So, how should we interpret Solomon's reign?

Solomon's wisdom and his construction of the temple were two very important achievements. In fact, his prayer at the dedication of the temple (1 Kings 8:22-53) is one of the most moving prayers recorded in the Bible. Furthermore, under Solomon's rule, Israel achieved its golden age. During this time, Solomon extended Israel's boundaries to their furthest points, and the people enjoyed unprecedented riches. Yet in spite of these positive accomplishments, his violation of the laws for kings shows us that all was not well beneath the surface. The author of Kings uses these laws to drop little hints throughout Solomon's story. These hints show us that Solomon had a divided heart throughout much of his reign. Let's look at the specific laws and their function in Solomon's story.

Since Solomon inherited his father's kingdom, neither he nor the people had the power to obey or disobey the first law for kings. Solomon was an Israelite and, more importantly, the son of David. David thus ensured that his son would take over his kingdom (1 Kings 1). When it comes to the other laws, Solomon had more control over his faithfulness to them. Therefore, these laws relate more pertinently to the author's assessment of Solomon's faithfulness.

In some of my classes, I ask students to read Deuteronomy 17 before we discuss Solomon's reign. The parallels between these laws and Solomon's reign often shock my students. If they are even remotely familiar with Solomon's story, they immediately see Solomon's reflection in the mirror of Deuteronomy 17. Take for example the second law, which forbids the king from multiplying horses, especially from the land of Egypt. In this regard, Solomon failed miserably. First Kings 4:26 reads, "Solomon also had 40,000 stalls of horses for his chariots, and 12,000 horsemen." Also, consider the words of 1 Kings 10:28: "And Solomon's import of horses was from Egypt and Kue, and the king's traders received them from Kue at a price." Not only did Solomon multiply horses, but one of the key locations from which he acquired these horses was none other than Egypt. The location of these references toward the beginning and the end of the Solomonic narrative highlights the author's purpose. Like parentheses around his story, Solomon's horses serve as a negation of a positive life.

The third law for kings forbids many wives. Do I need to say more? The author emphasizes Solomon's disobedience of this law the most explicitly. Solomon gave a new definition to polygamy with his seven hundred wives and three hundred concubines, and as a result, he ruined his life and the life of his descendants.

The fourth law prohibits the king from accumulating excessive silver and gold. At this point, we have to be careful in our assessment of Solomon because God promised him riches and honor when Solomon asked for wisdom instead of such things (1 Kings 3:10-13). Since God put his stamp of approval on Solomon's riches, God probably made an exception in the case of Solomon, who "made silver as common in Jerusalem as stone" (1 Kings 10:27).

Since the last two laws counter the negative laws for kings, Solomon's transgression of the negative laws implies that he did not obey the final laws. For this reason, the author of Kings did not need to allude to the fifth and sixth laws. Solomon's actions demonstrate that he failed to read the Book of the Law all of his days. Therefore, as 1 Kings 12 demonstrates, his children did not "continue long in his kingdom" (Deut 17:20).

When we add Solomon's worship at the high places into the mix, we quickly realize that Solomon was not as virtuous as many Christians assume. How then do we balance the positive and negative aspects of Solomon's life? I like to think of the author's negative hints as an undertow in Solomon's story. As a boy, my parents would warn me of the undertow whenever I swam in the ocean. Although I could not see the undertow on the surface, I could feel it pulling me away from the shore. Just like an undertow at the beach, the author uses the negative hints in Solomon's story to pull us back to the reality that Solomon had some major sins. The undertow does not negate the author's waves of positivity on the story's surface. However, it becomes a vicious riptide at the end of Solomon's story when the author emphasizes his apostasy. Without a knowledge of Deuteronomy 17, readers of the Solomonic narrative miss the undertow that lies beneath the surface of this story.

The examples I selected for this chapter demonstrate the important role the old covenant laws play in the biblical story. Specifically, many of the laws I discussed foreshadow Jesus, a phenomenon known as typology. The Pentateuch's focus on a future work of God does not stop with the typology of the old covenant tabernacle and sacrificial system; this focus is also present in the narrative portions of the book. In the next chapter, we will examine the Pentateuch's prophetic message.

NINE

CAN I HAVE THE GOOD NEWS?

THE HOPE OF THE PENTATEUCH

I have good news and bad news. Which would you like first?" Perhaps you have been on the receiving end of this statement. These words can have different levels of emotional impact depending on the situation. If a friend tells you this after your favorite team's baseball game, then these words likely create very little fear. If a car mechanic uses these words, they might have more impact. If a doctor uses this line, then most of our hearts skip a beat. In any of these situations, good news alone would put a smile on our faces, but the uncertainty of the bad news produces significant anxiety.

Which one do you pick? Do you pick the bad news first in order to alleviate your anxiety? Or do you pick the good news first in order to delay the disappointment? Many people prefer the road from bad news to good news because they hope that the good news provides a solution for the bad news or, at a minimum, a glimmer of hope in spite of the bad news. The biblical story often moves in this same trajectory, not because of God's character, but because of humanity's sinfulness. God's original creation was all good news! However, beginning in the garden, humanity has continually rebelled against its heavenly king, thus incurring his wrath and judgment, which is of course terrible news. Yet God has demonstrated grace and mercy repeatedly by promising salvation to those who love him, which is good—even wonderful and amazing—news. As we will see in a moment, this pattern appears in the garden after Adam and Eve's rebellion. In the midst of punishing the first couple, God offers them a glimmer of hope. The prophets also follow this pattern. They give oracle after oracle of judgment against rebellious people, but they also offer hope by describing God's future restoration. The numerous promises of salvation and restoration in the Hebrew Bible came to fruition when Jesus of Nazareth arrived and proclaimed the gospel (good news) of the kingdom.

My purpose in this chapter is to describe the good news of the Pentateuch. Throughout most of this book, I have focused on the negative outlook of the Pentateuch by showing how the old covenant increased Israel's sin and God's wrath. In chapter five I argued that the Pentateuch does not recognize the old covenant as Israel's ultimate hope, and on several occasions I have hinted at the ultimate hope of the Pentateuch. Finally, in this chapter I am going to discuss the Pentateuch's ultimate hope and briefly trace its echoes throughout the rest of the Bible. Broadly speaking, I identify this work as God's restoration of his people. The Pentateuch's description of this restoration includes three major items: heart change, a coming king, and Israel's return to the land.

HEART CHANGE IN THE PENTATEUCH

When teaching the Bible to young children, one of the most difficult tasks is explaining metaphorical language. Young children think in such concrete ways that we have to be very careful when teaching figurative expressions from the Bible. One word that the biblical authors frequently use in a nonliteral manner is *heart*. While sometimes the biblical authors use *heart* in reference to the actual organ in one's chest cavity, they most commonly use the word to refer to the entirety of the inner self. The word can refer to one's emotions, will, mind, or all of these things together. In short, *heart* usually refers to the core of one's inner life. This meaning is not strange for most of us. The word functions as a symbol of love in many societies. We commonly refer to someone "putting their heart and soul" into something, and we speak of "heartfelt" actions. In many ways, most of us naturally understand (and frequently use) the word *heart* in a figurative manner.

When it comes to a focus on the heart, few biblical books can compete with Deuteronomy, the fifth book in the Pentateuch. As Moses exhorted the new generation to follow Yahweh, he regularly urged them to whole-hearted devotion. The Shema (Hebrew for "hear") in Deuteronomy 6:4-5 serves as the premier example, wherein Moses commanded the people to love God "with all your heart and with all your soul and with all your might" (v. 5). Moses repeated similar sentiments in several other places (Deut 4:29; 5:29; 10:12; 11:13; 13:3; 26:16; 30:2, 10). He also commanded the Israelites to keep God's words and works in their hearts (Deut 4:9, 39; 8:5; 11:18; 32:46), told them that God had tested and would test their hearts (Deut 8:2; 13:3), and warned them against deceived (Deut 11:16) or proud (Deut 8:14-17; 9:4) hearts. Moses also used other expressions in Deuteronomy to emphasize Yahweh's expectation of his people's wholehearted devotion.

Yet in spite of all this urging, Moses expected disappointment. In a previous chapter, I explained Moses' (and God's) pessimism regarding the people's future obedience. The people had rebelled against Yahweh from the beginning (Deut 9:24), and they would continue to rebel after they entered the land (Deut 31:15–32:43). Moses attributed the people's rebellious nature to their hearts, but in doing so he gave an interesting twist to the problem. Deuteronomy 29:4 records his words to the people, "But to this day the LORD has not given you a heart to understand or eyes to see or ears to hear." Do you see the significance of this verse? Moses attributed the people's rebelliousness to their lack of an understanding heart, but even more, he focused on the need for Yahweh to work in their hearts. In other words, the people needed Yahweh to give them an understanding heart. Without Yahweh's work in their hearts, the people were lost!

Yet Moses did not leave the people with such a depressing forecast. He gave them hope for such a work in Deuteronomy 30. Moses begins this chapter by predicting Israel's future exile and dispersal among the nations (Deut 30:1). He then promises the people that God would bring them back to their land and bless them abundantly (Deut 30:2-10). In the middle of this wonderful prophecy, Moses describes how Yahweh will transform their hearts: "And the LORD your God will circumcise your heart and the heart of your offspring" (Deut 30:6a). Moses describes Yahweh's work figuratively, using imagery familiar to the Jews.

What exactly does it mean to have a "circumcised heart"? Physical circumcision played a significant role in Israel as the sign of the covenant that God made with Abraham (Gen 17). Yahweh required the circumcision of all males on the eighth day (Gen 17:12). The removal of the foreskin served as a sign of membership in the covenant community, and failure to obey the stipulation resulted in the death penalty (Gen 17:14). Thus, in Yahweh's eyes, a refusal to practice circumcision was a serious offense.

However, the requirement of circumcision does not end with physical circumcision. The Pentateuch also teaches the necessity of heart circumcision. In addition to Deuteronomy 30, the Pentateuch has two passages that mention heart circumcision. These passages both precede Deuteronomy 30 and help us understand the meaning of this metaphor. Leviticus 26 outlines the blessings and curses for covenant obedience and disobedience. At the end of this chapter, Yahweh describes the prerequisites for his restoration of Israel after judgment. In verses 41b–42 he states, "If then their uncircumcised heart is humbled and they make amends for their iniquity, then I will remember my covenant with Jacob, and I will remember my covenant with Isaac and my covenant with Abraham, and I will remember the land." Since humility is the "fix" for an uncircumcised heart, humility is thus one feature of a circumcised heart. Conversely, pride characterizes the uncircumcised heart. The second passage that mentions heart circumcision, Deuteronomy 10:16, consists of Moses' command to the people: "Circumcise therefore the foreskin of your heart, and be no longer stubborn." Here the positive command for heart circumcision equals a lack of stubbornness. The phrase "be no longer stubborn" actually reads, "no longer stiffen your necks." To put this in contemporary language, Moses told the people, "Quit being hardheaded!" Hardheadedness or stubbornness is not simply rebellion; it is willful, prideful rebellion. Therefore, a circumcised heart refers to a humble, obedient disposition.

Now that we understand the meaning of heart circumcision, let's turn our attention back to Deuteronomy 30:6. Unlike Leviticus 26:41 and Deuteronomy 10:16, both of which command the people to circumcise their own hearts, Deuteronomy 30:6 teaches that Yahweh will circumcise the people's hearts, thereby providing the solution for the people's rebellion problems. Since the people did not obey, Yahweh would transform his people from the inside out by giving them humble, obedient hearts. The efficacy of Yahweh's work comes to the forefront in the second half of Deuteronomy 30:6: "And the LORD your God will circumcise your heart and the heart of your offspring, *so that you will love the LORD your God with all your heart and with all your soul, that you may live."* Astonishing, right? Moses repeated the Great Commandment not as a command but as a factual statement. The people *will* love God after he circumcises their hearts. How many times have you heard lessons or sermons on the greatest commandment? How many of these lessons or sermons mentioned Deuteronomy 30:6? The implications of this passage are both astounding and comforting. God ensured his people's obedience by taking the initiative and changing their hearts. The converse is also true if we read this passage in light of Deuteronomy 29:4; unless God worked in their hearts, they would not change their actions.

Finally, Deuteronomy's heart circumcision passages demonstrate an additional insight into the role of circumcision in God's redemptive plan. When Moses commanded the people to circumcise their hearts (Deut 10:16), the males standing before him were uncircumcised. How do we know this? Joshua 5 records the circumcision of the second generation of Israelites (i.e., the generation Moses addressed in Deuteronomy), who had remained uncircumcised until they entered the Promised Land. Shockingly, nowhere in Deuteronomy does Moses command the physical circumcision of this generation. Such silence does not mean that Moses considered physical circumcision unnecessary or unimportant, but his emphasis on spiritual circumcision indicates that he considered spiritual circumcision as important as, or perhaps more important than, physical circumcision. Obedience begins in the heart, and if the people did not have circumcised hearts, their physical circumcision would not protect them from rebellion and the subsequent judgment.

Before moving on, I would like to address a common struggle that many Christians have. Since Moses stated that the "fix" to Israel's heart problem would come after their exile, we could easily interpret this to mean that Yahweh was not loving and gracious to Israel. If they needed Yahweh's help to obey, then why did he wait for so long before helping them? In dealing with this question, we must remember two things. First, we need to remember the authors' purposes in writing their stories. Much of the Hebrew Bible gives a negative assessment of Israel in order to create hope for a better covenant. Because of this negative focus, the Hebrew Bible often does not emphasize the faithful among the Israelites, which brings me to my second point. The Hebrew Bible indicates that

Yahweh always had a faithful remnant within Israel throughout their history. The story focuses so much on Israel as a nation that this faithful remnant does not get as much attention. However, we do get a glimpse of this remnant in one of the darkest times of Israel's history. During the reign of King Ahab in Israel (1 Kings 16:29–22:40), Baal worship was at an all-time high, thanks to Ahab's wicked wife, Jezebel. After Elijah killed all her prophets of Baal on Mount Carmel, she set her sights on Elijah, so Elijah ran for his life! Ironically (or, rather, providentially), Elijah ran to Mount Sinai. While there, God gave him an important revelation to remind him that he was not alone. God told him that he had left "seven thousand in Israel, all the knees that have not bowed to Baal, and every mouth that has not kissed him" (1 Kings 19:18). Much to our surprise as readers, God had seven thousand faithful followers during the time of Ahab. This one verse gives the only hint that a faithful remnant existed among God's people during this time. We may therefore assume that this was a common feature throughout the Hebrew Bible's story. Yet the authors do not emphasize this remnant because it does not suit their agenda in writing their narratives.

THE COMING KING IN THE PENTATEUCH

Deuteronomy 30 is not the only passage in which Moses predicts a restoration after God's judgment of his rebellious people. Deuteronomy 4:25-30 has very similar themes. Moses warned the people of exile because of their rebellion and assured the people that Yahweh would restore them if they returned to him. Deuteronomy 4:30 identifies the time of this restoration as "the latter days." A common phrase in the Hebrew Bible, "the latter days" does not refer to what Christians commonly identify as "the end times" (i.e., the end of human history). The phrase refers to a broad period in the distant future. One could paraphrase it as "at a later time" or, if you prefer, "down the road a little." The other appearance of this phrase in Deuteronomy supports such a broad interpretation. Moses uses this phrase in Deuteronomy 31:29 to describe the time during which Yahweh would judge his people for their sins. Therefore, in Deuteronomy "the latter days" refers to the time of God's judgment and restoration.

How does this phrase help us understand God's future restoration? It appears two other times in the Pentateuch, and both times it identifies the arrival time of Israel's future king, the second major component in God's salvation plan. Before looking at what this king will do in "the latter days," let's look at how he relates to the beginning.

Genesis 3:15. Our minds cannot fathom how good Adam and Eve had it in the Garden of Eden. God had abundantly provided them with all good things and had appointed them as rulers over his unspoiled creation. Like all of us, Adam and Eve failed to trust God's perfect plan and decided to take matters into their own hands. Tricked by a scheming serpent, Adam and Eve ate the forbidden fruit and immediately ruined their chances of enjoying Eden's ideal conditions.

Soon after Adam and Eve's sin in the garden, God began cursing his good creation. He first targeted the snake who tricked the first humans into disobeying their Creator's instructions. After informing the serpent that he would be on his belly and eat dust, he gave him some more bad news, news that actually was good news for the human race. He states, "I will put enmity between you and the woman, and between your offspring and her offspring; he shall bruise your head, and you shall bruise his heel" (Gen 3:15). On the surface, this verse seems to refer to the continual struggle between snakes and humans.

However, upon deeper reflection, the verse appears to have a more significant event in mind. Two things in this passage push readers in such a direction. First, this snake is no ordinary snake. Besides the fact that he talks, as the antagonist of God, he has introduced evil into God's good creation. With the serpent, there is more than meets the eye. Second, while there is enmity between the woman's offspring and the serpent's offspring, the ultimate battle is between one of the woman's offspring and the serpent himself. How do we arrive at this interpretation?

The Hebrew word for "offspring" (*zera*) can refer to a singular descendant or plural descendants. *Deer* serves as a good English example. If I see a deer on the side of the road, I might say, "Look at the deer." If I see a group of deer, I say, "Look at the deer." Besides looking at the deer, the only way to know how many deer I see is by the context of my statement. If I follow up with "He's a big buck," you would know that I am referring to one deer. When God refers to the woman's offspring in Genesis 3:15, we know how many of the woman's descendants he has in mind by looking for clues in the context. The second part of the verse provides us with the clue we need because God refers to a singular "he." Therefore, a particular descendant of the woman will one day battle the serpent himself (not one of his offspring). Moreover, the bad news for the serpent (and good news for humans) is that the woman's offspring (singular) will deal a fatal blow (crush the head) to the snake, even though the snake will injure (bruise the heel) the woman's offspring.

Because of the promise regarding the woman's offspring, Christians have traditionally called Genesis 3:15 the *protoevangelium* (first gospel). As one of my seminary professors often argued, this title is an overstatement since the passage raises more questions than it answers. But the fact that the passage raises questions is the very reason that it is so important. Coming on the heels of Adam and Eve's sin, it provides a glimmer of hope in God's great story. Although humanity had failed to obey the Creator's command and as a result had experienced God's judgment, God gives hope for his creation by alluding to the victory of one of the woman's offspring, a victory that will result in the defeat of the sin-introducing serpent. While the passage does not answer all of our questions, it does give us a key guiding question as we conclude the story of Eden and prepare to read the rest of the biblical story: Who is the offspring who will crush the serpent's head?

In film and literature, we refer to such an unresolved, dramatic moment as a cliffhanger. The old TV show *Dallas* provides one of the best examples of a cliffhanger's effectiveness. The slogan "Who shot J. R.?" was part of an advertising campaign between two seasons of *Dallas* in 1980. In the final episode of the season (March 21, 1980), someone walks into J. R. Ewing's office and shoots him. However, the camera only shows the shooter's arm, thus concealing his or her identity. The next season did not premiere until November 21 of the same year, thus providing CBS eight months to play up the revelation of J. R.'s shooter. The story took off as the question "Who shot J. R.?" became a staple phrase across the country. The show even made the cover of *Time* magazine (August 1980). As November 21 drew near, the anticipation built, and on that day 83 million Americans watched *Dallas* to discover who the culprit was. Many of these people watched the show just for that reason. The unanswered question drew them into the show and gave them something to anticipate. The cliffhanger question in Genesis 3:15 does the same thing. It draws us into the biblical story and gives us something to look for as we continue reading—namely, the one who will destroy the serpent.

As we continue our journey through Genesis, we meet numerous forks in the roads. These forks present us with a line of God's blessing (favor) and a line of God's cursing (judgment). If one follows the line of God's blessing, one of the key recipients is a man named Abraham, with whom God makes an important covenant, a covenant intended to reverse the effects of the fall by restoring God's blessing to the nations (Gen 12:1-3). Because of the restorative purposes of the Abrahamic covenant, one can conclude that the serpent crusher would come from Abraham's line. One of Abraham's descendants would carry out this task, but not all his descendants were in the line of the promised blessing. Even after Abraham, God narrows the line of promise among Abraham's descendants. The promise goes from Isaac to Jacob and then to Jacob's sons. At the end of Genesis, attentive readers should question which of Jacob's twelve sons would ultimately provide the line for the coming serpent crusher. Genesis 49 provides an answer to this question, and to return to our earlier discussion, it reorients us toward the "latter days."[1]

Genesis 49. Genesis 49:1-28 records Jacob's final words to his sons. After gathering his sons, Jacob informed them of what would happen to them "in days to come" (Gen 49:1, literally "in the latter days"). As he moved from son to son, he prophesied about many things that happen in later books of the Hebrew Bible. Judah and Joseph received the most significant promises, which is not surprising after one reads Genesis 37–50 (Judah plays an important part in the Joseph narrative). What is surprising and most important for our purposes is Jacob's prophecy regarding Judah's future in Genesis 49:8-12:

> Judah, your brothers shall praise you;
>> your hand shall be on the neck of your enemies;
>> your father's sons shall bow down before you.
> Judah is a lion's cub;
>> from the prey, my son, you have gone up.
> He stooped down; he crouched as a lion
>> and as a lioness; who dares rouse him?

---

[1]John Sailhamer, *The Pentateuch as Narrative: A Biblical-Theological Commentary* (Grand Rapids: Zondervan, 1992), 35-37, discusses the importance of this phrase in relation to the structure of the Pentateuch.

The scepter shall not depart from Judah,
> nor the ruler's staff from between his feet,

until tribute comes to him;
> and to him shall be the obedience of the peoples.

Binding his foal to the vine
> and his donkey's colt to the choice vine,

he has washed his garments in wine
> and his vesture in the blood of grapes.

His eyes are darker than wine,
> and his teeth whiter than milk.

Sensitive readers will immediately notice the irony of verse 8. Genesis 49 comes after Joseph's story, which has as one of its key themes Joseph's rule over his brothers. The story begins with Joseph informing his brothers of his dreams, in which his brothers and parents bow down to him (Gen 37:1-11). This results in Joseph's brothers' selling him into slavery and Joseph's eventual rise to governor of the land. Even though his brothers thought they had successfully removed Joseph from their lives, Joseph's dreams come to fruition on several occasions throughout the story when his brothers bow before him in homage (Gen 42:6; 43:26, 28; 44:14).

In his blessing of Judah, Jacob took this motif of the Joseph story and applied it to Judah's future. Just as the brothers had bowed down before Joseph in Egypt, so also they would one day (in the latter days) bow down before Judah. Just as Judah had addressed Joseph as his lord (Gen 44:18-34), so also Judah would rule over the tribes of Israel. In other words, Joseph's past would become Judah's future.

Genesis 49:9-10 clarifies and expands on this idea. Verse 9 describes Judah as a fierce lion who devours his prey and whose sleep no one dares to disturb. The lion was (and still is) a common image for royalty. Such a royal role for Judah gets more attention in verse 10, where Jacob mentions the royal symbols of a scepter and a ruler's staff. Particularly important in verse 10 is the second part, which mentions the time of Judah's reign. The Hebrew in verse 10b ("until tribute comes to him" [ESV]) is hard to translate, and thus the English translations differ in their translations of the phrase.[2]

---

[2]For a discussion of the translation issues and options, see Gordon J. Wenham, *Genesis 16–50*, Word Biblical Commentary 2 (Waco, TX: Word, 1994), 477-78. Regarding the interpretive significance of this verse, Wenham writes, "Whichever of these interpretations is adopted . . . all

The NIV, which reads, "until he to whom it belongs shall come," translates this passage best.[3] If such a translation is correct, then this verse predicts the rule of Judah's line over a period of time that ends with an ultimate king to whom belongs "the obedience of the peoples" (v. 10c).

The final two verses of Judah's blessing (Gen 49:11-12) emphasize the prosperity of this future king and his kingdom. The use of choice vines as hitching posts and wine as laundry water is similar to the value of silver in Solomon's kingdom (as common as stones [1 Kings 10:27]) and gold in the new Jerusalem (as paving stones [Rev 21:21]). In times of unprecedented wealth, people use expensive things in ways that shock those with less means. The king's enjoyment of such prosperous conditions is the focus of verse 12. Jacob describes the king's eyes and teeth in relation to wine and milk, two symbols of affluence in the ancient world (the Promised Land is often described as "a land flowing with milk and honey"). Whether Jacob is comparing the color of the king's eyes and teeth to wine and milk (ESV), or whether the wine and milk produce the condition of his eyes and teeth ("his eyes are dull from wine, and his teeth white from milk" [NASB]), the focus of the passage remains the same: under this king's rule, the wine and milk flow abundantly. The prophets, in their descriptions of God's restoration of his people, use similar imagery to describe God's abundant blessings (cf. Joel 3:18; Amos 9:13-15).

Jacob's prophecy concerning Judah's future does not explicitly connect Judah's tribe to the woman's offspring, but Genesis 49:8-12 does give some indication that the line of Judah and the ultimate ruler from Judah play a pivotal role in the fulfillment of Genesis 3:15's prophecy. Judah's victory over his enemies (v. 8) and rule over the nations (v. 10) echo God's promise to Abraham that he would bless the nations through him. If, as I argued earlier, Abraham's line is the source of blessing for all the nations, then Judah's rule becomes the means by which this happens. If Judah rules the nations and his kingdom is a prosperous kingdom, then the nations under his rule partake of such prosperity and blessing. Genesis 49 does not

---

at least agree that this line is predicting the rise of the Davidic monarchy and the establishment of the Israelite empire, if not the coming of a greater David. And if the primary reference is to David, traditional Jewish and Christian exegetes would agree that like other Davidic promises it has a greater fulfillment in the Messiah."

[3]For support, see Kenneth A. Mathews, *Genesis 11:27–50:26*, NAC 1B (Nashville: Broadman & Holman, 2005), 893-96.

contain the last word on Israel's future victorious king; Numbers 24 also gives us a glimpse of this king and his victories.

Numbers 24. Toward the end of Israel's forty-year wilderness wanderings, they eventually camped in the plains of Moab (Num 22:1). The Moabite king Balak had seen Israel defeat the Amorite kings Og and Bashan and grew terrified of their presence in his land. To alleviate his fear, he hired Balaam, a pagan prophet, to curse Israel. After putting the fear of God in Balaam with a little help from Balaam's donkey, God permitted Balaam to go with Balak's messengers, but he commanded Balaam only to speak what he commanded. Balaam obeyed Yahweh and on three occasions blessed Israel, much to the consternation of Balak. After the third blessing, Balak had had enough, so he ordered Balaam to return home. Nevertheless, Balaam gave the king several more oracles before returning home. Balaam's third and fourth oracles both contain references to Israel's coming king. The first reference to Israel's king comes halfway through his third oracle. In Numbers 24:7b-9 he prophesies:

> His king shall be higher than Agag,
>> and his kingdom shall be exalted.
> God brings him out of Egypt
>> and is for him like the horns of the wild ox;
> he shall eat up the nations, his adversaries,
>> and shall break their bones in pieces
>> and pierce them through with his arrows.
> He crouched, he lay down like a lion
>> and like a lioness; who will rouse him up?
> Blessed are those who bless you,
>> and cursed are those who curse you.

Did you notice the echoes of earlier passages in these words? The last two sentences are identical to two key passages in Genesis, one of which I just discussed. The comparison of Israel's king to a fierce lion connects this king to Jacob's prophecy regarding the tribe of Judah (Gen 49:8-12). Like Genesis 49, these verses emphasize the king's victories over his enemies and his rule over the nations. The last sentence connects this king to God's promises to Abraham in Genesis 12:1-3. These connections confirm my conclusions in the previous section regarding the relationship between the king from Judah and the fulfillment of the Abrahamic covenant. The pivot point for God's blessings and curses will be Israel's future king. Yahweh will bless those who bless the king, and he will curse those who curse the king.

Balaam's description of this king also echoes Balaam's second oracle in which, speaking of Israel's exodus from Egypt, he announces, "God brings them out of Egypt / and is for them like the horns of the wild ox" (Num 23:22). Balaam repeats this phrase almost verbatim in his third oracle with one key exception. He changes the pronoun from "them" (in reference to Israel [Num 23:22]) to "him" (in reference to Israel's king [Num 24:8]).[4] Just as God had brought Israel out of Egypt, so he would also bring Israel's king out of Egypt. Much like Jacob's prophecy in Genesis 49:8-12, in which Jacob casts Judah's future in the imagery of Joseph's past, Balaam portrays the future of Israel's king as a reflection of Israel's past.

Balaam's description of Israel's king in his third oracle lacks one thing: any mention of when the king will come. Balaam's fourth oracle provides the missing piece to the puzzle. Like Genesis 49 and the Deuteronomy passages (chaps. 4 and 30) we have already examined, Balaam's fourth oracle (Num 24:15-24) relates to events that will occur "in the latter days." Balaam introduces this fourth oracle with these words: "Come, I will let you know what this people will do to your people in the latter days" (Num 24:14). Ironically, the only thing Balaam says about the people of Israel in his prophecy is that they are "doing valiantly" (Num 24:18). The prophecy focuses primarily on Israel's coming king who will defeat the Moabites and other nations. With no intention of downplaying the other verses in this prophecy, I will limit my discussion to Numbers 24:17-19, verses that continue the thematic trajectory of Genesis 3:15, Genesis 49:8-12, and the previous oracle. They read:

> I see him, but not now;
>> I behold him, but not near:
> a star shall come out of Jacob,
>> and a scepter shall rise out of Israel;

---

[4]Unfortunately, the NIV does not draw out this difference. See Gary Edward Schnittjer, *The Torah Story* (Grand Rapids: Zondervan, 2006), 431, for a comparison of Balaam's second and third oracles as well as evidence from the context that supports reading Num 24:8 as an individual king.

it shall crush the forehead of Moab
> and break down all the sons of Sheth.

Edom shall be dispossessed;
> Seir also, his enemies, shall be dispossessed.

> Israel is doing valiantly.

And one from Jacob shall exercise dominion
> and destroy the survivors of cities! (Num 24:17-19)

Balaam's vision of the future (i.e., "not now" and "not near") king reiterates the themes we have already noticed. Balaam uses common royal symbols (the star and scepter) to designate the king, the second of which also appears in Genesis 49. Additionally, Balaam focuses on the king's victory over his enemies, particularly Israel's neighboring enemies, Moab and Edom. These nations were hostile to Israel on their journey to the land (Num 20:14-21; 22:1–25:18) and maintained such hostility throughout Israel's history (cf. Judg 3:14; 1 Sam 12:9; 14:47; 2 Kings 3; Obad).

Another phrase in Numbers 24:17 helps us put the pieces of the puzzle together. Balaam says that Israel's king will "crush the forehead of Moab." If we place our ears close enough to the text, we may hear echoes from another key verse, Genesis 3:15. As you recall, that verse predicts that the woman's offspring would crush the serpent's head. Although the passages contain different phrases, these phrases have similar meanings.[5] I have already argued that the coming king from Judah is the woman's offspring, but now the issue becomes the relationship between Moab and the serpent. Much like the serpent, Moab, in the context of Numbers 22–25, stands in direct opposition to the purposes of God. Not only does Balak attempt to curse Israel, but Numbers 25 also records Moab's seduction of Israel into the sensual worship of their gods, much like the serpent tempted Eve to disobey the Lord's command.[6] Although not the serpent himself, Moab—along with all nations that stand against the purposes of God—qualifies as one of the serpent's offspring.

---

[5]Sailhamer, *Pentateuch as Narrative*, 409. See also Schnittjer, *Torah Story*, 433.

[6]Concerning the Moabite's seduction of Israel, see Num 25:18; 31:16. Seth Postell, *Adam as Israel: Genesis 1–3 as the Introduction to the Torah and Tanakh* (Eugene, OR: Wipf and Stock, 2011), 99-107, 121-24, argues that the serpent serves as a prototype for the Canaanites. I extend this prototypical significance to the Moabites and Midianites. In addition to the seduction motif, Moses prescribes a punishment for the Midianite women (Num 31:13-20) that parallels God's commands for Israel when they entered Canaan (Deut 20:10-20).

As he will do to the serpent, the woman's offspring will one day deal a blow to the "head" of the Moabites.

Some scholars identify the king of Numbers 24 as King David because of the references to the defeat of Moab and Edom. Second Samuel 8 does support such an interpretation as it mentions Moab and Edom in the list of David's victories (2 Sam 8:2, 12-14). As an extension, some of these same scholars also identify the king of Genesis 49 as David. Such an interpretation does not contradict a messianic (Israel's ultimate king) interpretation of these passages, since 2 Samuel 7 narrows the messianic line to David's line. In other words, this interpretation identifies the trajectory rather than the intent of these early passages as messianic.

However, these passages push us beyond David's reign to a time of even greater prosperity and a more extensive rule over the nations. David serves as another step toward and even as a type (as he is in the Psalms) of this coming king, but in the end David is not Israel's ultimate hope. Why do I argue this? First, although Balaam limits the king's rule to Israel's neighbors in his fourth oracle, Jacob's blessing (Gen 49:8-12) does not limit the king's rule. According to Jacob, "the obedience of the peoples" belongs to this king (v. 10). If we consider how these prophecies connect with the Abrahamic covenant and the serpent crusher of Genesis 3:15, the king's rule becomes the means by which God restores his creation blessings. As a result, we would expect the king's kingdom to be universal in scope, thus delivering the kingdom blessings to "all the families of the earth" (Gen 12:3). David's dominance over his neighboring enemies is simply a foretaste of the dominance of Israel's final king, the Messiah.[7]

ISRAEL'S RETURN TO THE LAND

The third and final component of the Pentateuch's restoration plan is Israel's return to the Promised Land. God's promise of the land served as a key component of the Abrahamic covenant, and as we have observed, it plays a significant role in the old covenant. Not only do many of the old covenant

---

[7]Timothy R. Ashley, *The Book of Numbers*, New International Commentary on the Old Testament (Grand Rapids: Eerdmans, 1993), 503, shows how both Moab and Edom "regained their independence" after David, thus concluding that it could have only been "a temporary fulfillment."

laws (especially those in Deuteronomy) deal with Israel's life in the land, but the blessings and curses for covenant obedience and disobedience respectively culminate in either abundant prosperity in the land (blessings) or expulsion from the land (curses) (see Lev 26 and Deut 28).

I have emphasized in several places that Moses' outlook for the people was not positive at all. In fact, he was certain that Israel would receive the curses for disobedience and find themselves captives in a foreign land (Deut 4:25-28; 30:1; 31:17) as part of God's judgment "in the days to come" (Deut 31:29, literally "in the latter days"). Since the starting point for God's restoration of Israel was exile, God's restoration includes the people's return to the land. Two key passages in Deuteronomy highlight this return, passages that I have already discussed in this chapter. That we continue to return to the same passages shows the close relationship between the three restoration components.

Deuteronomy 4:25-31 and 30:1-10 both emphasize Israel's repentance as the prerequisite for God's restoration plans. Both passages teach that God would bring Israel back to their land when they returned to him and looked for him with all their heart and soul (Deut 4:29; 30:2, 10). Deuteronomy 30 gives a more detailed description of what their return will look like. Moses lists unprecedented prosperity (vv. 5, 9), victory over their enemies (v. 7), and heart change that results in obedience (vv. 6, 8) as accompanying aspects of Israel's return. The prerequisite of repentance and obedience demonstrates that Israel's return to the land will bring the covenant blessings that they would forsake because of disobedience during their first stint in the land. Yahweh ensures that this obedience would not be temporary by changing their hearts.

SUMMARY OF GOD'S PLAN OF RESTORATION
IN THE PENTATEUCH

The Pentateuch's restoration prophecies assume a period of judgment for the people of Israel. As noted above, the phrase "in the latter days" connects the periods of God's judgment and restoration. Furthermore, this key phrase also connects the three components of God's restoration. Israel's exile would come because of their rebellion against Yahweh and would make it impossible for Israel's king (Deut 17:14-20) to rule over them. God's salvation plan provided solutions for all three of these problems. First, Yahweh had to correct the root problem: Israel's sin. He would do this by changing their hearts so that they would obey him (Deut 30:6). Second, he would bring them back to the land in fulfillment of his promises to Abraham (Deut 4:25-31; 30:1-10). Because of their new hearts, their time of restoration would be permanent. Finally, God would raise up a king from Israel to judge the nations and bring his creation blessings to all the peoples of the world (Gen 49:8-12; Num 24:7-9, 17-19). Israel's king is the central component of God's restorative plans. In some mysterious way, this king would also defeat the serpent with a crushing blow (Gen 3:15). The Pentateuch therefore gives us some significant clues as to how God would turn the tide of sin and restore his world to its blessed beginnings in Eden. Furthermore, these three components reflect the three major components of the Abrahamic covenant (land, blessing, and offspring),[8] thus highlighting the Abrahamic covenant as the ultimate hope of the Pentateuch. Regarding the implicit contrast between the Abrahamic and old covenants in the Pentateuch, Dempster writes, "The note of hope found in the Abrahamic covenant is the larger context for the more pessimistic covenant of Sinai."[9]

GOD'S RESTORATION IN THE PROPHETS

The future work of God outlined in the Pentateuch continues as a central theme in the prophetic books of the Hebrew Bible. Much like Moses in the Pentateuch, the prophets highlight Israel's transgression of the covenant as evidenced in the nation's idolatry and social injustice. Just as Moses had predicted, the prophets foresaw a day when God would judge Israel and drive them out of their land by means of foreign invaders. The prophets urged the people to repent of their sins and turn to the Lord for healing and forgiveness, yet the people continued in their persistent disobedience. Moses was right. These people, like their fathers with whom Moses dealt, were stiff-necked and rebellious. Fortunately, the prophets (again, like Moses) did not leave the people with the bad news of judgment; they continually reminded the people of a better day after judgment, a day of hope!

---

[8] The people receive Yahweh's blessings after he changes their hearts, and the promise of the offspring is ultimately fulfilled by Israel's king, who would "possess the gate of his enemies" (Gen 22:17; cf. Gal 3:16).

[9] Stephen G. Dempster, *Dominion and Dynasty* (Downers Grove, IL: IVP Academic, 2003), 117.

The amount of material in the Prophets concerning God's future work of restoration is significant, so I am going to synthesize the key prophetic teachings regarding God's future restoration by briefly examining each of the major restoration components.

Heart change in the Prophets. Jeremiah 9:25-26 and Ezekiel 44:7 both mention circumcision in a way that echoes a twist Moses put on the concept in Deuteronomy. Earlier in this chapter, I pointed out that Moses' focus on heart circumcision and his lack of focus on physical circumcision in Deuteronomy shows that at minimum he regarded them as equals and at a maximum he considered heart circumcision more important. Jeremiah 9:25-26 and Ezekiel 44:7 follow Moses' teaching, the former by highlighting that physical circumcision alone is not enough to stop God's judgment against sin and the latter by equating the uncircumcision of flesh *and* heart. In addition to these passages, two other prophetic passages describe the heart change God would bring about during his future restoration of Israel.

Jeremiah 31:31-34. This passage is one of the most important prophecies in the Hebrew Bible and accords well with the Pentateuch's message. It characterizes Yahweh's future work as a covenant and terms this future covenant the "new covenant." While this covenant receives other designations in the Prophets,[10] Jeremiah 31 contains the only occurrence of the phrase "new covenant" in the Hebrew Bible. As one would expect, Jeremiah uses this term to highlight the contrast between the future "new covenant" and the "old covenant" that his people were transgressing at the time of his prophetic ministry (cf. Jer 11:10; 22:9). Because of its importance, I have chosen to quote the entire passage.

> Behold, the days are coming, declares the LORD, when I will make a new covenant with the house of Israel and the house of Judah, not like the covenant that I made with their fathers on the day when I took them by the hand to bring them out of the land of Egypt, my covenant that they broke, though I was their husband, declares the LORD. For this is the covenant that I will make with the house of Israel after those days, declares the LORD: I will put my law [instruction] within them, and I will write it on their hearts. And I will be their God, and they shall be my people. And

---

[10]Jeremiah and Ezekiel both designate it "an everlasting covenant" (Jer 32:40; 50:5; Ezek 16:60; 37:26). Ezekiel also labels it "a covenant of peace" (Ezek 34:25; 37:26).

no longer shall each one teach his neighbor and each his brother, saying, "Know the LORD," for they shall all know me, from the least of them to the greatest, declares the LORD. For I will forgive their iniquity, and I will remember their sin no more.

Whenever someone compares or contrasts two items, as interpreters we should identify the specific points of comparison and contrast. Jeremiah identifies two key points of contrast between the old and new covenants. The first and most significant contrast between these covenants relates to the place and manner of writing. Unlike the old covenant, which God (and later Moses) wrote on stone tablets, the new covenant consists of God writing his instruction on his people's hearts. Instead of an external imposition of laws, the new covenant is an internal transformation of heart and mind, so that Yahweh's instruction becomes part of the very fabric of his people.[11] In describing the new covenant's internal bull's-eye (mind and heart), Jeremiah uses different language to designate what Moses calls heart circumcision. Both passages underscore the centrality of the heart in the people's service to Yahweh.

You may have noticed that I put "instruction" in brackets after "law" (ESV) in verse 33. As I noted in an earlier chapter, the Hebrew word *torah* can mean general instruction or specific laws. I have translated the word as "instruction" in verse 33 in order to avoid confusion. If we translate the word as "law," we must define the law we are referencing. Although Jeremiah does not specify which *torah* he is referencing in verse 33, we can clarify this ambiguity when we consider this passage in light of the entire biblical story. It cannot refer to the old covenant legislation[12] since, as I have argued, Christ abolished these laws at the cross. The meaning of Jeremiah's prophecy did not change at the cross. Therefore, we must conclude that the *torah* of Jeremiah 31:33 refers to God's instruction and not to a specific law code (i.e., the old covenant). Under the new covenant, neither Jews nor Gentiles are under the Sinai legislation.

Jeremiah includes a second contrast between the covenants when he emphasizes Yahweh's forgiveness of Israel's sins (v. 34). Instead of receiving

---

[11]Jeremiah also teaches heart-transformed obedience in two other passages: Jer 24:7 and 32:39-41.

[12]For support, see F. B. Huey Jr., *Jeremiah, Lamentations*, New American Commentary 16 (Nashville: B&H, 1993), 287.

forgiveness of sins under the old covenant, Israel's sin increased, and they continually experienced God's wrath for their sins. Under the new covenant, Yahweh's removal of his people's sins provides the basis for their knowledge of Yahweh, a knowledge that is personal ("they shall all know me") and extensive ("from the least of them to the greatest"). Because Yahweh forgives their sins, their relationship with Yahweh no longer depends on priestly and prophetic mediation.[13] Such knowledge was not, and could not be, experienced under the old covenant.

Ezekiel 36. Deuteronomy 30 described God's future "heart work" as heart circumcision, whereas Jeremiah 31 portrayed it as God's writing his *torah* on people's hearts. Now we are going to turn our attention to a third passage that focuses on God's heart work: Ezekiel 36:16-38. Because of the length of this passage, I have chosen to quote the key section we will examine, Ezekiel 36:24-30:

> I will take you from the nations and gather you from all the countries and bring you into your own land. I will sprinkle clean water on you, and you shall be clean from all your uncleannesses, and from all your idols I will cleanse you. And I will give you a new heart, and a new spirit I will put within you. And I will remove the heart of stone from your flesh and give you a heart of flesh. And I will put my Spirit within you, and cause you to walk in my statutes and be careful to obey my rules. You shall dwell in the land that I gave to your fathers, and you shall be my people, and I will be your God. And I will deliver you from all your uncleannesses. And I will summon the grain and make it abundant and lay no famine upon you. I will make the fruit of the tree and the increase of the field abundant, that you may never again suffer the disgrace of famine among the nations.

Ezekiel 36 has several key parallels with the new covenant passage of Jeremiah 31, two of which are pertinent to this discussion. First, Ezekiel 36 predicts the cleansing and subsequent forgiveness that Israel would experience when the Lord worked on their behalf (vv. 25, 29). Second, both passages stress the internal work of the Lord, presenting the people's hearts as the target for Yahweh's work of restoration. Ezekiel 36 describes this heart work in a different manner and moves beyond Jeremiah 31 in one key

---

[13]C. F. Keil and F. Delitzsch, *Jeremiah, Lamentations* (Peabody, MA: Hendrickson, 2011), 283-84.

way; it states that the Lord will give his people a new heart *and* a new spirit. Ezekiel describes the new heart as "a heart of flesh" in contrast to the stony hearts the people possessed at the time of Ezekiel's prophecy. He identifies the new spirit that Yahweh would give his people as Yahweh's Spirit. In other words, God is going to give his people his very own Spirit.

This leads us to the way Ezekiel moves further than Jeremiah in his prophecy of the Lord's heart work. Ezekiel informs us that when the Lord puts his Spirit within his people, he will produce obedience in their lives. This truth corresponds to Deuteronomy 30 where the Lord's circumcision of his people's hearts causes them to love him. Here Yahweh's Spirit produces obedience in his people. Such obedience serves once again as a key contrast between the old and new covenants. Those who lived under the old covenant did not obey because they had a heart problem. However, those who live under the new covenant can obey because God has fixed this heart problem by giving his people a new heart and a new spirit.

The coming king in the Prophets. In the book of 2 Samuel, Yahweh made a key promise regarding the king from Judah. Yahweh narrowed this king's lineage from Judah to David by means of the Davidic covenant (2 Sam 7:8-16). The trajectory from the serpent crusher to the king from Judah finds its ultimate expression in a future king from David's line. The prophets therefore regularly connect this king to David instead of Judah (e.g., Is 9:7; 11:1; Jer 23:5; Ezek 34:24; 37:24-25; Hos 3:5).

Several components of the prophetic portrait of this Davidic king correspond to the Pentateuch's portrait of the coming king. First, Isaiah describes this king as a child who will be born (Is 9:6). The birth of this king makes him an eligible candidate for the woman's offspring who will crush the serpent's head. Second, the prophets state that this king will rule over Israel (Is 9:6-7; Jer 23:6; 33:16; Ezek 34:23-24; 37:24-25) and the nations (Is 11:10), a theme that echoes the rule of the king in Genesis 49 and Numbers 24. Third, Ezekiel emphasizes the prosperity of this king's reign (Ezek 34:25-30), much like Genesis 49 highlighted the prosperity of the coming king from Judah.

The prophetic testimony regarding the Davidic king adds several more components that were not part of the Pentateuch's descriptions. At the heart of these additional components is the description of this king's reign as one marked by righteousness and justice (Is 9:7; 11:1-5; Jer 23:5-6; 33:15-16). Unlike Israel and Judah's numerous unrighteous kings, this king will rule the people in perfect justice, caring for the poor and weak of society. Because of such righteousness, those who live under his reign relish in peace and joy (Is 9:3-7; 11:6-9).

Israel's return to the land in the Prophets. The third and final component of the Pentateuch's vision of God's restoration also comes to the surface on numerous occasions in the Prophets. Just as the Pentateuch described Israel's return to the land as a time in which they would receive the covenant blessings that they had forsaken during their first stint in the land, so the prophets describe Israel's restoration to the land by using language and imagery from Deuteronomy's list of blessings (chap. 28). For example, Ezekiel emphasizes Israel's safety in the land as well as the fertility of their fields, cattle, and wives (Ezek 34–37). Israel would no longer bear the reproach of their enemies; instead, the nations would serve them (Is 60:10-18; 61:4-7).

When it comes to the nations, the prophets emphasize an additional feature of Yahweh's restoration. They teach that the nations will join Israel in their worship of Yahweh. Isaiah and Micah prophesy that the nations will flow to Yahweh's mountain in the latter days (our key phrase from the Pentateuch) to hear Yahweh teach (Is 2:2-4; Mic 4:1-3). Isaiah also teaches that the knowledge of Yahweh will fill the earth (Is 11:9) and that the nations will seek the Davidic king (Is 11:10), and he even goes so far as to say that Egypt and Assyria, two of Israel's greatest enemies, will be Yahweh's people alongside of Israel (Is 19:22-25). Furthermore, Isaiah predicts that Yahweh's servant (who is the Davidic king) would be a light to the nations and thereby bring salvation to the nations (Is 42:1-9; 49:1-7).

THE PENTATEUCH'S PLAN IN THE NEW TESTAMENT

To complete our survey of the Pentateuch's three restoration themes— heart change, the coming king, and the provision of the land—let us briefly examine the New Testament's reiteration and application of these restoration themes. By way of reminder, everything we have discussed in this chapter comes directly from the Hebrew Bible. By the time we get to the New Testament, we know a significant amount about God's restoration plans. Such detailed information underscores the continuity of the Hebrew

Bible and the New Testament. Additionally, the continuity of the Hebrew Bible and the New Testament finds further confirmation when we remember that the apostles preached Jesus on the basis of the Hebrew Bible since many of the New Testament books were not written until much later.

Since the coming king served as the centerpiece of Yahweh's restorative plans, the New Testament authors emphasize this king's arrival more than the other two restoration themes. Such an emphasis does not indicate that the other two components are unimportant; on the contrary, this emphasis demonstrates that all three components find their fulfillment in the coming king. Paul says it best when he writes, "For all the promises of God find their Yes in him. That is why it is through him that we utter our Amen to God for his glory" (2 Cor 1:20).

The first words of the New Testament identify Jesus as the Messiah, the Son of David, and the Son of Abraham, thus establishing Jesus as the fulfillment of the Old Testament prophecies regarding the coming king, the Davidic covenant, and the Abrahamic covenant. From Matthew on, the New Testament authors assert, assume, and announce the coming of God's kingdom in the person and work of Jesus Christ.

When it comes to heart change, Paul in his Epistles shows how Christ's work has accomplished what God had promised to his people in the Hebrew Bible. Paul mentions non-fleshly circumcision in Colossians 2:11 and labels such circumcision "the circumcision of Christ." He associates this circumcision with the believer "putting off the body of the flesh." Paul also refers to God cleansing and transforming believers in several other passages (cf. 2 Cor 5:17; Gal 4:6; Tit 3:4-7). Finally, he continues the trajectory of the Pentateuch and the Prophets by teaching that heart circumcision is more important than physical circumcision. In fact, Paul goes so far as to say that the one who has merely fleshly circumcision is not a true Jew. For him, "a Jew is one inwardly, and circumcision is a matter of the heart, by the Spirit, not by the letter" (Rom 2:29). Like Ezekiel, Paul associates the work of God's Spirit with heart circumcision. Such heart change occurs when one enters the new covenant by the blood of the Davidic king.

The component of the Pentateuch's restoration passages that is the most difficult and controversial is the land promise. Attentive readers of the New Testament will notice that this component gets very little attention in the New Testament. Why is this topic less prominent in the New Testament?

What has happened? Are we still waiting for God to fulfill his promises and restore Israel to their land? Or did Jesus fulfill this promise?

The New Testament teaches that God has expanded both the land promise and the heirs to the land promise. Regarding the heirs, the New Testament teaches that God has grafted Gentiles into his people. Paul uses the illustration of a wild olive tree to explain this concept (Rom 11:16-24). Because of their unbelief, God broke off some of the natural branches (Israel) from the tree and replaced these branches with wild branches (Gentiles). Thus, in another place Paul can say that Jews and Gentiles are one body in Christ (Eph 2:11-22). The beauty of the Gospel is that God has brought together peoples from all nations into one body under one head, Jesus Christ.

Since God has expanded the heirs to the promise (see Gal 3:13-14), he has also expanded the land promise to include more than the land of Canaan. Because of Christ's work, the land promise now includes the whole world. This expansion corresponds to the vastness of the Messiah's reign as emphasized in the Prophets. Just as the Messiah's reign will be universal, so those who are coheirs with Christ will reign with him over the entire world (1 Cor 6:2; Rev 2:26-27; 3:21; 5:10). God has not broken his promise to restore Israel to the land; he has simply expanded his promise to give true Israelites (those who embrace Christ as their Messiah), as well as Gentiles who are grafted in, the true land (the entire world) as an inheritance. The author of Hebrews confirms that the land promise has moved beyond the land of Canaan. In Hebrews 11:16, he teaches that the early saints (Abraham, Isaac, and Jacob) had a heavenly country and that God prepared a city for them. In Hebrews 12:22-24, he identifies the heavenly Jerusalem, which he calls "Mount Zion" and "the city of the living God," as the homeland of his Jewish readers. All of these passages culminate in Revelation 21–22, wherein God creates a new heaven and earth with the new Jerusalem, which comes down from heaven, as its capital. As believers, "we are waiting for new heavens and a new earth in which righteousness dwells" (2 Pet 3:13).[14]

---

[14]See Peter J. Gentry and Stephen J. Wellum, *Kingdom Through Covenant: A Biblical-Theological Understanding of the Covenants* (Wheaton, IL: Crossway, 2012), 703-16, and Oren Martin, "The Land Promise Biblically and Theologically Understood," in *Progressive Covenantalism*, ed. Stepen J. Wellum and Brent E. Parker (Nashville: B&H, 2016), 255-74, for good explanations of the land promise's fulfillment in the new creation that also interact with a dispensational interpretation of the land promise. For a fuller treatment of this topic, see Oren R. Martin, *Bound for the Promised Land: The Land Promise in God's Redemptive Plan* (Downers Grove, IL: IVP Academic, 2015).

As you may recall, while outlining my position in chapter two, I distanced myself from No-Old-Law Christians who do not treat the Hebrew Bible as Christian Scripture. My survey of the Pentateuch's ultimate hope has demonstrated the centrality of messianic and new covenant themes in the message of the Hebrew Bible. When we couple these positive themes with the negative assessment of the old covenant, we can conclude that the Hebrew Bible and the New Testament are more similar than many Christians understand. I therefore have no problem affirming that the Hebrew Bible is Christian Scripture. Since our king serves as the ultimate hope on which God's complete restoration rests, an underemphasis or neglect of the Hebrew Bible results in an incomplete portrait of Jesus' first coming and a skewed understanding of the events that will take place at his second coming. The Hebrew Bible is Christian Scripture because our Messiah is the ultimate hope and solution for the sinfulness of Israel and all humanity!

CONCLUSION: BACK TO THE BEGINNING

THE LAW IN THE EARLY CHURCH
AND THE CONTEMPORARY CHURCH

Throughout the history of the Christian church, each generation of Christians has sought to apply the truth of Scripture to their culture. This book represents my attempt to present the unchanging truth of Scripture to the present generation of believers. The issue of the Christian application of the old covenant laws has been a consistent topic of discussion throughout the ages. This is why I devoted chapter two to outlining the various approaches to the law. I have titled this chapter "Back to the Beginning" because I am going to conclude this book by briefly discussing the church's beginnings in the book of Acts. Specifically, we will examine the church's first official discussion of the application of these laws.

JERUSALEM COUNCIL

On the day of Pentecost, God filled the early Christians with the Holy Spirit. As a result, they proclaimed the good news of the Messiah with great boldness. On that day alone, three thousand Jewish pilgrims received the promised gift of salvation as they put their faith in Jesus the Messiah. The early church continued to proclaim the gospel in spite of intense opposition from the Jewish religious leaders. This opposition reached a boiling point when Stephen, a Spirit-filled follower of Jesus, gave his defense before the Sanhedrin. After Stephen spoke to them as Moses spoke to his generation ("You stiff-necked people, uncircumcised in heart and ears" [Acts 7:51]), they rushed him and stoned him to death.

Acts 1: 8

Stephen's stoning marks a turning point in the book. After his death, a widespread persecution of the Jerusalem Christians drove them out of the city and into Judah and Samaria (Acts 8:1). Of course, as they went, they continued to proclaim the good news of their king. Eventually, God revealed to his church that his plan of salvation extended beyond the Jews to the Gentiles. He did so by leading Peter to a Gentile named Cornelius (Acts 10). As Peter preached the good news of Jesus to Cornelius, the Holy Spirit filled Cornelius and those around him, thus convincing Peter that God had accepted the Gentiles as part of his people. Not all the believers were elated with this news, so Peter had to convince a group of naysayers that God had accepted the Gentiles just as he had accepted the Jews (Acts 11:1-18).

Although God first used Peter to take the message to the Gentiles, he chose Paul as his official apostle to the Gentiles (Gal 2:7-8). With Antioch as his launching point, Paul embarked on three missionary journeys, taking the gospel to Gentiles across the Roman world. After returning from his first missionary journey (Acts 13–14), Paul settled in Antioch with the believers there (Acts 14:26-28).

The influx of Gentiles into the church soon hit a bump in the road. During Paul's time in Antioch, some Pharisee believers came to Antioch and taught the Gentile believers that they had to undergo circumcision in order to be saved (Acts 15:1). In response, Paul and Barnabas took a group of believers to Jerusalem to meet with the apostles and elders regarding this issue. During this meeting, often called the Jerusalem Council, the Pharisee believers clarified their expectations more clearly. They not only demanded that the Gentile believers be circumcised, but they also wanted them to obey "the law of Moses" (Acts 15:5). Their challenge marks the first formal discussion of the application of the old covenant (notice that I interpret this reference to "the law" as the old covenant) to Gentile believers. Let's listen closely to their discussion.

As expected, the first keynote speaker at the council is none other than Peter. Peter begins his speech by affirming God's acceptance of the Gentiles by faith, an acceptance he himself witnessed when God sent the Holy Spirit on Cornelius and his household (Acts 15:7-9). Then he asks, "Now, therefore, why are you putting God to the test by placing a yoke on the neck of the disciples that neither our fathers nor we have been able to bear?" (Acts 15:10).

Peter acknowledges the very thing that the Pentateuch teaches us: the people of Israel could not keep the law. Furthermore, Peter uses the imagery of a yoke to describe the law. A yoke was a large wooden beam placed on the necks of oxen and came to symbolize a burden. Peter thus refers to the burdensome nature of the law and argues that neither the first-century Jews nor their ancestors were able to bear it. Peter concludes his speech by arguing that everyone, Jews and Gentiles alike, is saved through the grace of Jesus (Acts 15:11).

Paul and Barnabas speak to the council next and describe all the amazing works God did among the Gentiles during their missionary journey. James, Jesus' brother, brings the final resolution to the dilemma. He affirms the veracity of Peter's words, using the prophets as support for Gentile inclusion in the church (Acts 15:13-18). He then makes the following proposal for Gentile believers:

> Therefore my judgment is that we should not trouble those of the Gentiles who turn to God, but should write to them to abstain from the things polluted by idols, and from sexual immorality, and from what has been strangled, and from blood. For from ancient generations Moses has had in every city those who proclaim him, for he is read every Sabbath in the synagogues. (Acts 15:19-21)

Although much of the council's discussion revolved around Gentile salvation, James' proposal moves beyond Gentile salvation. The apostles had just agreed that Gentiles were saved by grace through faith. If James gave the Gentiles these four laws as a prerequisite for salvation or inclusion in the people of God, then he would have contradicted the council's primary, previous decision. James's proposal relates to the Gentiles adherence to the old covenant laws *after* salvation, the very topic of this book.

Notice that James did not tell them to obey the Ten Commandments or the old covenant moral laws. I think such silence is due to the argument I have made throughout this book: Christians are no longer under the authority of the old covenant. James certainly would not condone Gentile believers murdering, stealing, hating others, and the like. We do not know why James did not highlight other laws for the Gentiles. Perhaps he trusted the Spirit's work in their hearts and, like Paul, realized that one who lives by the Spirit "will not gratify the desires of the flesh" (Gal 5:16). Ultimately, we do not know why James did not give a longer list of laws, but he did highlight four laws, so we need to examine those laws.

James gave the Gentile believers four laws, a few of which appear rather strange to many modern readers. Why did James select those laws?[1] Verse 21 gives us the answer to this question. He selected these laws because Jews read the Pentateuch ("Moses" refers to the book, not the person) in the synagogues every Sabbath. But what does the synagogue have to do with the church?

The answer to this question revolves around one of the central themes in the New Testament: the unity of Jews and Gentiles in the church. The four laws that James listed are four activities of first-century Gentiles that would have offended first-century Jews. Therefore, the apostles commanded the Gentiles not to participate in these activities for the sake of unity. The church's unity and mission to the Jews required sensitivity from Gentile converts.[2] In fact, we know that one of these laws (and perhaps as many as three) was not inherently sinful, but the apostles still required the Gentiles to submit to it for the sake of unity.

First Corinthians 8 accords with this interpretation of Acts 15. Here Paul deals with the issue of strong and weak consciences among Christians and the related topic of gray areas. Specifically, he addresses the topic of meat sacrificed to idols (one of the laws found in Acts 15). What he says about this matter is instructive. He begins by underscoring that it is not inherently wrong to eat meat sacrificed to idols because an idol is nothing (1 Cor 8:4-6). However, he acknowledges that some believers have a weak conscience and therefore do not recognize the nothingness of idols. If these believers ate meat sacrificed to idols, they would defile their consciences before God (1 Cor 8:7). Therefore, Paul commands believers with strong consciences not to eat meat sacrificed to idols because it would cause weaker Christians to stumble (1 Cor 8:9-13). Although eating meat sacrificed to idols was not sinful in and of itself, the action became sinful when it caused a Christian with a weaker conscience to eat meat sacrificed to idols.

---

[1] For a summary of four proposed backgrounds for the four laws, see Craig S. Keener, *Acts: An Exegetical Commentary*, vol. 3 (Grand Rapids: Baker, 2014), 2260-69.
[2] For support, see Richard N. Longenecker, "Acts," in *The Expositor's Bible Commentary*, ed. Frank E. Gaebelein (Grand Rapids: Zondervan, 1981), 448.

Paul's teaching in 1 Corinthians 8 (cf. Rom 14) helps us better understand the laws of Acts 15. First, since Paul makes it clear that eating meat sacrificed to idols is not inherently sinful, we cannot interpret James's four laws to the Gentiles as universally binding on all people at all times. In this regard, we should not automatically assume that all these laws apply to modern believers. The apostles gave them to a particular people at a particular time for a particular reason. Second, Paul's focus on the weaker and stronger believers confirms that James's motive relates to preserving the unity of the church. In other words, Paul's weaker Christians in 1 Corinthians 8 correspond to the Jews in Acts, and Paul's stronger Christians correspond to the Gentiles.

The teachings of Paul and the other apostles demonstrate how the early believers applied the law of Christ to various situations. Even though Christ had freed believers from the law of Moses, the law of Christ demanded believers to sacrifice their freedoms for the sake of other believers. Such sacrificial love was more important than enjoying the freedom from the law that Christ purchased on their behalf. For the Jerusalem Council, the law of Christ meant forcing Gentiles to obey some laws that were not binding on them in order to preserve the unity of the body in love.

We should apply the lessons of the Jerusalem Council to our own day. Most modern believers do not have the occasion to eat meat sacrificed to idols, so this is not a major issue for most Western Christians. However, depending on the culture, other gray areas—activities some believers in certain contexts may participate in without sinning—are abundant. In my own context, Christians disagree over alcohol, tattoos, R-rated movies, and many other issues. Like the first-century church, modern believers must sacrificially love their fellow brothers and sisters in Christ by not causing them to stumble. In other words, our freedoms have a limit, and that limit depends on the context in which we live and move. Understanding how to navigate these various contexts requires Spirit-led wisdom, not a law code. At times, the law of Christ might demand that we give up something that is not inherently wrong in order to demonstrate the selfless, sacrificial love of Christ. In this and many other ways, the law of Christ demands more of us than the old covenant did the Israelites, but the new covenant offers us far more than the old covenant did the Israelites. As members of the new covenant community, we stand forgiven, uncondemned, and blessed by God because Christ has taken the curses of the law for us.

CONCLUDING THOUGHTS

Writing a book on a subject that has received so much attention throughout church history is an intimidating endeavor. I pray that this book provides an avenue for many believers to understand more fully the biblical story and the old covenant laws' role in it. Very few issues are more difficult to understand than the biblical teaching on the old covenant. At the same time, very few issues, when understood properly, shed light on the message of the biblical story like the old covenant's role in pointing beyond itself to the ultimate hope of the Bible: Jesus the Messiah.

As I have argued throughout the book, believers do not have to wait until the New Testament to understand the person, work, and message of Jesus the Nazarene. The Pentateuch begins painting a portrait of this coming king, and it does so by showing the inadequacies of the old covenant in the nation of Israel. Like a master painter, God has revealed the glorious radiance of the coming king against the backdrop of Israel's sinful hearts, which God fully exposed in giving the old covenant. In the end, the ethical overlap between the old and new covenants does not serve as the glue that binds the Hebrew Bible and the New Testament together; on the contrary, it is Jesus the Messiah who serves as that bond. For this reason, Jesus could look at his contemporaries and boldly proclaim, "For if you believed Moses, you would believe me; for he wrote of me" (Jn 5:46). Hopefully, I have made a convincing case that Jesus did not expect his followers to put on their magnifying glasses and look for miniscule clues about him in the Pentateuch. Instead, an engaged reading of the Pentateuch points to Yahweh's coming king as the one who will deal a defeating crush to the serpent who introduced sin into God's perfect creation. While this coming king has inaugurated God's kingdom on earth, we still await the full consummation and restoration of all things. Therefore, as we wait for the perfect restoration of all things, we cry out, "Come, Lord Jesus!" (Rev 22:20).

APPENDIX A

HOW SHOULD CHRISTIANS USE THE HEBREW BIBLE TO ADDRESS HOMOSEXUALITY?

In my introduction I used two illustrations to challenge modern Christians to be consistent in their use of the old covenant laws when discussing homosexuality and gay marriage. Since this is such a controversial topic, I want to give a fuller discussion of what the Hebrew Bible teaches regarding homosexuality.[1] I have selected this topic not because I think homosexuality is the unpardonable sin, but because this issue is currently one of the most discussed issues in American culture. As Christians, we must allow the Bible to inform our beliefs and practices, and this includes the issue of homosexuality. However, we cannot do so in a haphazard way that ignores the literary context and the development of the biblical story. Applying the Bible—especially the Hebrew Bible—to modern contexts requires diligence and wisdom. In what follows, I will examine three passages and outline ways believers should or should not use them in conversations about homosexuality.[2] Unfortunately, American Christians have not always done a good job of communicating the Bible's teaching on homosexuality in a biblical manner. Whenever we discuss this issue, we must do so in a

---

[1] The New Testament gives many clear statements regarding the sinfulness of homosexuality (Rom 1:26-27; 1 Cor 6:9; 1 Tim 1:10). These passages reaffirm and support the Hebrew Bible's consistent stance toward homosexuality.

[2] For a recent introductory treatment of the Bible's teaching on homosexuality, see Kevin DeYoung, *What Does the Bible Really Teach About Homosexuality?* (Wheaton, IL: Crossway, 2015). For a more thorough treatment of this topic, see Robert A. J. Gagnon, *The Bible and Homosexual Practice: Texts and Hermeneutics* (Nashville: Abingdon, 2001).

gentle, humble, gracious, and honorable manner (Col 4:5-6; 1 Pet 2:12; 3:15). Even when we suffer for our stance, we must suffer in a way that reflects the humble suffering of our Lord Jesus. I therefore offer this chapter as guidance for gracious interaction.

GENESIS 1–2

Genesis 1–2 provides the picture of God's original creation before the corrupting effects of sin. Since these chapters give a pre-fall portrait of God's design for all of creation, including marriage, discussions of sex and marriage should begin here. These two chapters give us different yet complementary descriptions of the first couple and their relationship to God and each other.

Genesis 1:24-31 narrates the events that transpired on day six of God's creation. When God created human beings, he set them apart from the other living beings by creating them in his own image. Both men and women reflect God's image, and God's image in humans allows them to exercise dominion over the rest of his creation. In the description of God's creation of humanity, two things are pertinent for our discussion. First, God created human beings "male and female" (Gen 1:27). Second, the gender differences—and thus complementary features of the male and female—enabled them to fulfill Yahweh's first command to them: "Be fruitful and multiply and fill the earth" (Gen 1:28). Much like his blessing of the birds and sea creatures (Gen 1:22-23), God's creation blessing of human beings enabled them to increase in number and fill the earth.

Genesis 2 zooms in on God's creative activity on the sixth day of creation in a specific location, the Garden of Eden. After describing the location and contents of the garden (Gen 2:4-17), Moses, the author of Genesis, turns his attention to the only not-good thing in God's good world: Adam's solitude (Gen 2:18). To remedy this situation, Yahweh brought the beasts and birds to Adam, who then gave names to the animals. Yet the animals were not sufficient remedies for Adam's problem, so Yahweh put Adam to sleep, took one of his ribs, and from it made a woman. When Yahweh presented her to Adam, Adam recited a poem (Gen 2:23).

Yahweh's creation of Eve for union with Adam serves as the climax of Genesis 2. This event is so important that an authorial explanation follows Adam's poem. Genesis 2:24 reads, "Therefore a man shall leave his father and his mother and hold fast to his wife, and they shall become one flesh." For two chapters, Moses has simply narrated the events of creation; now he in essence steps onto the stage to have a little conversation with the readers, basically telling them, "This is why we do what we do." The first marriage serves as the model and basis for all future marriages. The one-flesh union of a man and woman was Yahweh's intention for marriage from the beginning. A man and woman becoming one flesh includes sexual intimacy in the relationship, but it runs much deeper than that. It involves the complete union of two persons in a permanent relationship, which in turn becomes the context for the multiplication of God's image bearers.

As we continue reading the Hebrew Bible, this pattern becomes the criterion by which we should judge the morality of all marriages and sexual relationships. We do not have to read very far in the Hebrew Bible before we encounter polygamy. Although the authors are usually silent on their condemnation of polygamy (the biblical authors do not explicitly grade every moral action they narrate), we as readers already know that it fails to meet God's creational design of a one-flesh union of a man and a woman. When we read about the men of Sodom and Gomorrah asking to have sexual relations with Lot's guests, we already know that such activity runs counter to God's original design for sexual relations.

Not only do we evaluate later passages on the basis of God's creational pattern; we also find confirmation of God's creational pattern in some later passages. Christopher J. H. Wright notes that Yahweh's use of marriage as a metaphor for his "exclusive relationship" with Israel presupposes "monogamy as the theological and ethical ideal."[3] Wright makes this point in the context of polygamy, but by extension the ideal of heterosexual monogamy addresses all perversions of this ideal, including homosexuality and gay marriage.

The good news for all Christians who read Genesis 1–2 as God's pattern for sex and marriage is that God himself has given the authoritative interpretation of these passages. During his ministry, Jesus answered many questions regarding numerous passages in the Hebrew Bible. On one

---

[3]Christopher J. H. Wright, *Old Testament Ethics for the People of God* (Downers Grove, IL: InterVarsity Press, 2004), 330.

occasion, the Pharisees tested him by asking him to clarify the appropriate grounds for divorce. In his answer, Jesus quoted Genesis 1:27 and 2:24 to underscore the permanence of the one-flesh union of a man and woman. After the Pharisees retorted by referring to Deuteronomy 24:1-4, Jesus states, "Because of your hardness of heart Moses allowed you to divorce your wives, but from the beginning it was not so" (Mt 19:8). Deuteronomy 24's casuistic divorce law represented a concession based on the Israelite's sinfulness, not God's created design.

Although Jesus was dealing with the issue of divorce, his treatment of Genesis 1–2 as God's intention for sex and marriage affirms our use of these chapters in discussions of homosexuality and gay marriage.[4] Homosexual behavior violates the creation pattern in two particular ways. First, God made the woman for union with the man. He did not create another man. Second, Genesis 1–2 indicates that one of the key—but not exclusive—purposes of the one-flesh union of the man and woman is procreation. Paul indicates that procreation is not the only purpose for marital sex in 1 Cor 7:1-9. In these verses, he advises (see v. 6) Christian husbands and wives to maintain regular sexual intimacy in order to avoid temptation. Adam and Eve's primary task was to be fruitful and fill the earth. Such a task is impossible in homosexual relationships. The complementary nature of the reproductive systems underscores God's created intention for sexual relationships.

When discussing homosexuality and gay marriage, modern Christians should appeal to Genesis 1–2 as their primary passage when arguing for heterosexual, monogamous marriages. Such reasoning presents a positive case for the institution of marriage and avoids much of the logical foolishness that has resulted from Christians using other passages in the Hebrew Bible (e.g., Lev 18:22; 20:13). Furthermore, Jesus' affirmation that these passages represent God's original good intention for sex and marriage adds significant weight to our interpretation of them.

---

[4]Genesis 1–2 does not address the issue of singleness, but the New Testament highlights the legitimacy and superiority of the single, celibate life both implicitly (the examples of Jesus and Paul) and explicitly (1 Cor 7:25-40). Paul's reference to singleness as a gift (1 Cor 7:7-9) and his explanation of the benefits of the single life (1 Cor 7:32-35) demonstrate the unique role of single people in the church.

GENESIS 18-19

Sodom and Gomorrah. The very names of these ancient cities have become synonymous in the church with homosexuality, brimstone, and even salt. For many Christians, Sodom and Gomorrah are Exhibit A for God's hatred of homosexual behavior. The modern linking of homosexuality and Sodom is not a recent phenomenon. In fact, the biblical story of Sodom serves as the basis for the English word *sodomy*.

The story of Sodom and Gomorrah begins in Genesis 18 when Yahweh and two angels visit Abraham in the form of three men. After informing Abraham that Sarah would give birth to a son in a year's time, Yahweh revealed his plan for Sodom and Gomorrah to Abraham. He outlines his plans in verses 20-21, which read, "Because the outcry against Sodom and Gomorrah is great and their sin is very grave, I will go down to see whether they have done altogether according to the outcry that has come to me. And if not, I will know." In response to Yahweh's plan, Abraham asked Yahweh to spare the city because of the righteous (Gen 18:22-32). Abraham's bold appeal resulted in Yahweh agreeing not to destroy the city if he found ten righteous people in it (Gen 18:32).

Genesis 19 records the angels' visit to Sodom and the subsequent destruction of the city. After the angels (disguised as men) entered Lot's house, the men of the city surrounded Lot's house and asked for the men in the following manner: "Bring them out to us, that we may know them" (Gen 19:5). In this context, the word "know" (*yāda*) indicates sexual relations. Three clues support this conclusion. First, Lot identifies their actions as wicked in verse 7. Such a designation does not accord well with a friendly conversation. Second, Lot uses the same word to refer to his daughters' lack of sexual relations with a man—that is, their virginity (v. 8). Third, the word *yāda* commonly appears in the Hebrew Bible as a euphemism for sexual relations. For example, Genesis 4:1 and 25 use this word to describe Adam's sexual intimacy with his wife, Eve. We can therefore confidently conclude that the men of the city desired homosexual relations with the two angels (whom the people of Sodom believed to be men [v. 5]) who entered the city.

Some proponents of homosexuality argue that the men of Sodom were not guilty of homosexuality but of an attempted gang rape.[5] However, bib-

---

[5]For example, the Reformation Project argues that the Bible does not condemn same-sex

lical scholars have noted that *yāda* in Genesis 19:5 does not refer to the men's desire to rape the men, but it refers to their desire for homosexual relations. For support, Brian Neil Peterson building on the work of Richard Davidson and Victor Hamilton, notes that "when rape is referred to in the Bible a term showing a level of coercion accompanies the word [*yāda*] . . . or completely different terms are employed."[6] Although the men of Sodom eventually resorted to gang rape (v. 9), their initial desire appears to be a desire for homosexual activity.

By storming Lot's house in a lustful uproar, the men of Sodom clearly demonstrated the gravity of their sin before God. In other words, God had seen that their actions corresponded to the outcry that had come before him (cf. Gen 18:21). After the angels struck the men of the city with blindness, they explained their plan to destroy the city and took Lot and his family out of the city. The subsequent judgment of Sodom and Gomorrah becomes a picture of God's judgment that echoes through the rest of the Hebrew Bible and into the New Testament. The prophets often compare Israel to Sodom and Gomorrah when emphasizing the wickedness of Israel (e.g., Is 1:10), but one prophet, Ezekiel, outlines the sins of Sodom most clearly.

Ezekiel 16 is one of the most graphic chapters in the Hebrew Bible, wherein Ezekiel compares Jerusalem to Yahweh's bride and recounts all her adulterous relationships. In the second half of the chapter, he compares Jerusalem to two of her sisters: Samaria and Sodom. For the purposes of our discussion, we will examine what Ezekiel says about Sodom. Ezekiel accuses Jerusalem of being worse than Sodom and, in so doing, specifically outlines the sins of which Sodom was guilty. In Ezekiel 16:49-50 he states, "Behold, this was the guilt of your sister Sodom: she and her daughters had pride, excess of food, and prosperous ease, but did not aid the poor and needy. They were haughty and did an abomination before me. So I removed them, when I saw it." These verses may surprise some readers because Ezekiel does not explicitly mention homosexuality. Instead, he lists several other sins that the Genesis narrative does not mention: pride, gluttonous

---

relationships. In "A Brief Biblical Case," they state, "Sodom and Gomorrah involved an attempted gang rape, not a loving relationship" (2016, www.reformationproject.org/a_brief_biblical_case).

[6]Brian Neil Peterson, "The Sin of Sodom Revisited: Reading Genesis 19 in Light of Torah," *The Journal of the Evangelical Theological Society* 59, no. 1 (2016): 19.

luxury, and social injustice. Although Ezekiel's reference to "an abomination" could refer to homosexual behavior, the context of this passage does not give us enough information to interpret it dogmatically in such a manner. Ezekiel does use the word *abomination* to refer to sexual sins (Ezek 22:11), but he also uses the term to describe idolatry (Ezek 7:20; 16:36), defiling the temple (Ezek 43:8), and undefined sin (Ezek 18:12; 33:26).[7] Because the context of Ezekiel 16 does not specify the abomination of Sodom, it is probably best to leave it unspecified in our interpretation of the passage.

The lack of an explicit mention of sexual sin in Ezekiel's description of Sodom's sins contrasts with another passage that highlights the sexual sins of Sodom. In the tiny New Testament book of Jude, Jude identifies the sins of Sodom and Gomorrah as "sexual immorality" and pursuing "unnatural desire" (better: "strange flesh") (Jude 7). Here Jude highlights the sexual sins of Sodom and Gomorrah as examples of sins that receive God's judgment. Some scholars interpret Jude's reference to the men's pursuit of "strange flesh" as a reference to the Sodomites' desire for sexual relations with angels.[8] Although such an interpretation is possible, Genesis 19 indicates that the men of Sodom thought the angels were men. Nevertheless, we can conclude with certainty that Jude regarded sexual immorality (any sexual relations outside a monogamous, heterosexual relationship) as one of the primary sins of Sodom and Gomorrah.

The story of Sodom and Gomorrah and later biblical authors' explanation of their sins supply us with additional clarity on the issue of homosexuality in the Hebrew Bible. Based on the passages we have discussed, how should we use the story of Sodom and Gomorrah in discussions of homosexuality? First, homosexuality is not the be-all and end-all reason Yahweh judged the cities of Sodom and Gomorrah. Ezekiel makes it clear that their pride, gluttonous pleasures, and social injustice contributed to Yahweh's judgment of the city.[9] Second, the narrative of Genesis 18–19 does

---

[7]Ezekiel uses the singular form of this word four times (16:50; 18:12; 22:11; 33:26). Peterson, "The Sin of Sodom Revisited," 21, argues that "sexual sins are the focus when Ezekiel uses the singular" form. Unfortunately, Peterson overstates his case when we consider that in 18:12 and 33:26 abomination is not explicitly connected to sexual sin.

[8]See Peter H. Davids, *The Letters of 2 Peter and Jude*, PNTC (Grand Rapids: Eerdmans, 2006), 52, for a discussion of the interpretive options.

[9]Rosaria Champagne Butterfield, *The Secret Thoughts of an Unlikely Convert* (Pittsburgh: Crown and Covenant, 2012), in her chapter titled "Repentance and the Sin of Sodom," offers a unique perspective on how these sins lead to sexual immorality.

indicate that their desire for homosexual relations with the visitors was an expression of their wickedness. In addition to the author's use of *know*, we should also remember that the angels entered the city "to see whether they [had] done altogether according to the outcry that [had] come to [Yahweh]" (Gen 18:21). After seeing and experiencing the wicked desires of the city's men, the visitors moved forward with their planned destruction (Gen 19:13). This interpretation finds confirmation in Jude 7, in which Jude highlights sexual immorality as a reason for the fiery judgment. Consequently, the story of Sodom does contribute to the discussion of homosexuality in the Hebrew Bible, but it does so in a way that challenges how many modern Christians use the passage. Homosexuality is one of the sins committed in Sodom and Gomorrah, but it is not the *only* sin of Sodom and Gomorrah. Pride, gluttonous luxury, and social injustice—all of which get less emphasis in modern discussions of actions that incur God's wrath—also played a key role in God's judgment of the cities. Contemporary Christians would do well to emphasize these other sins as much as they typically do homosexual behavior.

LEVITICUS 18:22 AND 20:13

Leviticus 18 has become the favorite passage for both opponents of homosexuality and proponents of homosexuality. Why is this? Many Christians gravitate toward Leviticus 18:22 and 20:13 because both passages refer to homosexuality as an abomination. For these Christians, such language is conclusive. Since these passages provide some of the Bible's clearest condemnations of homosexuality, these verses have become the first choice for many Christians when discussing homosexual behavior.

However, using these verses is not that easy. Proponents of homosexuality have pointed out that when Christians appeal to these verses, they often don't actually read the context of these verses. The larger context contains some statements that make it difficult for Christians to use these verses in discussions. First, Leviticus 18:19 prohibits a man sleeping with a woman during her menstruation, and Leviticus 20:18 actually prescribes the death penalty for the man and the woman who violate this command. Are these same Christians willing to condemn modern couples who have sexual relations during the woman's menstruation? Some may, but many are mute on this point. Second, Leviticus 19, the chapter sandwiched between these two chapters, prohibits such things as breeding two different kinds of livestock, sowing a field with different seeds, mixing linen and wool in a garment, and shaving the edges of one's beard. Once again, modern Christians are not promoting these prohibitions. Third, Deuteronomy 14:3-21 outlines numerous unclean animals that God forbade the Israelites to eat. Interestingly, Moses designates these unclean animals as an "abomination" (Deut 14:3). If an abomination refers to something that is always sinful in God's eyes, then modern Christians appear hypocritical.

Should modern Christians use these verses to argue against homosexuality? I urge modern Christians not to use Leviticus 18 or 20 in modern discussions over homosexuality. Let me be clear: I absolutely believe that homosexuality and many other forms of sexual immorality listed in Leviticus 18 and 20 are sinful before God. However, since Yahweh gave these commands to Israel as part of the old covenant, using them as proof texts against homosexuality presents too many difficulties and inconsistencies. Although Leviticus's prohibitions against sexual immorality reflect the universal law of God, Yahweh contextualizes them in the old covenant, a covenant whose jurisdiction does not extend to Gentiles and Christians. The Bible's teaching on God's will for sex and marriage is so clear that Christians have many other passages to use in discussions (e.g., Gen 1–2; Rom 1:26-27; 1 Cor 6:9; 1 Tim 1:10). By using these other passages, Christians can clearly articulate God's will and avoid much confusion that results from inconsistent interpretation.

NATURAL LAW

The above discussion should profit Christians in discussions with people who assign some level of authority to the Bible. However, Western culture increasingly gives less weight to a "the Bible says so" approach of reasoning. Many people couldn't care less about what the Bible says, so when we engage these people (in a gracious and respectful manner!) regarding homosexuality, we must reason from a different starting point. I think that the best starting point for such discussions is natural law. God has created a moral order in the world and in the hearts of all human beings. By appealing to this innate sense of morality, we are able to find a common ground with others, and hopefully we can help them see how their actions violate the natural moral order of the universe. When it comes to discussions regarding homosexuality, we should appeal to the anatomical complementarianism of men and women, the purposes of sexual activity, and the psychological and sociological effects of sexual immorality in all its forms.[10]

In conclusion, I encourage Christians to keep a Christ-centered perspective when discussing homosexuality with unbelievers. The Western cultural climate makes it difficult to discuss homosexuality in the public square without falling into an us-versus-them mentality. As Christians, we must regularly remind ourselves that moralism is not the answer. If we convince every homosexual to give up their lifestyle, we have not fixed the problem. Homosexuals, just like everyone else, have a much greater problem, and the solution to that problem begins with them submitting to the lordship of Christ. We all have rebelled against our Creator, and we all need his forgiveness and grace.

---

[10]For a natural law argument supporting monogamous, heterosexual sexual relations, see J. Budziszewski, *On the Meaning of Sex* (Wilmington, DE: ISI Books, 2014). For a list of his other books on natural law, see the bibliography.

APPENDIX B

THE SECOND COMMANDMENT
AND IMAGES IN WORSHIP

Many American churches display the Ten Commandments in a prominent place for all to see. Whether they are in the church's foyer, sanctuary, or other gathering area, these displays communicate that the Ten Commandments provide the foundational ethical guidelines for the Christian life. For some of these churches, obedience to the second commandment affects the visual aids they employ in worship. The second commandment reads:

> You shall not make for yourself a carved image, or any likeness of anything that is in heaven above, or that is in the earth beneath, or that is in the water under the earth. You shall not bow down to them or serve them, for I the LORD your God am a jealous God, visiting the iniquity of the fathers on the children to the third and the fourth generation of those who hate me, but showing steadfast love to thousands of those who love me and keep my commandments. (Ex 20:4-6)

For many churches, obedience to this commandment means that they cannot have artwork that portrays God the Father in any form. These Christians argue that God forbids images of himself because it betrays his invisible and transcendent nature. Since images of God pervert our understanding of God, we should never create an image of God. Many of these same Christians also extend this to Jesus Christ. Even though Jesus exists as the God-man, we do not know exactly what he looks like, and therefore any image perverts his true image.

Churches that prohibit visual images of God typically believe that Christians are justified in appealing to the second commandment because they are under the jurisdiction of the Ten Commandments, whether or not this is explicitly stated. But if, as I have argued in this book, we are not under the Ten Commandments, how does this affect our use of images in worship and, more generally, our portrayal of God in any context? The purpose of this appendix is to answer this question and, by so doing, to offer an example of how Christians can use the Hebrew Bible to address certain issues even though we are not directly under the jurisdiction of the old covenant.

If the Ten Commandments do not serve as our primary foundation for ethics, then on what basis should we approach the question of images in worship? As with all the issues that the Ten Commandments address, we must determine if the second commandment reflects something in God's universal natural law or if it relates directly to God's being and character. Even though we are not under this commandment, it may overlap with God's universal standards for all people.

As with most of the Ten Commandments, Moses repeats and further defines this commandment throughout the remaining sections of the Pentateuch. In these later clarifications, Moses specifies two activities that this command prohibits: (1) making idols of other gods and (2) making images of Yahweh. The command for the people not to make idols of other gods (Ex 20:23; 34:17; Lev 19:4; 26:1)[1] builds on the first commandment and echoes throughout the Hebrew Bible and the New Testament. In fact, the prohibition against worshiping other gods/idols finds its basis in Yahweh's uniqueness as the one true God. Israel's ancient neighbors and the Greco-Roman world of the New Testament represented their gods with images that they believed embodied the gods they worshiped. Throughout the Hebrew Bible, Israel constantly worshiped these foreign gods instead of Yahweh, and ultimately Yahweh judged them for their worship of the nations' idols (2 Kings 17:14-20). Since this aspect of the commandment builds on the uniqueness of Yahweh as the one true God and thereby reflects God's eternal, universal law, Christians should never worship an idol

---

[1]Patrick D. Miller, *The Ten Commandments* (Louisville, KY: Westminster John Knox, 2009), 48, argues that "the use of the plural 'gods' in several of [these] texts . . . tends to confirm [this] interpretation."

in any form. In fact, many of the New Testament's prohibitions against idolatry relate to this activity.

Moses explains the second prohibited activity most clearly in Deuteronomy 4:11-24. In explaining to the Israelites why God prohibited carved images, Moses underscores Yahweh's theophany (an appearance of God) on Mount Sinai. Twice (vv. 12 and 15) Moses informs the people that they did not see any form but only heard a voice. Although the people saw a fire, Moses makes it clear that the fire did not represent God; instead, he emphasizes that God spoke "out of the midst of the fire" (vv. 12 and 15). As we have already seen, the people's construction of the golden calf at Sinai directly violated this aspect of the commandment, since the people built the idol to represent Yahweh.

Since Yahweh's theophany at Sinai serves as the foundation for the second commandment's prohibition of representing Yahweh visually, we should ask how Yahweh's theophany at Sinai relates to other theophanies in the Hebrew Bible. Attentive readers will recall that Yahweh appeared to the patriarchs (Abraham, Isaac, and Jacob) in the form of a man (Gen 18:1-2; 32:22-32). Yahweh also appeared to Moses on Mount Sinai after the golden calf incident. In the description of this theophany, Yahweh describes himself using human characteristics (Ex 33:19-23). Later in the Hebrew Bible, both Isaiah and Ezekiel have visions of Yahweh in which Yahweh appears with human features. Isaiah sees "the Lord sitting upon a throne, high and lifted up" (Is 6:1). Ezekiel has a vision of the chariot throne of Yahweh and in his description states that "seated above the likeness of a throne was a likeness with a human appearance" (Ezek 1:26). These other passages demonstrate that Yahweh's theophany at Sinai was not the only way he revealed himself in the Hebrew Bible; he sometimes appeared to individuals in human form.

Alongside these visions and theophanies, numerous other passages in the Hebrew Bible speak of Yahweh's hands, arms, eyes, feet, and face. These descriptions are a literary device called an anthropomorphism. An anthropomorphism occurs when an author attributes a human quality or feature to God. Since God the Father is spirit, he does not have these physical features. Thus, when the biblical authors attribute these physical features to God, they are communicating something about God in a way that we can understand. Theologians typically call this "accommodation language," since God accommodates himself to us in human terms so that we can better understand him. For example, when the biblical authors describe God bringing Israel out of Egypt with "a mighty hand and an outstreched arm" (Deut 5:15), they are highlighting his power. Today, we might say that God "flexed his muscles" when he brought Israel out of Egypt. Nevertheless, by using anthropomorphic language, the biblical authors paint a mental image of God that reflects human features.[2]

The various theophanies and anthropomorphisms in the Hebrew Bible should give us pause when considering whether portraying God visually reflects God's universal moral law. Although God the Father is an invisible spirit, he does frequently reveal himself in the Hebrew Bible with human features. The Hebrew Bible's theophanies culminate in the greatest theophany of the Bible: the incarnation. When God became flesh in the person of Jesus Christ, God imaged himself as a human being. In this regard, one may argue that God brought an end to the second commandment's prohibition of representing God visually by making himself in "the form of [a] figure, the likeness of male" (Deut 4:16). The New Testament emphasizes that Jesus Christ perfectly represents God in the incarnation (Jn 12:45; 14:9; Heb 1:3). In particular, Colossians 1:15 reads, "He is the image of the invisible God." And because Christ rose from the dead physically, he exists at the right hand of God the Father as the God-man, fully divine *and* fully human. Thus, when we portray Christ as a human being, we are portraying him as he actually exists. We do not know his specific features, but we do know that he exists in the form of a human being.

Our brief analysis has demonstrated that one activity prohibited by the second commandment reflects God's universal moral law, but the other activity does not. Because God has imaged himself in Jesus Christ as a man,

---

[2]Martin Luther, in a response to his critics regarding his position on images, writes concerning the relationship between mental images and visual images: "For whether I will or not, when I hear of Christ, an image of a man hanging on a cross takes form in my heart, just as the reflection of my face naturally appears in the water when I look at it. If it is not a sin but good to have the image of Christ in my heart, why should it be a sin to have it in my eyes? This is especially true since the heart is more important than the eyes, and should be less stained by sin because it is the true abode and dwelling place of God." *Luther's Works*, vol. 40, *Church and Ministry II*, trans. Bernhard Erling and Conrad Bergendoff, ed. Conrad Bergendoff (Philadelphia: Fortress, 1958), 99-100. Taken from Gesa Elsbeth Thiessen, ed., *Theological Aesthetics: A Reader* (Grand Rapids: Eerdmans, 2004), 134.

the prohibition against making images of God solely because of his invisible nature seems to have been a temporary, and even preparatory,[3] measure for the nation of Israel under the old covenant.

Some Christians still apply the prohibition against images to God the Father since he is spirit (Jn 4:24). Such a practice may be a wise decision for these believers, especially if they are in a context where people worship images of deities, but such a practice does not appear to be an absolute requirement after the incarnation. Regardless of one's position on this issue, we must emphasize that the incarnation does not give us the freedom to portray God arbitrarily. In what follows, I will outline three areas of caution for Christians.

First, Christians who choose to portray God visually must only use images as an aid in their worship of God. If portrayals of God ever become the object of worship, these portrayals become an abomination before him and deserve immediate condemnation. Unfortunately, for some Christians, the slip from an image as a window through which we view God's character to the image as an object of worship happens quickly. Therefore, anytime Christians venerate or associate spiritual power with an image, they have moved into the realm of idolatry.

Second, whenever Christians make or view visual images of God, they must accompany such images with clear teaching regarding the limited nature of these visual images. For example, church leaders must emphasize and Christians must understand that portrayals of Jesus—whether in paintings or films—do not equal the historical Jesus. The biblical text gives us very limited knowledge regarding Jesus' physical features, and we must make sure that we do not base our images of Jesus more on our culture than on first-century Jewish culture. Also, because the Bible consistently teaches that God the Father is spirit (Deut 4:15; Jn 4:24; 1 Tim 1:17), any representation of the Father is purely anthropomorphic (i.e., symbolic). I am always amazed at how many of my students think of God the Father as a human being. When I ask them why, they commonly cite anthropomorphic

---

[3]William A. Dyrness, *Visual Faith: Art, Theology, and Worship in Dialogue* (Grand Rapids: Baker, 2001), 84, writes regarding the preparatory function of the visual signs that accompanied Yahweh's presence in the Hebrew Bible: "If, as Hans Urs von Balthasar has pointed out, one of God's purposes in the Old Testament is to prepare his people for the actual appearance of God in the incarnation, we can see how vital the visible aspects of God's presence had to be."

passages in the Hebrew Bible. They do not attribute a body to God the Father because of church art; they do so because no one has taught them about anthropomorphisms in the Bible. Whenever Christians view an artistic representation of God the Father, they must ask what the representation teaches about God's nature. Furthermore, I am not comfortable with artists representing God outside of any categories given in the Bible. By tying representations of God the Father to the biblical text, Christians have a context by which to interpret the anthropomorphic expression.

Finally, since Christians throughout the centuries have disagreed on this issue,[4] we must always remember the principle of love in our interactions with other believers. If one's visual portrayal of God causes another brother or sister to stumble and fall into idolatry, then one should exercise great care when using visual art. We all can agree that idolatry is thoroughly condemned throughout the Bible. In order to prevent idolatry, some Christians refuse to use visual images in worship, whereas other Christians enjoy using visual art as a symbol that aids in worship. Christians on both sides of the debate should exercise love and grace and, in so doing, reflect Christ's law of love.

---

[4]For a brief historical survey of the church's uses of visual arts, see ibid., 25-67.

APPENDIX C

CHALLENGES TO MY POSITION

I have discussed many scriptural passages in this book. However, I have not dealt directly with some common objections to my position. Although I won't be able to address all such objections, I want to consider briefly some of the major challenges to my view by discussing two passages, one from the Hebrew Bible and one from the New Testament, which people often present as objections to my position.

PSALMS 19 AND 119

Psalms 19 and 119 contain numerous positive statements about the old covenant laws. For example, Psalm 19:7-9 reads:

> The law of the LORD is perfect,
>   reviving the soul;
> the testimony of the LORD is sure,
>   making wise the simple;
> the precepts of the LORD are right,
>   rejoicing the heart;
> the commandment of the LORD is pure,
>   enlightening the eyes;
> the fear of the LORD is clean,
>   enduring forever;
> the rules of the LORD are true,
>   and righteous altogether.

Because this passage contains such positive affirmations regarding the old covenant laws, some scholars argue that David's praise of the law and his emphasis on the law's benefits support their argument that Christians are still under some of the old covenant laws.

This argument carries very little weight for a few reasons. First, if we consider David's historical context, his praise of the old covenant laws is completely appropriate and reflects his righteousness. As I have argued in this book, God intended the Israelites who lived in the land to obey the old covenant laws. As a faithful king, David delighted in obeying God and thus delighted in God's will for the nation as expressed in the old covenant laws (cf. Deut 17:14-20). David also recognized the benefits and blessings of obeying the law, which Moses had outlined in the Pentateuch. In this regard, David's delight in God's law prepares us for the true king who would "fulfill all righteousness" (Mt 3:15).

Second, David's affirmation of the law's goodness fits perfectly with Paul's understanding of the law's goodness (Rom 7:12) and with what I have argued throughout this book. God's laws were good; the problem was with the Israelites' hearts. In contrast to much of what we see in the Hebrew Bible, David exemplifies a faithful Israelite, and therefore as an expression of his faith he delighted in God's laws.

Third, to argue that David's positive comments regarding the law means that Christians are under the old covenant laws demonstrates a misunderstanding of the law's jurisdiction. I may affirm that many of Germany's laws are good, but I would never argue that I am under the jurisdiction of those laws as an American citizen unless I visited Germany. As Christians, we can recognize that the old covenant laws were good and useful in Israel's national life without arguing that everyone is under the jurisdiction of those laws.

MATTHEW 5:17-20

Matthew 5:17-20 provides one of the New Testament's most explicit statements concerning the continuity between the Hebrew Bible and Jesus' ministry. Located in the early portion of Jesus' Sermon on the Mount, this passage serves as an introduction to Jesus' six "You have heard . . . but I say to you" sayings. In these sayings, Jesus gives his authoritative interpretation of several old covenant commands, both correcting some traditional Jewish interpretations of these commands and modifying some of the old covenant laws themselves (Mt 5:38-42). Since Jesus offers a different, yet not contradictory, interpretation of several laws, he prefaces his interpretive sayings with these important verses in order to avoid the accusation that he was abolishing the Hebrew Bible. The passage reads,

> Do not think that I have come to abolish the Law or the Prophets; I have not come to abolish them but to fulfill them. For truly, I say to you, until heaven and earth pass away, not an iota, not a dot, will pass from the Law until all is accomplished. Therefore whoever relaxes one of the least of these commandments and teaches others to do the same will be called least in the kingdom of heaven, but whoever does them and teaches them will be called great in the kingdom of heaven. For I tell you, unless your righteousness exceeds that of the scribes and Pharisees, you will never enter the kingdom of heaven.

These verses have traditionally been a battlefield on which Christians with different approaches to the law have fought. Christians who argue that we are under the jurisdiction of some of the old covenant laws typically cite this passage to support their position. Before outlining my interpretation of the passage, I will outline some common theological conclusions that most Christians hold. This common ground provides a starting point for proper interpretation of the passage.

First, all the Christian positions on the old covenant laws agree that we are not required to obey many of the old covenant laws. For example, God does not require Christians to offer sacrifices, bring offerings to a temple, establish a priesthood, keep the Jewish festivals, and so on. Therefore, in order to be consistent with many other passages of Scripture, we cannot hold that Jesus' words in this passage mean that every law requires obedience until "heaven and earth pass away" (Mt 5:18).

Second, Jesus' teaching and actions in Matthew indicate that his kingdom citizens are no longer under the jurisdiction of several old covenant laws. For example, after the Pharisees questioned Jesus over ceremonial hand washing before meals, Jesus proclaimed to the crowds, "It is not what goes into the mouth that defiles a person, but what comes out of the mouth; this defiles a person" (Mt 15:11). The implication of Jesus' words is clear, and just in case we missed it, Mark gives an explicit interpretation of the passage, writing, "Thus he declared all foods clean" (Mk 7:19). By declaring the old covenant dietary restrictions obsolete, Jesus sheds more light on the meaning of his words in Matthew 5:17-20.

Another example from the book of Matthew will help us responsibly interpret Matthew 5:17-20. Matthew records several phenomenal events that occurred when Jesus surrendered his spirit on the cross. The first event is arguably the most important. Matthew 27:51 records the rending of the temple's veil into two pieces. This rending demonstrates that Jesus' death opened the Most Holy Place to people other than just the high priest. It indicates that Jesus' death allows unrestricted access to God's presence through Jesus. Such a change indicates that Christians no longer approach God according to the old covenant prescriptions. Jesus' fulfillment of the roles of the priesthood and the temple indicate a change in the way God's people approach him.

From the Gospel of Matthew and, more specifically, Jesus' teaching, we can conclude that Matthew 5:17-20 cannot mean that Christians should obey every old covenant law. The larger context of Matthew's Gospel indicates that Jesus brought an end to the dietary laws and the temple system as known in first-century Judaism. Recognizing this teaching protects us from overinterpreting Matthew 5:17-20 to mean that every old covenant law is binding on believers until the end of the present age. Now that I have outlined what the passage cannot mean, let's look at what the passage does mean.[1]

Matthew 5:17 contains the statement that governs the rest of the passage. Jesus teaches that he came not "to abolish the Law or the Prophets . . . but to fulfill them." By pairing the Law and the Prophets, Jesus indicates that his referent is the entire Hebrew Bible. A little later in the Sermon on the Mount, Jesus states that the golden rule serves as an apt summary of "the Law and the Prophets" (Mt 7:12). Jesus did not come to get rid of the Hebrew Bible; rather, he came to fulfill the Hebrew Bible.

---

[1]Numerous interpretive difficulties accompany this passage, and a detailed discussion of these issues falls beyond the scope this appendix. For good discussions of these issues, I recommend the commentaries of Donald A. Hagner and D. A. Carson. My own interpretation of this passage has much in common with their analyses. See Donald A. Hagner, *Matthew 1-13*, Word Biblical Commentary 33a (Nashville: Thomas Nelson, 2000), 102-10; and D. A. Carson, "Matthew," in *Expositor's Bible Commentary*, vol. 8, ed. Frank E. Gaebelein (Grand Rapids: Zondervan, 1984), 140-47.

Commentators have debated extensively over the meaning of the word *fulfill*. This word is one of Matthew's favorite words to describe Jesus' relationship to the Hebrew Bible. At this point in his Gospel, Matthew has already used the word in reference to Jesus five times (Mt 1:22; 2:15, 17, 23; 4:14). In each of these cases, Matthew quotes a specific prophecy from the Hebrew Bible to indicate that Jesus was the ultimate focus of these prophecies. These prophecies thus find their meaning in Jesus. In other words, the prophecies serve as road signs that point us to the Bible's ultimate destination. Jesus does not quote a specific prophecy in Matthew 5:17 but speaks generally of fulfilling the entire Hebrew Bible. In this regard, we may interpret Jesus' words as stating that the entire Hebrew Bible finds its ultimate meaning in the Messiah, an interpretation that corresponds with what I have argued throughout this book.

After establishing his broad point, in Matthew 5:18 Jesus narrows his attention to a specific portion of the Hebrew Bible—that is, the Law. Once again, we face the question of the referent of *law*. What "law" does Jesus have in mind in verse 18? In light of verse 17, Jesus is most likely referencing the Pentateuch.[2] Since he is about to address specific commands from the Pentateuch in verses 21-48, he leaves the Prophets behind and focuses only on the Pentateuch. Additionally, he moves one step further in his specificity and highlights the smallest letters and strokes (iota and dot) of the Pentateuch.

Jesus emphasizes the abiding authority of the Pentateuch's iotas and dots with two "until" phrases: "until heaven and earth pass away" and "until all is accomplished." The first phrase designates the end of the present world and the beginning of the new heaven and earth. The interpretation of the second phrase hinges on the referent of *all*. Many scholars identify these phrases as synonymous expressions.[3] With this interpretation, *all* refers to all of God's eschatological plans, thus indicating that the iotas and dots remain until the consummation of all things. Such an interpretation, however, seems to indicate that every law has binding authority until the end of the present age. A better way to interpret the second phrase is to

---

[2]The ESV indicates this referent by capitalizing "Law" in this verse. In contrast, the NKJV uses "law" in v. 18 but "Law" in v. 17.

[3]For example, Hagner, *Matthew 1-13*, 108; David Turner, *Matthew*, Baker Exegetical Commentary on the New Testament (Grand Rapids: Baker, 2008), 163.

interpret *all* as the contents of the Pentateuch.[4] This interpretation allows for the possibility that some portions of the old covenant may pass away once Jesus "accomplishes" them in his life, death, and resurrection, yet it also acknowledges that the Pentateuch's message stands "until heaven and earth pass away." Therefore, the phrase "until all is accomplished" relates closely to "fulfill" in verse 17. Since Jesus fulfills the Pentateuch, we must interpret every part of the Pentateuch in light of that fulfillment. As Matthew makes clear, Jesus' fulfillment of the Pentateuch includes the end of certain laws contained therein. Although Matthew does not discuss this in detail, Paul and other New Testament authors teach that Jesus' fulfillment of the Pentateuch marked the end of the whole old covenant. Jesus (and the New Testament authors) restated some of the old covenant laws, but we must interpret the laws through the lens of Jesus' teaching and fulfillment. Even though Jesus ended the old covenant, the old covenant still plays a significant role in the Pentateuch's message. In this sense, its function as part of Scripture lasts "until heaven and earth pass away."

Verse 19 outlines the consequences of those who break the least of the Pentateuch's commandments. Again, all Christians have similar problems with this verse. On the surface, it seems like Jesus commands his followers to obey every old covenant law. However, as we have seen, Jesus dismisses the dietary and temple laws later in Matthew's Gospel, so any interpretation must consider this. The best way to approach this verse is to interpret it in light of Jesus' fulfillment of the old covenant and as a preparation for verse 20, where Jesus calls out the scribes and the Pharisees. As those who taught the law, the scribes and Pharisees fit the bill of verse 19. In Matthew 15, Jesus rebukes them for breaking God's command because of their traditions (Mt 15:3). Also, Jesus corrects many of their misinterpretations of the laws in the verses that follow (Mt 5:21-48). Thus, Jesus is warning Israel's legal experts of the danger of not keeping the laws and teaching others to do the same. As modern readers, we have to read Matthew 5:19 in light of the rest of Christ's ministry and, in particular, his death. As those who lived "under the law," the Pharisees were required to obey all the old covenant commandments, but as those whom Christ has set free from the law, we are not required to obey the old covenant commandments.

---

[4]For a similar interpretation, see Carson, "Matthew," 145-46, and Craig L. Blomberg, *Matthew*, New American Commentary 22 (Nashville: B&H, 1992), 104.

By emphasizing his fulfillment of the Hebrew Bible in Matthew 5:17-20, Jesus identifies himself as the lens through which we can observe the unity of the two major sections of the biblical canon. When we interpret the Hebrew Bible in a Christ-centered manner, we are able to employ it "for teaching, for reproof, for correction, and for training in righteousness, that the man of God may be complete, equipped for every good work" (2 Tim 3:16b-17). I pray that a proper understanding of the Hebrew Bible will permeate the global church, so that the Hebrew Bible may be restored—in word and deed—to its rightful place as an essential part of the biblical canon, a restoration that is only possible when we correctly identify Jesus the Messiah as the bond that holds the testaments together.

BIBLIOGRAPHY

Aland, Barbara, et al., ed. *The Greek New Testament*. 4th rev. ed. Stuttgart: United Bible Society, 1998.

Alexander, T. Desmond. *From Paradise to the Promised Land: An Introduction to the Pentateuch*. 3rd ed. Grand Rapids: Baker, 2012.

———. "Royal Expectations in Genesis to Kings: Their Importance for Biblical Theology." *Tyndale Bulletin* 49 (1998): 191-212.

Arnold, Bill T., and Bryan E. Beyer. *Readings from the Ancient Near East: Primary Sources for Old Testament Study*. Grand Rapids: Baker, 2002.

Ashley, Timothy R. *The Book of Numbers*. New International Commentary on the Old Testament. Grand Rapids: Eerdmans, 1993.

Bahnsen, Greg L. *By This Standard: The Authority of God's Law Today*. Powder Springs, GA: American Vision, 2008.

———. "The Theonomic Reformed Approach to Law and Gospel." In *Five Views on Law and Gospel*, edited by Wayne G. Strickland, 93-143. Grand Rapids: Zondervan, 1996.

Baker, David L. *Two Testaments, One Bible: The Theological Relationship Between the Old and New Testaments*. 3rd ed. Downers Grove, IL: IVP Academic, 2010.

Barrs, Jerram. *Delighting in the Law of the Lord: God's Alternative to Legalism and Morality*. Wheaton, IL: Crossway, 2013.

Barton, John. *Understanding Old Testament Ethics: Approaches and Explorations*. Louisville, KY: Westminster John Knox, 2003.

Bauckham, Richard J. "Sabbath and Sunday in the Post-Apostolic Church." In *From Sabbath to Lord's Day*, edited by D. A. Carson, 221-50. Eugene, OR: Wipf and Stock, 1999.

Bauer, Walter, Frederick W. Danker, William F. Arndt, and F. Wilbur Gingrich. *A Greek-English Lexicon of the New Testament and Other Early Christian Literature.* 3rd ed. Chicago: University of Chicago Press, 2000.

Blaising, Craig A., and Darrell L. Bock. *Progressive Dispensationalism.* Wheaton, IL: Victor, 1993.

Block, Daniel I. *The Book of Ezekiel: Chapters 25–48.* Grand Rapids: Eerdmans, 1998.

———. *Deuteronomy.* NIV Application Commentary. Grand Rapids: Zondervan, 2012.

———. *Judges, Ruth.* New American Commentary 6. Nashville: B&H, 1999.

Blomberg, Craig L. *Matthew.* New American Commentary 22. Nashville: B&H, 1992.

Briggs, Richard S., and Joel N. Lohr, eds. *A Theological Introduction to the Pentateuch: Interpreting the Torah as Christian Scripture.* Grand Rapids: Baker, 2012.

Brown, Francis, S. R. Driver, and Charles A. Briggs, *The Brown-Driver-Briggs Hebrew and English Lexicon.* Peabody, MA: Hendrickson, 1996.

Brown, Jeanine. *Scripture as Communication: Introducing Biblical Hermeneutics.* Grand Rapids: Baker, 2007.

Bruce, F. F. *The Epistle to the Galatians.* New International Greek Testament Commentary. Grand Rapids: Eerdmans, 1982.

Bruckner, James K. "Ethics." In *Dictionary of the Old Testament: Pentateuch,* edited by T. Desmond Alexander and David W. Baker, 225-41. Downers Grove, IL: InterVarsity Press, 2003.

Budziszewski, J. *The Line Through the Heart: Natural Law as Fact, Theory, and Sign of Contradiction.* Wilmington, DE: ISI Books, 2009.

———. *On the Meaning of Sex.* Wilmington, DE: ISI Books, 2014.

———. *Written on the Heart: The Case for Natural Law.* Downers Grove, IL: InterVarsity Press, 1997.

Carson, D. A., ed. *From Sabbath to Lord's Day.* Eugene, OR: Wipf and Stock, 1999.

———. *The Gospel According to John.* Pillar New Testament Commentary. Leicester, UK: Apollos, 1991.

———. "Matthew." In *The Expositor's Bible Commentary,* vol. 8, edited by Frank E. Gaebelein, 1-599. Grand Rapids: Zondervan, 1984.

Cassuto, Umberto Moshe David. *A Commentary on the Book of Exodus.* Translated by Israel Abrahams. Skokie, IL: Varda, 2005.

Christensen, Duane L. *Deuteronomy 21:10–34:12.* Word Biblical Commentary 6B. Nashville: Thomas Nelson, 2002.

Clines, David J. A. *The Theme of the Pentateuch.* 2nd ed. Journal for the Study of the Old Testament Supplement Series 10. Sheffield, UK: Sheffield Academic Press, 2001.

Cole, R. Dennis. *Numbers*. New American Commentary 3b. Nashville: B&H, 2000.

Craigie, Peter C. *The Book of Deuteronomy*. New International Commentary on the Old Testament. Grand Rapids: Eerdmans, 1976.

Davids, Peter H. *The Letters of 2 Peter and Jude*. Pillar New Testament Commentary. Grand Rapids: Eerdmans, 2006.

Dempster, Stephen G. *Dominion and Dynasty*. Downers Grove, IL: IVP Academic, 2003.

DeYoung, Kevin. *What Does the Bible Really Teach About Homosexuality?* Wheaton, IL: Crossway, 2015.

Dorsey, David A. "The Law of Moses and the Christian: A Compromise." *Journal of the Evangelical Theological Society* 34 (1991): 321-34.

Douma, J. *The Ten Commandments: Manual for the Christian Life*. Translated by Nelson D. Kloosterman. Phillipsburg, NJ: P&R, 1996.

Duguid, Iain M. *Ezekiel*. NIV Application Commentary. Grand Rapids: Zondervan, 1999.

Dyrness, William A. *Visual Faith: Art, Theology, and Worship in Dialogue*. Grand Rapids: Baker, 2001.

Enns, Peter. *Exodus*. NIV Application Commentary. Grand Rapids: Zondervan, 2000.

Gagnon, Robert A. J. *The Bible and Homosexual Practice: Texts and Hermeneutics*. Nashville: Abingdon, 2001.

Gentry, Peter J., and Stephen J. Wellum. *Kingdom Through Covenant: A Biblical-Theological Understanding of the Covenants*. Wheaton, IL: Crossway, 2012.

Gieschen, Charles A., ed. *The Law in Holy Scripture*. St. Louis, MO: Concordia, 2004.

Greengus, Samuel. "Law." *Anchor Bible Dictionary*, vol 4, edited by David Noel Freedman, 245-51. New York: Doubleday, 1992.

Hagner, Donald A. *Matthew 1–13*. Word Biblical Commentary 33a. Nashville: Thomas Nelson, 2000.

Hamilton, Victor P. *Handbook on the Pentateuch*. 2nd ed. Grand Rapids: Baker, 2005.

Harrison, Ronald K. "Bible." *International Standard Bible Encyclopedia*, vol. 1, edited by Geoffrey W. Bromiley, 482-92. Grand Rapids: Eerdmans, 1979.

Hartley, John E. "Holy and Holiness, Clean and Unclean." In *Dictionary of the Old Testament: Pentateuch*, edited by T. Desmond Alexander and David W. Baker, 420-31. Downers Grove, IL: InterVarsity Press, 2003.

———. *Leviticus*. Word Biblical Commentary 4. Nashville: Thomas Nelson, 1992.

Hays, Christopher B. *Hidden Riches: A Sourcebook for the Comparative Study of the Hebrew Bible and Ancient Near East*. Louisville, KY: Westminster John Knox, 2014.

Hays, J. Daniel. "Applying the Old Testament Law Today." *Bibliotheca Sacra* 158 (2001): 21-35.

Horton, Michael S. *God of Promise: Introducing Covenant Theology*. Grand Rapids: Baker, 2006.

Huey, F. B., Jr. *Jeremiah, Lamentations*. New American Commentary 16. Nashville: B&H, 1993.

Kaiser, Walter C., Jr. "Exodus." *The Expositor's Bible Commentary*, vol. 2, 287-487. Grand Rapids: Zondervan, 1990.

———. "The Law as God's Gracious Guidance for the Promotion of Holiness." In *Five Views on Law and Gospel*, edited by Wayne G. Strickland, 177-99. Grand Rapids: Zondervan, 1996.

———. *Toward Old Testament Ethics*. Grand Rapids: Zondervan, 1983.

Keener, Craig S. *Acts: An Exegetical Commentary*. Vol. 3. Grand Rapids: Baker, 2014.

Keil, C. F., and F. Delitzsch. *Ezekiel, Daniel*. Vol. 9 of *Commentary on the Old Testament*. Translated by James Martin and M. G. Easton. 1866–1891. Reprint, Peabody, MA: Hendrickson, 2011.

———. *Jeremiah, Lamentations*. Vol. 8 of *Commentary on the Old Testament*. Translated by David Patrick and James Kennedy. 1866–1891. Reprint, Peabody, MA: Hendrickson, 2011.

———. *Pentateuch*. Vol. 1 of *Commentary on the Old Testament*. Translated by James Martin. 1866–1891. Reprint, Peabody, MA: Hendrickson, 2011.

Koehler, Ludwig, and Walter Baumgartner. *The Hebrew and Aramaic Lexicon of the Old Testament*. Leiden: Brill, 2002.

Leiter, Charles. *The Law of Christ*. Hannibal, MO: Granted Ministries Press, 2012.

Levine, Baruch A. *Leviticus*. JPS Torah Commentary. Philadelphia: Jewish Publication Society, 1989.

Loader, William. *Jesus' Attitude Toward the Law: A Study of the Gospels*. Grand Rapids: Eerdmans, 2002.

Longenecker, Richard N. "Acts." In *The Expositor's Bible Commentary*, edited by Frank E. Gaebelein, 207-573. Grand Rapids: Zondervan, 1981.

Longman, Tremper, III, and Raymond B. Dillard. *An Introduction to the Old Testament*. 2nd ed. Grand Rapid: Zondervan, 2006.

Luther, Martin. *A Commentary on the Epistle to the Galatians* (1535). Translated by Theodore Graebner. Accordance electronic ed. Grand Rapids: Zondervan, 1949.

Mann, Thomas W. *The Book of the Torah: The Narrative Integrity of the Pentateuch*. Louisville, KY: Westminster John Knox, 1988.

Martens, Elmer. "How Is the Christian to Construe Old Testament Law?" *Bulletin for Biblical Research* 12, no. 2 (2002): 199-216.

Martin, Oren R. *Bound for the Promised Land: The Land Promise in God's Redemptive Plan*. Downers Grove, IL: IVP Academic, 2015.

Martin, Ralph P. *Worship in the Early Church*. Rev. ed. Grand Rapids: Eerdmans, 1974.

McConville, J. G. *Deuteronomy*. Apollos Old Testament Commentary 5. Downers Grove, IL: IVP Academic, 2002.

McKeown, James. *Genesis*. Two Horizons Old Testament Commentary. Grand Rapids: Eerdmans, 2008.

Mendenhall, George E., and Gary A. Herion. "Covenant." In *Anchor Bible Dictionary*, vol. 1, edited by David Noel Freedman, 1179-202. New York: Doubleday, 1992.

Merrill, Eugene H. *Deuteronomy*. New American Commentary 4. Nashville: B&H, 1994.

Meyer, Jason C. *The End of the Law: Mosaic Covenant in Pauline Theology*. Nashville: B&H, 2009.

Milgrom, Jacob. *Numbers*. JPS Torah Commentary. Philadelphia: Jewish Publication Society, 1990.

Millar, J. Gary. *Now Choose Life: Theology and Ethics in Deuteronomy*. Downers Grove, IL: IVP Academic, 2000.

Miller, Patrick D. *The Ten Commandments*. Louisville, KY: Westminster John Knox, 2009.

Mohler, R. Albert, Jr. *Words from the Fire: Hearing the Voice of God in the 10 Commandments*. Chicago: Moody, 2009.

Moo, Douglas J. *The Epistle to the Romans*. New International Commentary on the New Testament. Grand Rapids: Eerdmans, 1996.

Murray, Scott R. *Law, Life, and the Living God: The Third Use of the Law in Modern American Lutheranism*. St. Louis, MO: Concordia, 2002.

Niehaus, Jeffrey J. "God's Covenant with Abraham." *Journal of the Evangelical Theological Society* 56:2 (2013): 249-71.

Packer, J. I. *Keeping the Ten Commandments*. Wheaton, IL: Crossway, 2007.

Peterson, Brian Neil. "The Sin of Sodom Revisited: Reading Genesis 19 in Light of Torah." *Journal of the Evangelical Theological Society* 59:1 (2016): 17-31.

Postell, Seth. *Adam as Israel: Genesis 1–3 as the Introduction to the Torah and Tanakh*. Eugene, OR: Wipf and Stock, 2011.

Pritchard, James B. *The Ancient Near East: An Anthology of Texts and Pictures*. Princeton, NJ: Princeton University Press, 2011.

Rooker, Mark F. *Leviticus*. New American Commentary 3a. Nashville: B&H, 2000.

———. *The Ten Commandments: Ethics for the Twenty-First Century*. Nashville: B&H, 2010.

Rosner, Brian S. *Paul and the Law: Keeping the Commandments of God*. Downers Grove, IL: IVP Academic, 2013.

———. *Paul, Scripture and Ethics: A Study of 1 Corinthians 5–7*. Grand Rapids: Baker, 1999.

Ryken, Philip Graham. *Written in Stone: The Ten Commandments and Today's Moral Crisis*. Wheaton, IL: Crossway, 2003. Reissued, Phillipsburg, NJ: P&R, 2010.

Sailhamer, John. *Introduction to Old Testament Theology: A Canonical Approach*. Grand Rapids: Zondervan, 1999.

———. *The Meaning of the Pentateuch: Revelation, Composition and Interpretation*. Downers Grove, IL: IVP Academic, 2009.

———. *The Pentateuch as Narrative: A Biblical-Theological Commentary*. Grand Rapids: Zondervan, 1992.

Sarna, Nahum M. *Exodus*. JPS Torah Commentary. Philadelphia: Jewish Publication Society, 1991.

Schnittjer, Gary Edward. *The Torah Story*. Grand Rapids: Zondervan, 2006.

Schreiner, Thomas R. *40 Questions About Christians and Biblical Law*. Grand Rapids: Kregel, 2010.

———. *The Law and Its Fulfillment: A Pauline Theology of Law*. Grand Rapids: Baker, 1993.

———. *Romans*. Baker Exegetical Commentary on the New Testament. Grand Rapids: Baker, 1998.

Selman, Martin J. "Law." In *Dictionary of the Old Testament: Pentateuch*, edited by T. Desmond Alexander and David W. Baker, 497-515. Downers Grove, IL: InterVarsity Press, 2003.

Sprinkle, Joe. *Biblical Law and Its Relevance: A Christian Understanding and Ethical Application for Today of the Mosaic Regulations*. Lanham, MD: University Press of America, 2005

Strickland, Wayne G., ed. *Five Views on Law and Gospel*. Grand Rapids: Zondervan, 1996.

Stuart, Douglas K. *Exodus*. New American Commentary 2. Nashville: B&H, 2006.

Thielman, Frank. *Paul and the Law: A Contextual Approach*. Downers Grove, IL: InterVarsity Press, 1994.

Thompson, J. A. *The Book of Jeremiah*. New International Commentary on the Old Testament. Grand Rapids: Eerdmans, 1980.

Tigay, Jeffrey H. *Deuteronomy*. JPS Torah Commentary. Philadelphia: Jewish Publication Society, 1996.

Turner, David. *Matthew*. Baker Exegetical Commentary on the New Testament. Grand Rapids: Baker, 2008.

VanGemeren, Willem A. "The Law Is the Perfection of Righteousness in Jesus Christ." In *Five Views on Law and Gospel*, edited by Wayne G. Strickland, 13-58. Grand Rapids: Zondervan, 1996.

Vogt, Peter T. *Interpreting the Pentateuch: An Exegetical Handbook.* Grand Rapids: Kregel, 2009.

Walton, John. *Ancient Near Eastern Thought and the Old Testament: Introducing the Conceptual World of the Hebrew Bible.* Grand Rapids: Baker, 2006.

Wells, Tom, and Fred Zaspel. *New Covenant Theology.* Frederick, MD: New Covenant Media, 2002.

Wellum, Stephen J., and Brent E. Parker. *Progressive Covenantalism: Charting a Course Between Dispensational and Covenant Theologies.* Nashville: B&H, 2016.

Wenham, Gordon J. *The Book of Leviticus.* New International Commentary on the Old Testament. Grand Rapids: Eerdmans, 1979.

———. *Genesis 1–15.* Word Biblical Commentary 1. Waco, TX: Word, 1987.

———. *Genesis 16–50.* Word Biblical Commentary 2. Waco, TX: Word, 1994.

———. *Numbers: An Introduction and Commentary.* Tyndale Old Testament Commentaries. Downers Grove, IL: InterVarsity Press, 1981.

———. "Sanctuary Symbolism in the Garden of Eden Story." *Proceedings of the World Congress of Jewish Studies* 9 (1986): 19-25.

———. *Story as Torah: Reading Old Testament Narratives Ethically.* Grand Rapids: Baker, 2000.

Westbrook, Raymond. "The Character of Ancient Near Eastern Law." In *A History of Ancient Near Eastern Law*, vol. 1, edited by Raymond Westbrook, 1-90. Leiden: Brill, 2003.

Westbrook, Raymond, and Bruce Wells. *Everyday Law in Biblical Israel: An Introduction.* Louisville, KY: Westminster John Knox, 2009.

Williamson, Paul R. "Covenant." In *Dictionary of the Old Testament: Pentateuch*, edited by T. Desmond Alexander and David W. Baker, 140-55. Downers Grove, IL: InterVarsity Press, 2003.

———. *Sealed with an Oath: Covenant in God's Unfolding Purpose.* Downers Grove, IL: InterVarsity Press, 2007.

Wright, Christopher J. H. *Old Testament Ethics for the People of God.* Downers Grove, IL: InterVarsity Press, 2004.

SCRIPTURE INDEX

OLD TESTAMENT

Genesis
1, *48, 186*
1-2, *184, 185, 186, 191*
1-3, *165*
1-11, *41*
1-15, *136*
1:1, *53*
1:22, *184*
1:24, *184*
1:26, *113*
1:27, *184*
1:28, *14, 184*
1:31, *53*
2, *96, 184*
2:1, *96, 101*
2:2, *96*
2:4, *184*
2:16, *14*
2:18, *184*
2:23, *184*
2:24, *185*
3-5, *80*

3:8, *130*
3:15, *158, 159, 162, 164, 165, 166, 168*
3:24, *130*
4, *117, 136*
4:1, *187*
4:3, *136*
4:4, *136*
4:5, *136*
5:28, *16*
6:5, *137*
6:8, *80*
6:9, *80, 128*
6:11, *117*
8:21, *137*
9:1, *14*
9:3, *14*
9:4, *14*
9:5, *117*
11:27-50:26, *162*
12, *58*
12:1, *163*
12:1-3, *160*
12:3, *60, 166*

12:15, *58*
12:17, *58*
13:16, *58*
14:18, *60*
15, *15, 58*
15:1, *59*
15:4, *58, 82*
15:5, *58*
15:6, *82*
15:13, *94*
16-50, *161*
17, *58, 154*
17:12, *155*
17:14, *155*
17:19, *58*
18, *81, 187*
18-19, *187, 189*
18:1, *195*
18:10, *58*
18:21, *188, 190*
18:22, *187*
18:25, *81*
18:32, *187*
19, *141, 187, 188, 189*

19:5, *187, 188*

19:13, *190*

20, *81*

20:4, *81*

20:6, *81*

21:1, *16*

21:31, *15*

22:13, *137*

22:17, *58, 168*

25:24, *74*

25:25, *16*

26:5, *12*

26:8, *64*

35:14, *137*

37–50, *160*

37:1, *161*

39:14, *64*

39:17, *64*

42:6, *161*

43:26, *161*

43:28, *161*

44:14, *161*

44:18, *161*

49, *160, 161, 162, 163, 164, 165, 166, 172*

49:1, *160*

49:8, *160, 162, 163, 164, 166, 168*

49:9, *161*

49:11, *162*

Exodus

1–15, *15*

2:1, *74*

2:24, *58*

3:1, *17*

3:12, *57*

3:14, *19*

4:27, *17*

6:3, *58*

12, *96*

12:48, *114*

13–19, *73*

14:10-12, *74*

14:13-31, *78*

15:22-26, *78*

15:22–17:7, *57*

15:22–18:27, *74*

15:24, *74, 75*

16–17, *74*

16:2, *75*

16:2-3, *74*

16:4-5, *78*

16:6, *75*

16:20, *74, 78*

16:21, *96*

17:3, *74, 75*

17:5-7, *78*

17:8, *57, 73, 77*

18, *60*

18:5, *17*

19, *21, 57, 61, 119, 122*

19–24, *15*

19:1, *57*

19:3, *48, 57, 119*

19:4, *57, 122*

19:5, *59, 60, 120, 122, 140*

19:6, *43, 61*

19:8, *59, 79*

19:11, *1*

19:16, *64*

20, *14, 21, 22, 38, 46, 91, 92, 117*

20–23, *23*

20–24, *16*

20:1, *38, 66*

20:1–23:33, *22, 23*

20:2, *64, 94, 120*

20:4, *64, 193*

20:8, *37, 96*

20:12, *94*

20:13, *117*

20:18, *22*

20:22, *66, 105*

20:22–23:33, *28*

20:23, *92, 194*

21:7, *5*

21:12, *92*

21:15, *92*

21:17, *92*

21:23, *28*

21:28, *27, 28*

22, *36*

22:1, *92*

22:20, *92*

23:1, *92*

23:7, *92*

23:12, *37, 92*

23:13, *92*

23:19, *2*

23:22, *59*

23:24, *92*

23:33, *92*

24, *66*

24:3, *59, 66, 79*

24:4, *22*

24:7, *22, 59, 66, 79*

24:8, *138*

24:9, *67*

24:12, *67*

24:13, *17*

24:18, *63*

25–31, *1, 23, 63, 67, 129*

25:3, *129*

25:8, *129*

25:10, *129*

25:23, *129*

25:31, *129*

26:33, *129*

27:1, *129*

27:9, *129*

29, *48, 68*

29:38, *67*

29:45, *129*

30:1, *129*

30:17, *129*

31:12, *37, 92, 96*

31:13, *96*

31:14, *3*

32, *64*

32–34, *63*

32:1, *63*

32:4, *63, 64*

32:5, *63, 64*

32:6, *63*

32:7, *65*

32:8, *63*

32:9, *65*

32:10, *65*

32:11, *65*

32:13, *58, 65*

32:15, *63, 66*

32:16, *38*

32:19, *65*

32:21, *67*

32:25, *65, 67*

32:35, *65*

33:3, *65*

33:5, *65*

33:19, *195*

34, *23, 65*

34:6, *65*

34:9, *65*

34:10, *66*

34:11, *66, 70*

34:14, *92*

34:17, *92, 194*

34:26, *2*

34:28, *22, 93*

35–40, *1, 23, 63, 129*

35:2, *5*

35:3, *97*

39:42, *23*

40, *67, 130, 131*

40:34, *23, 129*

40:35, *129*

Leviticus

1–7, *23, 25, 60, 134*

1:1, *47, 48*

1:1–6:7, *23*

1:4, *134, 135*

3:2, *135*

3:8, *135*

3:13, *135*

4:4, *135*

4:15, *135*

4:20, *134*

4:24, *135*

4:26, *134*

4:29, *135*

4:31, *134*

4:33, *135*

4:35, *134*

5:5, *137*

5:6, *134*

5:10, *134*

5:13, *134*

5:16, *134*

5:18, *134*

6:7, *134*

6:8–7:38, *23*

8, *48*

9, *68*

9:22, *68*

10, *67, 68*

10:1, *68*

10:3, *68, 76*

10:8, *70*

10:10, *24*

11, *2, 4*

11–15, *23, 25*

11:7, *5*

12, *2*

14, *2*

15:31, *24*

16, *24, 25, 70, 134*

16:1, *70*

16:2, *70*

16:3, *70*

16:11, *135*

16:21, *135*

16:22, *135*

16:33, *134*

17–26, *24, 25*

17:10, *114*

17:11, *135*

18, *35, 190, 191*

18–19, *36*

18:1, *35*

18:19, *190*

18:22, *4, 186, 190*

19, *36, 190*

19:2, *24*

19:3, *92*

19:4, *92, 194*

19:9, *2, 140*

19:11, *92*

19:12, *92*

19:13, *92*

19:18, *36, 39, 110*

19:19, *2, 4*

19:27, *2*

19:28, *37*

19:30, *92*

19:32, *37*

20:7, *24*

20:9, *92*

20:10, *92*

20:13, *186*

20:18, *190*

20:26, *24, 140*

21:8, *24*

22, *69*

22:17, *136*

22:32, *24, 69*

23:3, *92, 97*

24, *69*

24:8, *97*

24:10, *69*

24:11, *69*

24:12, *70*

24:13, *70*

24:15, *70, 92*

24:23, *69*

25, *97*

25:1, *97*

25:8, *97*

26, *24, 59, 120, 121, 155, 167*

26:1, *92, 194*

26:2, *92*

26:41, *155*

27, *24, 25*

Numbers

1–10, *25*

6:22, *60*

10, *21, 22*

10–21, *73*

10:11, *72*

10:11–36:13, *74*

11–25, *79*

11:1, *74, 75, 78*

11:4-6, *74*

11:31-34, *78*

12, *76*

12:1-2, *74*

12:3, *20*

12:9-12, *78*

13–14, *21, 74, 76*

13:26, *77*

13:33, *77*

14:1, *77*

14:11, *76, 79, 82*

14:18, *66*

14:26-38, *78*

15–36, *21, 22, 25*

15:32, *73, 92, 96, 97*

15:32-34, *74*

15:32-36, *69, 78*

16, *76*

16–17, *70*

16:1-3, *74*

16:31-35, *78*

16:41, *74*

16:46-50, *78*

17:10, *70*

17:12-13, *70*

18, *70*

20, *76*

20:2-5, *74*

20:9-12, *78*

20:12, *76*

20:14, *165*

21, *75*

21:1, *73, 77*

21:4-5, *74*

21:5, *75*

21:6, *78*

22–25, *165*

22:1, *163*

23:22, *164*

24, *163, 172*

24:7, *163, 168*

24:8, *164*

24:14, *164*

24:15, *164*

24:17, *164, 165*

24:18, *164*

25, *165*

25:1-3, *74*

25:9, *78*

25:18, *165*

28:9, *97*

31:13, *165*

31:16, *165*

35:15, *114*

Deuteronomy

1:5, *12*

1:6, *17*

1:19, *17*

1:37, *76*

2–3, *120*

2:7, *120*

4, *83, 92*

4:8, *13, 17, 120*

4:9, *154*

4:10, *17*

4:11, *92, 195*

4:13, *22, 38, 93*

4:14, *93*

4:15, *92, 197*

4:16, *196*

4:20, *120*

4:21, *76*

4:25, *157, 167, 168*

4:29, *154, 167*

4:30, *157*

4:34, *120*

4:39, *154*

5, *38, 92*

5:2, *17*

5:6, *94*

5:15, *196*

5:16, *92, 94*

5:29, *154*

5:31, *93*

6:4, *36, 110, 154*

6:5, *83*

6:14, *92*

8:2, *120, 154*

8:5, *154*

8:14, *154*

9:24, *83, 154*

10:12, *83, 154*

10:16, *155, 156*

11:13, *154*

11:16, *154*

11:18, *83, 154*

11:26, *120*

12, *146, 147*

12–26, *22, 26*

12:1, *26, 93*

13, *3*

13:3, *154*

14:3, *191*

14:21, *2, 115*

17, *149, 150, 151*

17:1, *136*

17:2, *92*

17:14, *148, 167, 200*

17:19, *149*

17:20, *149, 150*

19:14, *140*

20:10, *165*

21:5, *60*

21:18, *3*

22:5, *2*

22:8, *2, 140*

22:20, *3*

24, *186*

24:1, *186*

26:16, *154*

27:26, *17*

28, *59, 120, 121, 167*

28:13, *121*

28:58, *17*

29:4, *124, 154, 156*

29:7, *120*

30, *155, 157, 167, 171, 172*

30:1, *18, 124, 154*

30:2, *154, 167*

30:6, *154, 155, 156, 168*

30:10, *154, 167*

30:15, *121*

31, *83*

31:15–32:43, *154*

31:16, *83*

31:19, *83*

31:27, *83*

31:29, *157, 167*

32, *83*

32:46, *154*

33, *120*

33:10, *17*

34, *48*

34:1, *20*

Joshua

1:7, *20*

1:8, *143*

5, *156*

Judges

3:14, *165*

13:24, *74*

19, *140*

1 Samuel

3:21, *146*

11:14, *146*

12:9, *165*

14:47, *165*

16:13, *125*

20:16, *15*

2 Samuel

2:1, *146*

7, *166*

7:2, *130*

7:8-16, *172*

7:13, *130*

8:2, *166*

8:12, *166*

1 Kings

1, *149*

1–11, *149*

3:3, *147*

3:10, *150*

8, *131, 146*

8:9, *17, 38*

8:22, *149*

10:27, *150, 162*

10:28, *150*

11, *146, 149*

12, *146, 150*

12:28, *147*

15:11, *147*

16:26, *147*

16:29–22:40, *157*

19:18, *125, 157*

2 Kings

3, *165*

12:1, *147*

14:6, *20, 49*

16:7, *15*

17:13, *28*

17:14, *194*

18:3, *148*

22:8, *49*

22:11, *49*

1 Chronicles
23:31, *100*
29:3, *59*

2 Chronicles
2:4, *100*
6:16, *17*
14:4, *17*
17:9, *49*
25:4, *20, 49*
31:3, *100*
34:14, *20, 49*
36:21, *28*

Ezra
6:18, *49*
7:6, *48*
7:10, *48*
9–10, *141*

Nehemiah
8:1, *48, 49*
8:3, *49*
8:18, *49*
9:3, *49*
9:8, *58*
13, *141*
13:1, *49*

Psalms
19, *199*
20:7, *148*
62:10, *148*
86:15, *66*
103:8, *66*
105:9, *58*
106:19, *17*
147:19, *87, 115*

Proverbs
1:8, *12*
4:1, *12*

Isaiah
1:10, *137, 188*
1:15, *137*
2:2, *173*
5:24, *28*
6:1, *195*
9:3, *173*
9:6, *172*
9:7, *172, 173*
11:1, *172, 173*
11:9, *173*
11:10, *172, 173*
13:11, *115*
14:4, *115*
14:12, *115*
19:1, *115*
19:22, *173*
31:1, *148*
42:1, *173*
60:10, *173*

Jeremiah
6:19, *137*
6:19-20, *137*
9:25, *169*
11:2, *28, 115*
11:10, *169*
22:9, *169*
23:5, *172, 173*
23:6, *172*
24:7, *170*
31, *169, 171*
31:31, *18, 124, 169*
31:32, *42*
31:33, *170*
32:18, *66*
32:40, *169*
33:16, *172*
34:18, *59*

48:7, *115*
48:26, *115*
48:27, *115*
48:29, *115*
48:35, *115*
48:42, *115*
49:4, *115*
49:16, *115*
50:2, *115*
50:5, *169*
50:11, *115*
50:29, *115*
50:32, *115*
50:33, *115*
50:38, *115*
51:13, *115*
51:24, *115*
51:34, *115*
51:44, *115*
51:47, *115*
51:52, *115*

Ezekiel
1, *189*
1:26, *195*
1:28, *131*
2:3, *115*
7:20, *189*
10, *121*
10:15, *131*
16, *188, 189*
16:49, *188*
16:59, *28, 115*
16:60, *169*
18:12, *189*
20:10, *115*
22:11, *189*
25:3, *115*
25:6, *115*
25:8, *115*

25:12, *115*

25:15, *115*

26:2, *115*

27:3, *115*

28:2, *115*

28:16, *115*

30:13, *115*

31:11, *115*

32:23, *115*

33:26, *189*

34–37, *173*

34:23, *172*

34:24, *172*

34:25, *169, 172*

34:25-31, *18*

36, *171*

36:16, *171*

36:24, *18, 124, 171*

37:24, *172*

37:26, *169*

40–48, *131*

43:1, *131*

43:8, *189*

44:7, *169*

Hosea

3:5, *172*

Joel

2:12, *66*

3:18, *162*

Amos

1:3–2:3, *115*

1:11, *115*

2:4, *115*

9:13, *162*

Obadiah

3, *115*

10, *115*

Jonah

1:2, *115*

4:2, *66*

Micah

4:1, *173*

7:18, *66*

Nahum

1:3, *66*

1:14, *115*

3:1, *115*

3:4, *115*

Habakkuk

1:11, *115*

2:5, *115*

2:6, *115*

2:8, *115*

2:9, *115*

2:12, *115*

2:17, *115*

2:18, *115*

Zephaniah

2:8, *115*

2:10, *115*

2:15, *115*

Malachi

1:6, *136*

1:6-14, *137*

1:8, *136*

1:14, *136*

4:4, *17*

NEW TESTAMENT

Matthew

1–13, *202, 203*

1:21, *138*

1:22, *203*

2:1–4:1, *74*

2:15, *203*

2:17, *203*

2:23, *203*

3:15, *200*

4:14, *203*

5:17, *40, 200, 202, 203, 205*

5:18, *201, 203*

5:19, *204*

5:21, *8, 204*

5:38, *201*

7:12, *202*

15, *204*

15:1, *34*

15:3, *204*

15:11, *201*

19:8, *186*

19:16, *39*

19:18, *38*

19:19, *39*

21:12, *131*

22:36, *36*

23:23, *36, 37*

26:17, *138*

26:28, *138*

27:51, *132, 202*

28:1, *102*

Mark

2:23, *98*

2:25, *98*

2:27, *98*

3:4, *98*

7:1, *34*

7:19, *202*

10:17, *39, 106*

10:19, *38, 39*

12:26, *20, 48, 49*

12:28, *36, 110*

12:29, *110*
12:31, *110*
16:9, *102*

Luke
4, *103*
10:25, *36, 110*
13:10, *98*
13:15, *98*
16:31, *49*
18:18, *106*
22:20, *112*
24:1, *102*
24:27, *49*
24:44, *18*

John
1:14, *131*
1:29, *138*
2:19, *35, 131*
4:24, *197*
5:45, *20*
5:46, *48, 182*
10:34, *51*
12:45, *196*
13, *110*
13:34, *110, 111*
13:35, *110*
14:9, *196*
14:15, *13*
14:16, *110*
15:12, *111*
15:25, *51*
17:6, *111*
17:21, *111*
19:31, *138*
20:1, *102*

Acts
3:25, *58*
7:51, *177*

8:1, *178*
10, *35, 178*
11:1, *178*
13–14, *178*
13:14, *103*
14:26, *178*
15, *8, 180, 181*
15:1, *178*
15:5, *178*
15:7, *178*
15:10, *178*
15:11, *179*
15:13, *179*
15:19, *179*
15:21, *49*
17:28, *107*
20:7, *102*

Romans
1, *62, 113*
1–2, *113*
1:7, *141*
1:13, *98*
1:18, *62, 114, 128*
1:26, *183, 191*
1:32, *114*
2, *62, 114*
2:5, *114*
2:7, *114*
2:12, *62, 114*
2:14, *62, 114*
2:16, *114*
2:17, *114*
2:21, *106*
2:29, *174*
3:19, *17, 52, 88*
3:20, *42*
3:21, *48, 51, 52, 124*
3:25, *138*
3:27–4:25, *82*

3:28, *31*
4:13, *59, 124*
4:15, *42, 80*
5:20, *77*
6, *125*
6:1, *121, 125*
6:2, *125*
6:14, *34, 39, 124*
6:15, *125*
6:22, *125*
7:5, *42*
7:7, *106*
7:12, *35, 40, 78, 200*
8:1, *119, 123*
8:3, *138*
8:4, *125*
8:5, *125*
8:15, *125*
8:23, *123*
11:16, *175*
12:1, *139*
13:8, *36*
13:9, *38, 106*
14, *98, 99, 100, 105, 181*
14:1, *99*
14:2, *99*
14:3, *99*
14:4, *99*
14:5, *38, 99, 104*
14:8, *99*
14:10, *99, 105*
14:13, *99, 105*
14:19, *99*
15:1, *100*
15:16, *139*

1 Corinthians
3:16, *133*
5–7, *50*
5:7, *138*

6:2, *123, 175*

6:9, *183, 191*

7:1, *186*

7:7, *186*

7:19, *13*

7:25, *186*

7:32, *186*

8, *98, 100, 181*

8:4, *180*

8:7, *180*

8:9, *180*

9, *109*

9:20, *52, 109*

9:21, *109*

9:22, *109*

10:1, *88*

14:21, *51*

15:57, *124*

16:2, *102*

2 Corinthians

1:20, *174*

3, *8*

3:4, *124*

3:14, *18*

5:10, *119*

5:17, *174*

5:21, *123, 128, 138, 141*

Galatians

2:7, *178*

3, *82*

3:7, *82*

3:13, *122, 123, 175*

3:16, *168*

3:17, *17*

3:19, *70*

3:21, *33*

3:23, *52*

3:24-25, *39*

3:25, *34*

4:4, *52, 98*

4:5, *98*

4:6, *174*

4:8, *98*

4:21, *48, 52*

5:14, *110*

5:16, *125, 179*

5:18, *34*

5:23, *125*

6, *111*

6:2, *109, 110*

6:7, *123*

6:10, *112*

Ephesians

1:1, *141*

1:3, *123*

1:7, *138*

2:11, *99, 132, 175*

2:11-22, *8*

2:12, *59*

2:13, *132*

2:14, *34, 40*

2:19, *132*

2:21, *133*

4:1, *141*

4:25, *106*

5:2, *138*

5:18, *125*

6:2, *36, 107*

Philippians

1:1, *141*

2:17, *139*

4:18, *139*

Colossians

1:15, *196*

2, *100*

2:8-23, *8*

2:11, *101, 174*

2:14, *34, 40*

2:16, *38, 98, 100*

2:17, *34*

4:5, *184*

1 Timothy

1:8, *40, 71*

1:8-11, *8*

1:10, *183, 191*

1:17, *197*

2 Timothy

3:16, *205*

4:6, *139*

Titus

1:12, *107*

3:4, *174*

Hebrews

1:3, *196*

3:16–4:10, *101*

4:3, *101*

4:9-10, *101*

4:15, *132, 138*

6:19, *132*

7:6, *59*

7:26, *132, 138*

7:27, *138, 139*

8:6, *18*

8:7, *59, 78*

9–10, *35*

9:1–10:18, *138*

9:8, *135*

9:11, *138, 139*

9:28, *138*

10:1, *34*

10:18, *139*

10:19, *132*

11:16, *119, 175*

12:3, *119, 123*
12:22, *175*
13:15, *139*
13:16, *139*

James
2:8, *107*
2:8-13, *8*
2:10, *107*

1 Peter
1:3, *122*
1:15, *142*
1:19, *138*
2:4, *133*

2:5, *139*
2:9, *122*
2:11, *119*
2:12, *184*
2:22, *138*
3:15, *184*
4:2, *142*
4:3, *142*
4:4, *142*

2 Peter
3:13, *175*

1 John
2:2, *138*

Jude
7, *189, 190*

Revelation
1:10, *102*
2, *175*
2:26, *123*
14:13, *101*
21–22, *175*
21:1, *133*
21:2–22:5, *133*
21:3, *133*
21:21, *162*
21:22, *134*
22:20, *182*

Finding the Textbook You Need

The IVP Academic Textbook Selector
is an online tool for instantly finding the IVP books
suitable for over 250 courses across 24 disciplines.

ivpacademic.com